Anxiety Free

Anxiety Free

How to trust yourself
and feel calm

Sam Owen

First published in Great Britain in 2018 by Orion Spring
an imprint of The Orion Publishing Group Ltd
Carmelite House, 50 Victoria Embankment
London EC4Y 0DZ

An Hachette UK Company

1 3 5 7 9 10 8 6 4 2

A CIP catalogue record for this book is
available from the British Library.

ISBN (Trade Paperback) 9781409171393
ISBN (eBook) 9781409171409

Printed and bound by CPI Group (UK) Ltd, Croydon, CR0 4YY

MIX
Paper from
responsible sources
FSC® C104740

www.orionbooks.co.uk

This book is dedicated to all of my sweet, kind clients.

Health Advice and Caution

Contents

Part 1:
Anxiety Free, Easily

Why Anxiety Is Your Friend
Rather Than Your Enemy

'Success isn't measured by money or power or social rank.
Success is measured by your discipline and inner peace.'
Mike Ditka

Angela's day-to-day life is becoming increasingly burdensome as she finds herself frequently caught up in her own head, listening to a barrage of self-doubting, self-criticising and worrisome thoughts. Her thoughts are sapping her energy, her self-confidence and her happiness. She's not sure how she got here to Miseryville, but she's desperate to leave; she just doesn't know how.

Jane on the other hand enjoys her life but has recently started getting anxious about work meetings. She's not sure why she's suddenly started feeling nervous and nauseous, but she does, every – single – time another meeting is called. She's been working at this company for years, and her recent anxiety does not make any sense to her; all she knows is, her heart starts racing when she even thinks about work meetings.

Then there's Rob, sweet, gentle Rob. Rob has always been popular but now he gets worried about social situations – so much so that he's started avoiding them, even those with his close friends. His social life is dwindling and he now struggles to interact with friends and strangers alike. He wants to get out and start living his life again because it feels on hold at the moment but he is feeling increasingly nervous around other people.

Lastly we have Gillian who now finds herself feeling tearful much of the time. She worries a lot about things that haven't happened and may never happen, especially when it comes to dating. Sometimes she loses thirty minutes or even an hour and a half of her day – and her life – as she sits there staring into space, worrying about 'what ifs'. She knows what she wants from her future, but is now struggling to take productive steps towards achieving it because of the self-doubt and worry that are consuming her.

Anxiety can punch you in the stomach occasionally or wrap itself around you from morning to night, daily. It can make you feel self-conscious, nervous, foggy-headed, frustrated, tearful, dizzy; the list goes on. It can also make you feel panicked about the future, whether that's the next hour or the next four years.

Anxiety can also be such a different experience for each person, which makes the topic so confusing for both sufferers and bystanders. You may be one of those people who had heard others talking about anxiety in a certain way and so when *you* suddenly experienced it first hand as something quite different, it was unidentifiable at first. The confusion doesn't help because if you can't even identify the problem you're experiencing, you can't solve it. It can make your mind run wild, too, with concerns about illness, for example. 'Does this constant nausea and pain in my stomach mean there's something physically very wrong?' It can also make you sound melodramatic – even hypochondriacal – when you say things such as, 'I feel like my heart is thumping all the time but I don't know why and sometimes I just wake up feeling so worried and panicky...' and your friends and family look at you as though you just had one too many coffees or maybe you just need to get a grip.

Anxiety is a huge umbrella term, though, and it can manifest in so many different ways and for so many different reasons. When it becomes a constant overhanging shadow in your life it can fall into one of several categories of anxiety 'disorders'. To name most, there is generalised anxiety disorder, social anxiety disorder, obsessive compulsive disorder, phobia, health anxiety, perinatal anxiety and post-traumatic stress disorder. Whether you suffer from anxiety from time to time or an anxiety disorder, you can always identify some of the symptoms you tend to experience.

Typical Psychological Symptoms of Anxiety:

◊ Feeling tense, nervous, uneasy or unable to relax
◊ A sense of dread – impending doom
◊ Feeling 'on edge'
◊ Difficulty concentrating
◊ Irritability
◊ Feeling like the world is speeding up or slowing down
◊ Feeling like you can't stop worrying
◊ Feeling that bad things will happen if you stop worrying
◊ Worrying about anxiety itself and that it might occur
◊ Feeling the need for lots of reassurance from others
◊ Worrying a lot about how others feel towards you
◊ Worrying that you're losing touch with reality
◊ Thinking obsessively about a bad experience or about a situation
◊ Feeling disconnected from yourself or from the world
◊ Worrying a lot about the future
◊ Feeling panicky

Typical Physical Symptoms of Anxiety Include:

◊ Shortness of breath
◊ Increased heart rate
◊ Shaking or trembling
◊ Palpitations
◊ Faster breathing
◊ Feelings of nausea
◊ Dizziness or light-headedness

◊ Stomach aches and pains
◊ A feeling of 'butterflies' or churning in your stomach
◊ Excessive sweating or sweaty palms or hot flushes
◊ Headaches, backache or other aches and pains
◊ Tension in your body such as your back or neck
◊ Difficulty falling asleep or staying asleep
◊ Wanting to go to the toilet more often
◊ Pins and needles
◊ Dry mouth
◊ Tiredness
◊ Feeling restless or unable to sit still
◊ Grinding your teeth
◊ Reduced sex drive

The great news is, you're going to learn how to solve and resolve your anxiety quickly, whether it's a one-off bout or if you suffer from an anxiety disorder, and regardless of whether you have had an official diagnosis.

Since the day my coaching practice began, I have watched clients fix long-standing and/or deep issues in their life with just a few 60-minute coaching sessions, issues that they would normally spend months or years in traditional counselling or psychotherapy for and whilst these lengthy approaches still help people, there's usually a much quicker way. There is a really simple reason for this. Until recently, we have been predominantly led to believe that long-standing mental health or personal problems require difficult solutions and/or a long time to fix. There are various industries that have benefited from this belief even though many of those working within them are as innocent as the rest of us, as they too have this belief. Yet I have helped the vast majority of my clients achieve their goals, or be well on their way to doing so, in just three to six sixty-minute coaching sessions; many in just two to three. Some of these clients resolved chronic anxiety in just two to three coaching sessions, some in just one. Some clients have overcome a lack of confidence in just two to three coaching sessions, whether in general or specific to an upcoming event, and gone on to achieve their important goals as a result. Some clients have transformed low self-esteem in as little as three coaching sessions. Some have discovered what new direction of life they want to go in and have taken great strides towards it in just three coaching sessions, having held themselves back for years. Some have overcome their self-sabotage to go on and find and/or create the romantic relationship of their dreams after just three to four coaching sessions. Some couples have overcome long-standing relationship problems and averted potential divorce, after just three coaching sessions. Some clients even come to me whilst on antidepressants and have reduced or completely ended their reliance on antidepressants during our coaching journey.

My clients have proved time and time again that changing even the most chronic, long-standing, painful situations takes relatively little time and effort when the approach is solution-focused, proactive and logical. The simplest solutions are usually the most powerful and when my clients understand both how their brain and body function and why – based on research and common sense – they can achieve seemingly miraculous changes in their life in astoundingly little time! Such is the power of getting to the heart of a problem quickly and then using proactive solutions to resolve those issues at their root, for once and for all.

In order that you can do the same, let's look at what anxiety actually is and how you can overcome it in four weeks or less.

The Definition of Anxiety

A good definition of anxiety is: **an uneasy feeling of nervousness or worry about something that is happening or might happen.**

So if that's the definition, how do we solve the anxiety?

What I am about to share with you is how I have helped all of my clients to solve and resolve their anxiety, usually within a couple of coaching sessions, sometimes in just one.

I've had people come to me for anxiety help either because their doctor has suggested they seek psychological help after checking for physical illness or because they have found their anxiolytic (anti-anxiety) drugs have helped ease symptoms but not resolved their anxiety. Other times clients have been trying to tackle their anxiety themselves with the help of books or other self-help methods but still haven't resolved it. And sometimes people just know that something is bothering them but they don't know what, let alone how to resolve it, whether they identify it as anxiety, stress, or just not feeling clear about their future and like they are nervously stuck at a crossroads in their personal or professional life.

I am going to show you an easy way to resolve your anxiety completely, every time it turns up in your life. I am so excited to be able to share this with you because despite what you may think you know about anxiety, you can usually solve it very quickly, whether within a few minutes or within a few weeks. Anxiety will happen from time to time because, as you will see, it is there to serve you; you are meant to use anxiety to your advantage (as intended by your brain) and once you have done, you can extinguish it from your life quickly and easily.

In my practice, I have consistently come across two themes which have helped me to understand what anxiety is and how I can help clients solve it for themselves, within just minutes, hours, days or a few weeks:

◊ Theme 1: there is *always* a reason you're experiencing anxiety.
◊ Theme 2: the moment you identify the cause and resolve it, the anxiety will always disappear, as quickly as you can click your fingers.

This is the case however short- or long-lived your anxiety has been. After all, anxiety is a feeling of worry or nervousness about something, so before you even get into the science, it makes sense to think, 'What might I be worried or nervous about?' and 'What can I do about it?

To give you just a few examples right now, I've helped clients who had anxiety because:

◊ they felt their life was at a standstill and important life goals might be missed;
◊ they had an upcoming groom's speech they didn't feel they could perform;
◊ their physical safety was being threatened;
◊ they felt out of control of their dating life;
◊ they felt unable to get their parents' approval;
◊ they were pretending to be someone they were not;
◊ they'd become extremely afraid of social situations;
◊ a significant relationship undermined their self-esteem;
◊ they wanted to save their marriage but didn't know how;
◊ they hadn't put clear guidelines in place for a long-distance relationship.

There is always a reason you're experiencing anxiety, and I'll shortly give you eight simple categories that will help you to identify the cause.

Dispelling Myths and Making Changes

Before we continue, if what I have just said confuses you a little because you have read from credible sources that your anxiety can have a genetic basis or stem from a chemical imbalance, don't worry. Those statements do not mean that your genes or brain chemicals are the actual *cause* of your anxiety or that you are helpless in changing how your brain is currently functioning. Far from it. For example, whilst the research literature suggests that we can inherit genes that make us more likely to suffer from anxiety, it is noted that environmental factors also play a role in whether or not you will actually develop anxiety.[1] This makes sense because we now know that that the human brain continues to develop throughout our lifetime based on how we use it. That's how we are able to adapt to new situations and learn new skills. Whenever you do something new, your brain rewires itself to reflect the new skill. When you create a habit through repetition, this is also wired into your brain. So whilst your genes may predispose you to a higher chance of being more anxious or developing an anxiety disorder, you still have control over how you use your brain from today onwards. You can **maintain** the way it currently works or **retrain** it to work differently, and thus restructure itself, much like how you change your brain's structure when you learn how to drive a car, play a musical instrument, improve your memory or improve your dancing skills. More on how you control how your brain rewires itself in the chapter on thoughts in Part 2.

You also needn't worry about the theory of neurochemical imbalances for anxiety, depression and other mood disorders.[2] If there are any such chemical imbalances in your brain, unless you've had them from birth, they likely occurred for a reason, such as your response to a very stressful or traumatic life event at a certain point in your life. For example, looking at brain structure for a moment, women with depression have been found to have a smaller hippocampus (brain region involved in memory) compared with non-depressed women[3] but that is more likely the result of the effect stress had on the size of their hippocampus and/or the way they repeatedly used/trained their brain in the face of stressful events, rather than the size of the hippocampus being the actual cause of the depression. So two things being present at the same time doesn't necessarily tell you which came first or, indeed, if one even caused the other or has any connection with the other.

Why We Get Anxious

So back to the two themes I discussed on p.8. I have never had a client who had anxiety who didn't have a reason for its presence. The tricky part is that you can have this uneasy feeling of nervousness or worry without knowing why; but rather than let the uneasiness unnerve you, know that it is there to serve you. Anxiety is both a mental health and physical health feedback loop. It exists because your brain is trying to alert you to a threat to your mental or physical well-being or survival, whether a definite threat or a potential threat[4] and whether that threat is:

a. real or imagined,
b. major or minor,
c. generated by ourselves or generated by something else.

Anxiety is just our brain's way of trying to keep us alive and well; it is simply, and fortunately, one of our many in-built survival mechanisms. Just as we feel pain when we burn our skin which tells us to move away from the cause of the pain, we experience anxiety when the brain perceives a threat to our well-being and is telling us to prevent or extinguish the threat/danger.

When the brain experiences what it perceives as a threat, it initiates the fight-or-flight response to help us stay alive. This brain–body response causes near instantaneous physiological changes that help us to fight a threat or flee from it. For example, the heart beats faster to push blood to our muscles for strength, extra oxygen is sent to our brain to increase alertness, and our airways widen and we breathe faster to draw in more oxygen. The thinking part of our brain, the prefrontal cortex, also stops working at its optimum level because if we stop to think in times of perceived immediate danger, we can get hurt or killed. As a result, we act more instinctively (rather than thoughtfully) so that we can react to things quickly *just in case* they are a serious threat.

Have you ever overreacted or acted a little 'crazy' in the midst of an argument? You can thank your fight-or-flight response for that. When you're not able to think so well, you can end up saying and doing silly things. Plus, acting crazy can actually be helpful in a genuinely dangerous situation as it can scare off your opponent, but when you're just having an argument with your mum or spouse, you probably don't really want to frighten them off!

The threat to our well-being nowadays, though, isn't usually as obvious as that which our ancestors would have faced – being chased by a lion, for example. But our body responds in a similar way. So anxiety is an alerting system that is making us aware of a threat to our mental or physical well-being or survival. Our job is to use this alerting system to our advantage, not get anxious about our anxiety, but be grateful that our anxiety is telling us that something is not quite right and needs addressing.

In my experience, most people don't naturally think this way; they tend to be worried that there may be something 'wrong' with them. But with my clients, once I've explained this to them and asked a few simple questions about how they think their anxiety might be serving them, i.e. what threat it's alerting them to, we're already closer to completely resolving their anxiety.

Your Outlook Determines How Quickly You Become Anxiety Free

How you view anxiety will determine how you set about eliminating it from your life and how quickly you become anxiety free. You will find your current outlook on anxiety either serves you or sabotages you because you either view anxiety as your friend or your enemy. Let's first look at what happens to you and your life when you view anxiety as your friend.

When you view anxiety as your friend, alerting you to a potential threat to your mental or physical well-being or survival, you view anxiety as:

◊ **guiding you towards your goals, health, happiness and survival**.

As a result, you embrace your anxiety:

◊ **optimistically, thoughtfully and proactively**.

This outlook that anxiety is your friend becomes self-serving because it produces emotions, behaviours and outcomes like:

◊ **feeling grateful** for the anxiety, despite its undesirable symptoms, as it is seen as nudging you towards your health and happiness;
◊ **being proactive** as you would if you had a bleeding wound on your arm;
◊ **resolving your anxiety**, often quickly and easily.

Now let's look at what happens to you and your life when you view anxiety as your enemy, sabotaging your inner peace, goals, health and happiness. You view anxiety as:

◊ **blocking you from your goals, health, happiness and survival**.

As a result, you recoil from your anxiety:

◊ **pessimistically, without thinking clearly and without taking actions that will truly help you**.

This outlook that anxiety is your enemy becomes self-sabotaging because it produces emotions, behaviours and outcomes like:

◊ **feeling ungrateful** for the anxiety, and feeling sad or miserable, as you see it as blocking you from your health and happiness;

◊ **being inactive or avoidant** and thus letting the anxiety continue;

◊ **living with anxiety**, often for the long term.

When I see clients who initially have a self-sabotaging outlook on anxiety because they don't know the reason anxiety exists, i.e. for our survival and well-being, I notice them panic about the presence of anxiety and being afraid of what it means about their mental health, or, if they're experiencing a lot of physical symptoms, what it means about their physical health. Things feel scary or stressful or they become unnerved by the sheer presence of their anxiety.

Once I've explained to my clients that there is an underlying issue that the anxiety is trying to alert them to (anxiety is self-serving), and then ask them questions to help them identify what the underlying issue might be that they need to address, **their facial expressions and body posture instantly relax, they feel calmer and they sound calmer, and they look optimistic and sometimes even excited**. It's so heart-warming and exciting to watch that unfold in front of you right there and then in that moment. The **instant relief** happens because the moment you know there is a reason there is a problem, you are on your journey to solving it.

For example, learning that your anxiety around your wedding stems from an underlying awareness that family dynamics threaten to sabotage your big day, not a fear of getting married, provides instant relief because now, aside from knowing you're not worried about marrying your future spouse, you've identified that if you sort family dynamics out before your wedding, you can prevent an issue that could ruin an important occasion.

So, anxiety is there to serve you and if you read this book and apply the approach outlined within it, you'll most likely never in your life need to see a therapist or coach about your anxiety because you'll solve it for yourself. Now let's take a look at potential causes of anxiety and what problem or problems we are being alerted to.

Self-Generated Anxiety or Externally-Generated Anxiety

When you experience anxiety it is either, what I call, (a) self-generated anxiety or (b) externally-generated anxiety:

◊ Self-generated anxiety stems from your thoughts and/or behaviours.
◊ Externally-generated anxiety stems from a person, object, situation or event.

Sometimes it can be both because though the source of your anxiety may be external, there may be things you are doing that are generating additional anxiety in the face of that externally-generated anxiety. For example, you are about to go to a job interview and you feel anxious because you really want the job. You have also met the interviewer in the waiting room and she does not seem very pleasant. However unpleasant she may seem, you have two options: in your own mind you can either talk yourself up or talk yourself down. For example: 'I'm perfect for this role and she will see it' or 'I'm scared I won't get the job because she won't see what I can bring to the table. She looks like she doesn't even want to interview me.' Do the first and you'll feel more confident and empowered regardless of the external situation or threat to your well-being. In this case, the anxiety is only externally-generated. Do the second and you will feel doomed and disempowered, regardless of how much control you actually have over the outcome of the job interview. In this case, the anxiety is both externally-generated and self-generated.

You could be perfect for the job, and the interviewer could already be thinking so, too. She may just be testing your resilience with a cold exterior. Or it might all be in your head. You may only need to walk in, smile and answer questions honestly and you'd get the job, but if you've made yourself more anxious than the situation warrants by talking yourself down, you may sabotage this opportunity. Why? Because when you've amped up your anxiety levels from moderate to high with your self-generated anxiety added to the already present externally-generated anxiety, your brain won't work as well as it could and so your performance won't be as good as it could be.

Either way, whether your anxiety is self-generated or externally-generated or both, your brain still needs to sound the alarm – and thank goodness it does! It's essentially telling you: 'Warning, something is sabotaging or might sabotage your goals, health, happiness and survival – find it, fix it!' to which your mental response should be, 'Gee, thanks, I'm on it!'

Anxiety Is Our Servant, Not Our Saboteur

Anxiety in moderation is a good thing, it helps ensure we survive and thrive in line with our goals – our survival goals and our life goals – whether those goals are, for example, to be happy, healthy, have a successful career, keep a roof over our head, retain self-respect, or find someone to spend our life with. When we let anxiety unnerve us by its mere presence, we have completely missed the point about its purpose. Anxiety is our friend, not our enemy. Even when anxiety is severe and out of control, it's *still* our friend because it's telling us something *seriously* needs addressing in order for us to survive and thrive, even if that severe anxiety is a sign that our alerting system is unnecessarily working overtime or even 'malfunctioning' of sorts. As we progress through this book, we'll look at how you can deconstruct and simplify the message your alerting system – your anxiety – is communicating to you and how to utilise your brain, body and behaviours to address the anxiety head on and resolve it instantly or over the space of a few days or a few weeks. Do also speak to a medical professional if you are concerned about your condition, as anxiety can occur with other mental health conditions, such as depression.

This book will show you how to:

◊ feel grateful for the warning;
◊ identify the source of your anxiety;
◊ instantly take action to quell the anxiety;
◊ feel calm and in control;
◊ with your doctor's approval, potentially ditch any anxiety pills you may be on;
◊ become completely anxiety free within minutes, days or weeks;
◊ achieve your goals, however big or small, with inner confidence.

As mentioned, I help most of my clients to resolve their anxiety in a handful of coaching sessions and I've had coaching clients come to me with really varied experiences of anxiety and completely different underlying causes of their anxiety. Whilst the anxiety-freeing solution is, therefore, equally different for each person, there are some really distinct common themes to solving anxiety relatively effortlessly and quickly.

All you have to do each time anxiety rears its ugly head is employ the upcoming Three Pillars of Calm (explained on the next page) and use the Five Calm Strengthening Habits to help you (explained on p.67).

What you are about to do is simple yet powerful. That's why it works: anyone can do it. I use this formula with every single coaching client who comes to me for help with anxiety and it works every time. All you have to do is:

◊ identify, solve and resolve your anxiety (Three Pillars of Calm),

◊ tweak things here and there to honour the Five Calm Strengthening Habits,

◊ and maintain those positive changes consistently.

It may take anywhere between a few minutes and four weeks to become anxiety free, depending on the cause of your anxiety and how seriously you honour the Three Pillars of Calm and the Five Calm Strengthening Habits. How exciting!

So, my little action-taker, let's put you back in the driving seat so you can give anxiety a smug goodbye grin and wave, as you speed off towards your goals, happiness and inner peace.

Three Pillars of Calm

'Every problem has in it the seeds of its own solution.
If you don't have any problems, you don't get any seeds.'
Norman Vincent Peale

What is coming up is the exact approach I use with success every single time I help a client with anxiety. For your sake I have termed this the Three Pillars of Calm, calm being the opposite of anxious, and an optimum state for your brain and body to be in, as we will explore throughout the book. From this moment on, you can recall this simple anxiety-busting formula to mind *every time* you experience anxiety, whether short-term or more long-term, minor or severe.

The Three Pillars of Calm are:

1. **Identify the cause** of your anxiety.
2. **Identify solutions** to overcome the threat.
3. **Take thoughtful action** to resolve the issue.

That is your simple three-point anxiety-busting formula.

Use this formula every time you experience anxiety and you will instantly experience a decrease in your anxiety symptoms, even if you're still a little anxious because the threat still needs fully resolving. Once Calm Pillar 3 has been honoured, if not even sooner, the anxiety will completely dissipate.

You will still experience anxiety in the future if something needs your attention because that is how your brain's survival mechanism works – you still need the alarm to warn you of a threat to your mental/physical well-being or survival. The difference is, you'll have retrained your brain, over time, to face anxiety in a calmer, grateful, empowered way, rather than be unnerved by it whenever something triggers it. **Grateful** that the anxiety is alerting you to something that threatens your well-being or safety and **empowered** because you're taking charge of your anxiety, and protecting your life and well-being, by seeking to solve and resolve the threat causing it (Calm Pillars 1, 2 and 3: identify the cause of your anxiety —> identify solutions to overcome the threat —> take thoughtful action to resolve the issue). Both feeling grateful and feeling empowered help us instantly to feel calmer, emotionally and physically, because our thoughts and subsequent emotions become less negative and more positive. Thus your bodily sensations of anxiety, such as palpitations and nausea, will also begin to subside and then fully dissipate once the anxiety-producing threat has been resolved (Calm Pillar 3).

I **see** the instant relief on clients' faces when they've correctly identified the cause of their anxiety (Calm Pillar 1) and they **feel** the relief. After all, when you know the cause of your anxiety, your starting point, you can then work out what you need to do to solve it. Not knowing what is causing your anxiety is only going to make you more anxious, especially if you've had anxiety over a period of months or years without no understanding of why.

Rebecca felt that she was either in the wrong career for her or was fooling herself into thinking that 'the grass was greener on the other side'. She felt anxious and confused about her future and this is what had brought her to me, but she also told me that anxiety was something that had plagued her for many years.

A few simple questions later and two themes had transpired at the start of the very first coaching session. (A) She recalled feeling that she wasn't always being herself, both in her school days and even now in her mid-thirties, and she felt as though she was hiding a part of who she was. (B) Certain circumstances in her career impacted how much she enjoyed her work and her inner peace.

Rebecca described herself as sensitive. I often find that means intuitive. Some people are naturally more intuitive than others, perhaps as a result of both genes and upbringing (nature and nurture), though we can all build the skill (as we'll see in the chapter on problem-solving). What we discovered was that her mother, whom she loved dearly, had unintentionally conveyed to her daughter (my client) that if she was to be wholeheartedly herself, her mother may not wholeheartedly accept her, just as she had struggled to wholeheartedly accept her son (Rebecca's brother) because he's gay. This made Rebecca want to be guarded about who she was, for fear of rejection.

Of course, if you learn these 'life skills' (i.e. survival techniques) within your home life, you are likely to repeat them outside the home around strangers because you have learned that this is how you keep yourself safe. However, now an adult, Rebecca was experiencing increasing self-awareness, albeit subconsciously 'at the back of her mind'. Living inauthentically day-to-day, aside from being exhausting because you are living behind a facade to some degree, can destroy your well-being directly and indirectly. Directly because you are telling yourself you are not good enough or somehow not acceptable as you are and so need to hide it from others to keep their love and/or compassion. Indirectly because you are forcing yourself, daily, into making decisions for your persona rather than for *you*, decisions that will often sabotage your happiness for the sake of keeping up appearances.

When discussing the circumstances in her career that were draining her enjoyment and making her second-guess a future in it, it transpired that Rebecca's clients would sometimes seek her services as a physiotherapist but then blame her for poor results when they had not done the work to ensure recovery. This just added to her anxiety about her daily career experience and a future in this career.

To be under psychological attack from others and not know how to protect yourself from being blamed for things that aren't your fault, but which make you look bad at your job, is a massive recipe for anxiety, too. We put two measures in place at the end of that first coaching session. Firstly, we looked at ways which she could manage her clients' expectations from the outset and secondly, she reappraised her mum's comments in a way that enabled her to feel empathic and compassionate towards her mum and also feel good about herself and confident about owning her own identity. By session two, her life was completely different. Her relationship with her mum had changed, she felt much calmer about that relationship and much more comfortable being authentic. She came to that second session with big, confident career goals for her current career and she was excited and optimistic about her future. She had so much clarity and she no longer felt under threat anymore. My work was done. Rebecca had become a great student of her own life, she'd got straight to fixing the problem with thoughtful action, and her anxiety was gone.

Before we look at how you resolve your anxiety with the Three Pillars of Calm...

1. **Identify the cause** of your anxiety.
2. **Identify solutions** to overcome the threat.
3. **Take thoughtful action** to resolve the issue.

...let's have a quick look at some of the methods that people with anxiety employ to either live with or overcome their anxiety so that you know whether they help or hinder.

Trying To Solve Anxiety with Endless Worry

There are two types of anxious clients that I encounter:

◊ One type listens to what I have to say, reflects upon it and

acts upon it, from the moment we begin exploring their anxiety issues.
◊ The other type wants to listen to and act upon what I have to say, but are too caught up in their worry to do so.

With respect to this latter group, although they're trying to take the right step by coming to see me, and know something needs to change, they struggle to listen to and act upon what I have to say because – whether or not they know yet what the cause of their anxiety is, i.e. Calm Pillar 1 – they have this fear that if they don't worry, they won't be able to remain prepared for, and prevent, any potential dangers on the road ahead. Research looking at the different brain regions employed by this type of worrier shows that they engage parts of their brain that keep them in a state of arousal, deployed on purpose of course, to keep them alert and ready.[5] One problem with this is that they think this is a useful strategy when in reality it isn't because they are wound up tight, worrying near constantly, feeling miserable and not enjoying their life as they could be.

Another major problem with this is that in a frequent state of fight-or-flight, you can't think clearly and you are much more likely, in a negative state of mind, to sabotage yourself and your goals by making poor decisions and silly mistakes. Remember that we're less likely to use our logic when we're in fight-or-flight mode? You are much more likely to invite or *create* potential threats or dangers to your well-being or someone else's, when you are thinking negative thoughts, because, as you'll see in the chapter on thoughts, negative thoughts tend to lead to negative emotions that lead to self-sabotaging 'negative' behaviours that lead to self-sabotaged 'negative' outcomes. What you focus on, you work towards. You're steering your mind with your thoughts; are you steering it towards positive outcomes or negative outcomes, towards your fears (the threats) or your desires (the absence of threats)?

A third problem with this 'keep worrying strategy' is that it's not resolving the threat itself, but simply keeping you hypervigilant, and so you're going to maintain your anxiety. Only when you identify, solve and resolve the anxiety threat (Calm Pillars 1, 2 and 3) will the anxiety diminish from your life.

So worrying as a response to anxiety itself (the feelings and sensations) or the source of it is definitely a flawed process that only keeps you in an aroused, anxious and dangerous state where you are much more likely to further sabotage your, or your loved ones', well-being and safety.

Trying To Solve Anxiety With Avoidance

Avoidance behaviour is also a flawed response because then you are not dealing with the very problem that your anxiety alert system is signalling you to, whether self-generated or externally-generated. The anxiety isn't going to go away if you don't resolve whatever it is alerting you to. Plus, when you avoid something you are essentially telling your brain, 'Affirmative; there is definitely danger ahead. I repeat: danger. Something to be afraid of ahead.' In reality you have no idea if you need to be as anxious or afraid as you feel because you have yet to find out. You allow your brain to second-guess from afar instead of finding out for real by getting up close and personal with the problem or perceived problem. Your avoidance, therefore, only strengthens your anxiety – the worry, fear, apprehension or panic. Avoidance makes it impossible for you to do anything positive about the source of your anxiety whether known or unknown.

Besides, there is only so much we can learn from speculating. You have to *do* things, take some action; only then can you learn all the answers you've been searching for, and usually way quicker than you would otherwise. Taking small steps to see what you can find out usually feels way better than you expect it to and progress always feel good.

So let's now look at how and why the Three Pillars of Calm do help you to resolve your anxiety completely and, often, quickly and easily.

Calm Pillar 1: Identify The Cause of Your Anxiety
This is where you work out what the threat is that your mind is alerting you to.

Our alerting system that is anxiety is telling us that we need to address a problem we're facing, a problem that is sabotaging or might sabotage our health, happiness, goals or survival. So the first step we need to take is identifying that problem – that threat or danger.

The quickest way to do this is to ask ourselves good questions that dissect which area of life we believe that anxiety is stemming from and then drill down to what specifically the exact source of the anxiety is. The answer may come to you instantly or after a bit of time. In coaching, I find clients are usually able to identify the exact source of their anxiety very quickly once prompted with straightforward questions. They usually know the answer already but just don't always recognise that the thing that they have been worrying about, albeit in the back of their mind sometimes, and sometimes for years, is the very thing that is causing their anxiety symptoms. Anxiety, like so many other mental conditions, is shrouded in so much mystery that people often just don't realise that the obvious answer is the right answer. It also doesn't help that so many people are prescribed drugs for anxiety as this takes the focus off the self-serving reason anxiety occurs. Anxiety instead becomes something that people simply resign themselves to living with. But not you. Don't choose to live with anxiety any more than you would choose to live with a bleeding arm. Also, though drugs may help you in the short-term to alleviate symptoms, so can plenty of research-based natural solutions, too, which we'll explore in this book. Besides, you still need to resolve the anxiety anyway (Calm Pillar 3 – take thoughtful action to resolve the threat) in order to delete the anxiety from your life.

Really, all you have to think is: my mind has identified something it is concerned about, what is that likely to be? Of course you need more questions than that and I will help you with them shortly, but you get the point. Once you know the source, the root cause, you simply need to work out what will alleviate your mind's concern (i.e. find the solution) and then take proactive steps to ensure that threat, whether imagined or real and whether self-generated or externally-generated, is prevented, resolved or at least minimised the best you can. A lot of resolving anxiety comes down to thoughts, using your thoughts to solve and resolve your anxiety until it's been completely eliminated. And let's face it, when you know what the problem is, you can usually work out what the solution is quite quickly and easily.

Even when those solutions are challenging in some way, the common-sense nature of those solutions you'll identify helps them to feel a lot easier to deal with, especially when those same solutions come with a sense of relief attached; relief that the anxiety will be quashed as a result of implementing those common-sense solutions.

I suspect one of the reasons some people don't address anxiety with common-sense solutions is the focus in society on prescribing medication. Anxiolytic medication, also known as minor tranquillizers, can help soothe symptoms but not the underlying cause of your anxiety...because they are tranquilizers. Also, a 2014 study, looking at 34,727 patients who had received at least two prescriptions for an anxiolytic or hypnotic drug between January 1998 and December 2001, found that after an average of 7.6 years since their first prescription, they were at double the risk of death from any cause compared with the 69,418 patients with no prescriptions for such drugs.[6] Wow! So anxiolytic drugs can result in premature death and in the meantime only suppress your anxiy symptoms but not actually resolve the anxiety at its root.

For those who believe medication is the only way, when the drugs don't successfully resolve their anxiety, this can make them feel panicked, fearful and worried about their future, whether for the next hour or the next few years. Significantly, they feel totally helpless and when we feel helpless, we stop looking for solutions because a helpless mindset tells the brain that searching for solutions is futile; hence that person then places zero focus on trying to solve their anxiety. They decide to live with it instead.

But anxiety is not intended for us to live with it. You use anxiety to your advantage to protect your mental and physical well-being and survival from a threat or danger. Back in prehistoric times you wouldn't say, 'Let the lion keep ramming his head into the wall of our mud hut, slowly breaking it down until he kills us and our children.' The same applies now. You don't ignore anxiety or live with it, you find the source of it – the cause of your anxiety (Calm Pillar 1), and then identify solutions and resolve the issue (Calm Pillars 2 and 3). In the case of the lion ramming his head, you might reinforce the walls of your mud hut to make them impenetrable, feed the lion some meat to satisfy his hunger through other means, or kill the lion to end the danger that the lion posed to you and your family, for once and for all. Similarly, you need to find a solution to your anxiety-inducing root cause and to do that, you must first identify the true cause of your anxiety. Is your anxiety caused by you, by external factors or by a combination of the two? Let's identify it now, and provide you with a way to identify it quickly and easily in the future, too, should you experience anxiety again.

Anxiety causes come down to one of eight categories of threat; four of them are self-generated and four of them are externally-generated. Let's look at each of those eight, now.

Self-Generated Anxiety

Self-generated anxiety can stem from our **thoughts**:

◊ **repetitive negative thinking** (e.g. self-criticism, worry and rumination);
◊ **our self-image** (i.e. how we view ourselves);

and our **behaviours**:

◊ **our authenticity** (i.e. whether we behave in line with our true inner self);
◊ **overload** (i.e. taking on too many tasks or processing too much information).

Repetitive negative thinking

Repetitive negative thinking, as we'll see in the thoughts chapter, is intimately linked to mood disorders including anxiety and depression and it also sabotages your ability to resolve your anxiety at its root cause, whether the source of your anxiety/ worry is real or imagined, self-generated or externally-generated.

You can go on a downward spiral with your negative thoughts and get stuck in a rut of negative thinking, whether directed at yourself, other people, a situation or an event, thoughts that make you feel negative emotions like sadness, anger, frustration, worry and panic. A large volume of negative thoughts can really slow down your progress day to day and your ability to focus on important tasks; thus they can slow down your life or take it completely off-track.

When you keep worrying about things that may never happen, you sap the joy out of the current moment and you miss out on living your life because you're so caught up in your head worrying. You can get stuck in a worry loop only to find out that you had been worrying for nothing and, therefore, wasted those minutes of your life for – nothing.

Similarly, when you keep ruminating or 'obsessing' over negative things that have happened, you force yourself into experiencing negative emotions a lot of the time without trying to learn from the situation with the goal of moving on and making a better, happier future for yourself. For example, you might find yourself so focused on how an ex-partner has treated you badly with thoughts of 'How could they treat me this way after all we've been through?', that you forget to be reflective and introspective and say, 'Okay, so they were awful to me, not what I want for my future, and I'm definitely not going to date someone like that again!' Rumination doesn't solve anything, reflection and introspection can solve all.

Another self-sabotaging thought process that we can fall into is self-criticism, accidentally and repetitively bullying ourselves, criticising our personality, our performance and our abilities. We wouldn't be friends with someone who spoke to us the way we can fall into a habit of speaking to ourselves, yet we can continue to attack ourselves in this way, sometimes constantly throughout the day. Not only do those self-critical thoughts and comments threaten our mental well-being, they make it near impossible for us to fulfil our potential.

Ongoing self-criticism, worry and rumination are enough to derail our inner peace on their own. Sometimes life gets stressful but if you keep thinking repetitive negative thoughts, you can create anxiety purely because of this focus. Negative thinking will also perpetuate anxiety that stems from some other cause, too. As we will see in more detail in the thoughts chapter, positive thoughts lead you towards positive outcomes whilst negative thoughts lead you towards negative outcomes through how your thoughts influence your emotions and behaviours. Repetitive negative thoughts also impact the physiology within our body; for example, our heart can beat faster or our breathing can quicken, and these internal bodily changes then influence our subsequent thoughts, emotions and behaviours, too. When repetitive negative thinking results in self-sabotaging behaviours such as ill-thought-out actions or complete inaction, it's those negative thoughts which are responsible for making the anxiety worse, either because we have made poor decisions which have led to a worsening of the problem or because we have got stuck in inaction and still haven't resolved the anxiety. Let's look at an example of inaction and ill-thought-out action in the same scenario and how these modes of behaviour keep people stuck in anxiety.

Scenario: Kate is meant to be going to a good friend's party but is feeling anxious about meeting people because she has social anxiety.

Ill-thought-out action: Kate is dreading going because she thinks it will be a horrible experience, she spends the whole time that she is getting ready mentally running over all the reasons she feels anxious and now believes it's a mistake to go. She promised her friend she would go, though, so because all the negative thinking has slowed her down whilst getting ready, she turns up late; by which point most guests have arrived and so now it feels even more overwhelming to walk into a crowded room and much more stressful making conversation with people. Had Kate turned up earlier when only a few guests had arrived, she would have felt less overwhelmed walking into the party and would have found it easier to get acquainted with people. Instead, now she is desperate to leave as soon as she has arrived.

Inaction: as she is dreading going because she thinks it will be a horrible experience, Kate spends the next hour when she should be getting ready, sat on her bed, staring at her wardrobe but really just absorbed in her own thoughts of worry. She runs through all the negative experiences she has had in the past, all the things that could go wrong tonight and all the things she hates about social events. She hears a car alarm going off in the street which brings her back to the present moment. She decides to stay home and make up an excuse for why she's not going. She crawls into bed and continues thinking about her social anxiety a little more and then switches the TV on and watches it until she falls asleep.

Remember also that when you indulge in self-sabotaging or goal-sabotaging behaviours as a consequence of negative thoughts, you tend to reinforce those negative thoughts because they become a self-fulfilling prophecy. For example, when Kate turns up late to the party and finds it difficult walking in and even more difficult making conversation with fellow guests, she may spend the rest of the party avoiding eye contact with others and sitting alone in a corner. Not only would her body language be saying, rightly or wrongly, that she doesn't want to speak to people and essentially stop anyone from approaching her, it would also make it difficult for her (and others) to naturally strike up a conversation when she's sat far out of the way. She would spend the evening mostly alone and mostly unhappy and then go home thinking thoughts like, 'See, it's so difficult and scary going to social events and people don't really make an effort with me and I'm bad at making friends and I probably should've just stayed home instead.'

The other problem with repetitive negative thinking is that you get stuck focusing on the problems instead of thinking about solutions; and whatever we focus our mind on we work towards, consciously or subconsciously, as we will see in the chapter on thoughts. Words are like instructions to the brain and work a bit like a Google search; the results you get are linked to what you focus it on. This is also how goal-setting works.[7] What instructions do you feed your brain minute to minute? Or, what are you telling your brain to work towards minute to minute? The problem or solutions? Misery or happiness? Mental health issues or mental well-being? Bad relationships or good relationships?

Being fat or being slim? Always being late for meetings or always being on time? Being good at remembering names or being bad at remembering names? It doesn't matter what you are now; what matters is what you tell your brain you are because that is what you will stay as or become as the result of how your thoughts influence your behaviours, immediately and over time. I've always said to clients that your brain will consciously and subconsciously spot, create and grasp opportunities to make what you are focusing on a reality. Goal-setting research indirectly supports this too.[8]

You can actually test this in your day-to-day life and see it work instantly sometimes. For example, next time you are brushing your teeth, silently or aloud, tell yourself, 'I take really good care of my teeth' or 'I brush my teeth rigorously', and notice how you end up brushing for longer or more meticulously than you normally do. Or when you're dressed up to go somewhere, tell yourself 'I have an elegant walk', and see how your walk suddenly becomes more poised. Or the next time you drive a car, as you get in, tell yourself, 'I'm a competent and safe driver', and notice how much more thoughtfully you drive off, checking the mirrors and out of the windows more often, driving slightly more slowly and patiently, etc. It's weird how much just one sentence uttered to yourself about the thing that you are doing, as you are doing it, can noticeably alter your behaviour right there and then. Just start watching how your thoughts play out.

Our self-image

Our self-image is how we view ourselves – our abilities, appearance, personality, identity (e.g. racial, cultural, sexual) – and is influenced by how we treat ourselves, how we allow others to treat us, what we think and what we do.

How we **view** ourselves in turn shapes:

◊ how we **feel** about ourselves:

◊ our **behaviours** minute to minute, and

◊ what we **achieve** day to day, week to week.

One study demonstrates this point well. Socially anxious individuals were asked to first have a conversation with a 'conversational partner' whilst holding a negative self-image in mind and then to have another conversation whilst holding a less negative self-image in mind.[9] When holding the negative self-image, the socially anxious individuals said they felt more anxious and used more safety behaviours such as avoiding eye contact and checking they were coming across well, than when they had held the less negative self-image in mind. They also vastly overestimated how poorly they had come across to the other person compared with how their conversational partner had rated them, i.e. they thought they had performed a lot worse than they had. Interestingly, the conversational partners also noticed a difference because they rated their socially anxious conversational partner's performance as poorer when they had held the negative self-image compared with when they had held the less negative self-image. So holding a negative self-image: makes an already anxious person feel more anxious and behave in ways that sabotage human interaction/relationships, affects their performance and their perception of themselves, and changes how others perceive and experience them. That's a lot of effects stemming from one thing – how you view yourself.

This research also demonstrates how our self-image, our thoughts about ourselves, are changeable and we can choose a self-serving self-image rather than a self-sabotaging self-image. In Part 2 where we'll cover the Five Calm Strengthening Habits – positive thoughts, positive emotions, positive relationships, good self-care and good problem-solving – you'll learn how to tweak some of your daily habits such as how you treat yourself, the sort of people you surround yourself with, and how easily you can problem-solve, so that you can create and maintain a positive self-image.

Our authenticity

Authenticity in the human sense is about being real, being genuine and being true to who you are.

Ralph Waldo Emerson once said, 'To be yourself in a world that is constantly trying to make you something else is the greatest accomplishment.' This quote probably makes more sense as you get older and start realising just how much pressure there is to conform when we are in fact unique individuals who must only conform with what we feel resonates with us and what motivates us, not with what others expect of us or are instructing us to follow. There are truly so many people telling us what to think, what goals we should have, what sort of materialistic possessions we should have, how we should be living our lives, what an ideal body looks like, which careers are considered valuable...the list is exhausting and so is the pressure.

What's more, trying to live a life that is not authentically aligned with who we feel we are on the inside, creates mistakes, discontent and inner unease, and drains energy because you're having to think about how to be rather than just being. We saw this earlier with my client Rebecca (p.20). Nothing feels better than being, and people allowing us to be, ourselves. Remember:

◊ The important people in our life (eventually) allow us to be our authentic selves when they see it makes us happy and more pleasant to be around.

◊ The people who don't have our best interests at heart will show us their true colours through their clear lack of support.

◊ When we are inauthentic we attract people who are not truly right for us.

◊ When we are authentic, we attract the right people into our life, the right friends, romantic partners, business associates and other well-wishers.

'Duties overload' and 'information overload'

If we take on too much in any given hour, day or week, physically or mentally, we're going to feel overwhelmed. Only you can know what too much is for you and thankfully, your body will tell you when you have taken on too much because you'll feel your tell-tale anxiety sensations within your body. Your mind may also tell you when you have taken on too much for your well-being because you may find it difficult to think clearly or find yourself talking negatively to yourself about the overload and overwhelm.

Duties overload may mean that you're constantly rushing from one task to the next and/or from one place to the next. I get that you may want to achieve something worthwhile but you're likely to underperform compared with your true abilities when you're in a heightened alert state because you'll be reacting more instinctively than thoughtfully. This isn't helpful when you need your logical thinking brain working at optimum level so you can think clearly, problem-solve and make great decisions. When you are frequently rushing from one thing to the next, you're also hindering your mental well-being. Once you've eroded your mental well-being and underperformed in tasks you could have performed much better in because you didn't give them the full attention they needed, you feel crappy about your performance and it can knock your self-esteem by compromising your self-image. I've seen it happen with clients. The reality is that people can be incredibly talented but just by the sheer act of taking on too many duties within a given space of time, they can unravel their own well-being and life.

We are also bombarding our brains with a lot of information simply because we can and we seem to have fallen into a habit of overwhelming ourselves, often unnecessarily. We're frequently on our mobile phones doing anything from surfing the internet, to responding to emails, to connecting with friends, to updating our business's social media to organising our family's lives, to watching videos on YouTube, to deciding which photo to post on social media...the list goes on. We order clothes online and then have the added job of returning the ones we don't want. Not only do we have to send the returns back, until we do, they sit there in the corner of the room reminding us of yet another task on our to-do list, weighing us down a little without us really thinking about the weight of responsibility no.137. We have several gadgets around the home, electrically buzzing, draining more energy unnecessarily because it's another sound for us to process. We go to a restaurant and just because we have a few minutes to sit and wait for our friend to arrive, we pick up our phone to do something whilst we wait.

Just because we can achieve so much in little pockets of time doesn't mean we should. Just because we can, doesn't mean it's good for us. Everything in moderation, right? Yet in our modern lives where we pile on the information overload and duties overload, we seem to think more is better while our brain and body may be telling us it's not. Are you paying attention to what your brain and body are yearning for or are you too distracted by the ping of your latest social-media notification?

Externally-Generated Anxiety

Externally-generated anxiety can stem from any one of these things that POSE a threat (notice that acronym I've thrown in there to help you easily remember them):

◊ People e.g. negative relationships;
◊ Objects e.g. clown dolls;
◊ Situations e.g. dark alleyways, life goals seeming out of reach;
◊ Events e.g. a presentation, job interview, social occasion, your own impending wedding.

People

People can be the source of our greatest pain and our deepest pleasure. People are powerful, intriguingly so. Some people have power over how we feel because, aside from us letting them, they are either someone important in our life and we want their approval, support or ongoing attention, or they are someone insignificant in our lives who is trying hard to hurt us for their own gains.

The important people in our life can be our partner, family, friends, boss, employees, colleagues and any person with whom our well-being, safety and security resides, such as a doctor, solicitor or government body. When we feel like the relationship isn't working harmoniously or we're not getting the approval, support, or ongoing attention we want or need, we can feel deflated, vulnerable, upset or worried. All of these can lead to anxiety because of the worry about the future that comes attached with those situations. For example, you want to pursue a new career but don't feel you're getting the support that you need from your spouse in terms of encouragement and practical help around the home. This may conjure thoughts like, 'If he/she doesn't encourage my personal growth, what's going to happen when I need a sounding board or a shoulder to cry on because I've had a bad day in this new career, or what if I need him/her to help out with the kids more so that I can concentrate on my increasing workload as I grow my career?' If you repeatedly encounter situations where this lack of support from your significant other is palpable, it could lead to feelings of anxiety about the future of the relationship itself and/or about your ability to pursue your dreams and goals. You might then also compound the anxiety by ruminating over it. In fact, even if you don't really need to worry about the relationship breaking down or your partner not supporting you when things get tough, if you keep focusing your mind on the idea that you do, you will think yourself into anxiety, anxiety about your future, and the future of your relationship and your career.

On the other hand, the significant and insignificant people in your life can sometimes cause you to get anxious. Sometimes this happens because, aside from giving them too much of our attention, we feel hurt by how they are maltreating us. Even though these are people in your life who try to sabotage your well-being as an attempt to elevate their own, or so they think, it can be easy to wonder, 'Why are they doing this to me?' In reality, people who treat you badly do so for themselves. About fifteen years ago I heard the phrase, 'People don't do things **to you**, they do them **for themselves**.' That is such a great way to put it; every time someone treats you badly, think about that, they do things because they want to achieve something for themselves. Even if that involves them sitting at night with a desk lamp on, pen in hand, scheming about how they can do something to you, they are still only doing so because they want an outcome that does something for them. Maybe they want to feel good about themselves by belittling or bullying you. Maybe they want to test their own sociopathic skills by seeing how far they can fool their new date. Maybe they want to get ahead in business and think that by sabotaging you they'll do so. You just have to focus on the threat part: what the threat is, how you can overcome it, and then do whatever it takes to resolve it (Calm Pillars 1, 2 and 3).

Objects

The brain, over time, builds associations between two things it frequently experiences together. For example, if I say the word 'apple' you may think of the colour green or an apple pie, or feel happy because the word reminds you of your beloved grandma who loves baking with apples...because you have frequently experienced the two together. One thing can conjure an associated thought, feeling or behaviour.

In the case of anxiety, for example, it might be that a playground swing elicits the emotional response of anxiety and panic. Maybe you had a nasty fall from a swing once where you broke your nose and this happened because you weren't swinging with due care and attention. Maybe now you always fear swings because your brain never moved on from the association with that incident. Perhaps, given the intensity of the trauma you personally experienced at that time, your brain placed extra emphasis on that association of swings equal danger and deep sadness, as though you underlined it and highlighted it with a yellow highlighter. Your brain might even start generalising its emotional response to similar objects; for example, playground slides and roundabouts. What you have to do is retrain your brain, through repeating, safe, positive experiences with swings, to recognise that swings per se are not anything to feel anxious about, when you use them with care. Retraining your brain takes time and repetition, which will make complete sense when we look at how to retrain your brain, on p.84.

Whilst such associations and responses may be understandable, they are not necessarily serving you. It doesn't serve you to generalise all circumstances as being a threat when they are not. This just places unnecessary stress on your brain and body and it can have further negative repercussions on your life, too, like never being able to enjoy time at the park with your child. We want our alerting system working properly, not malfunctioning all the time, draining our limited resources, such as energy and focus, unnecessarily. We also don't want negative past experiences to sabotage us from having positive future experiences.

Situations

Situations can cause anxiety for a number of reasons and they can be to do with your lifestyle or your surroundings. Maybe there is a situation you have found yourself in where you don't feel safe. Here are some examples to get you thinking about your life situations:

◊ You've turned up to a party and there seems to be a lot of aggression and so you don't feel physically safe.

◊ There is a lot of back-stabbing going on at your place of work and so you don't feel emotionally safe because you don't know who to believe and who to trust in conversations.

◊ The dynamic at your local gym causes you anxiety because all the bravado makes you feel nervous about going there and being judged for your fitness level.

◊ You're always indoors and never get to see any nature nor much daylight and you feel anxious because our surroundings also affect our well-being (see p.126).

◊ You live in a block of flats that the other residents litter and trash. Over time you begin to feel anxious every time you think about leaving your apartment or going back home after you've been out, because you know you will have to see that reminder of where you're living and that makes you feel worried about where your life is headed.

In anxiety-causing situations we either need to tend to a threat or need to retrain our brain so that it learns the 'threat' is imaginary.

Events

If there is an impending event that you're worried is going to threaten your physical or mental well-being or survival in some way, you may become anxious without knowing why. It might be, for example, a presentation you have to perform, a job interview, a social occasion, or your own impending wedding that you're having second thoughts about.

Let's say your wedding day is approaching but you're starting to have second thoughts. The finality of it may have alerted your brain to issues you have thus far ignored within the relationship or it may be that as the wedding day has approached, your soon-to-be spouse has begun treating you differently, in ways that have raised the alarm. If you keep explaining it away as 'I'm just getting nervous about the day itself', but the reality is that there is a much more serious, pressing issue that needs your urgent attention, you'll continue to feel anxious. Similarly, even if it is just wedding-day nerves because you want everything to be perfect for your guests but you keep mulling over everything that could go wrong, you'll still experience ongoing anxiety. Events can be easy to identify as the cause of your anxiety symptoms, like when you realise you've been feeling nauseous every day since that upcoming event turned up in your life.

Another example might be when you have an impending presentation to deliver. As the day approaches you realise you've been feeling somewhat light-headed every day for about a week. You then realise this light-headedness started when you began rehearsing your lines for the presentation. This helps you to identify that the cause of your anxiety (Calm Pillar 1) is your concern that you're not going to be able to memorise your lines in time for your presentation, rather than being worried about the content you are delivering during the presentation.

Calm Pillar 2: Identify Solutions To Overcome the Threat
This is where you work out how to solve the problem, the threat.

When you've identified the cause, the solutions are normally very easy to recognise. A lot of it will be common sense. Some of the solutions you'll instantly recognise, some may take a little more thought, some you'll execute on your own without any help from others, some you might need a helping hand with from others (family, friends, colleagues or professionals). Some solutions will involve you changing your behaviours, some solutions will involve getting other people to change their behaviours, and some will involve both as you can't force people to change but *you* can change and thus force them to respond differently.

In a moment, we'll run through examples of threats my clients have encountered and some example solutions for resolving those threats so that you can start visualising how Calm Pillars 1 and 2 work together (identify the cause of your anxiety, identify solutions to overcome the threat).

Throughout the chapters in Part 2, you'll find 'Over to You' exercises that enable you to:

◊ soothe your anxiety symptoms immediately,
◊ completely overcome your anxiety in a few minutes or a few weeks,
◊ prevent future anxiety,
◊ and become more resilient to life's stresses overall.

These exercises begin on p.62. In Part 3, you'll find a table that refers you to the 'Over to You' exercises that are most likely to be relevant for completely resolving each of the eight types of anxiety (four self-generated and four externally-generated). This way you'll always know the steps you need to take to resolve anxiety, no matter how different the threat is each time and no matter whether you're solving and resolving your own current anxiety, your friend's anxiety, your child's anxiety, your mum's anxiety, or any new and totally different type of anxiety you encounter in your future. In Part 3, you'll also find a list of every 'Over To You' exercise within the book so that you can instantly remind yourself what each exercise helps you to do and what sort of dose it requires, such as 'as and when required' and 'daily'.

Some examples of how to solve the cause of your anxiety:

◊ 'My new boss frequently tells me off in front of staff and that makes me feel anxious about going to work and even more anxious about making mistakes and potentially being demoted, humiliated and devastated. If I ensure I really swot up on my new job role and stay an extra ten minutes to ensure everything is as it should be, that should minimise my mistakes and minimise or eliminate embarrassment and knocks to my self-esteem and prevent me losing my job, which is incredibly important to me. As I'm going to spend extra time and energy to help me become competent and prevent complaints from my boss, I will indulge some self-care such as getting a good night's sleep (exercise 18), reducing mental overload (exercise 20) and carving out some me-time (exercise 23) to help recharge myself and replenish my resilience for this challenging work situation. I'll also indulge in some happiness- and resilience-building activities (exercise 11) such as socialising with loved ones to boost my self-esteem. I'll also do some dancing (exercise 9) or aerobic exercising or yoga (exercise 21) after work to soothe my anxiety symptoms and potentially help my brain to learn and memorise new skills. I'll also use nature by getting a fresh plant for my desk (exercise 19) to help soothe my anxiety symptoms at my desk.'

◊ 'Every time I see my parents, they muddy my self-image and knock my self-esteem by being so judgemental and patronising all the time and making me feel bad about the decisions I make. I'm a forty-year-old now, and I don't think they realise the effect their words and attitude have on me but they do – every time I'm with them, speak to them on the phone or am even thinking about visiting them. I'm going to let them know I appreciate their opinions when they are constructive but that they knock my self-esteem when they are purely critical; they wouldn't want to do that to me. To help change how they interact with me, I'll make sure I also reinforce their positive comments more by saying things like, 'Thanks, Mum, I really appreciate that', and 'You make me feel like I can achieve anything when you say things like that, Dad.' I'll also take back control by saying things like, 'I'm grateful for all your advice and help but I feel like I need to do this on my own and make my own mistakes.' I also recognise that I may need to bolster my self-esteem and confidence to enable me to make this change. So I will create a habit of talking positively to myself day to day (exercise 5) and take care to raise my self-image (exercise 13). I'll also listen to some soothing music (exercise 8) before I visit them so that I react to their comments in a calm and measured way. If I feel myself getting increasingly anxious mid-conversation with them and feel like I'm about to sabotage my efforts, I will use the quick breathing exercise (exercise 17) to help me achieve a calm mental and physical state.'

◊ 'Checking my ex's social media updates twenty times a day is making me worry more and more that I'm never going to move on and find someone else like she has. I know I'll feel instantly better by banning myself from checking her updates. I'm going to have a social media detox (exercise 15) to break this self-sabotaging habit of checking her updates. I'm also going to retrain my brain into better habits (exercise 3) so that every time I feel worried or sad about my love life, I immediately take proactive steps towards finding my life partner. I'm also going to invest more time in offline friendships (exercise 16) to get a balanced perspective on my situation, and boost my self-esteem, happiness and resilience, and prune away negative relationships that deflate me, like mine and my ex's mutual friends who are really just her friends.'

◊ 'I feel very anxious about dating now whereas I never used to. It's because I feel like every guy I date is really into me at first and then goes cold and stops calling after about three or four dates, once we've been intimate in the bedroom. I'm going to ensure I don't have too much physical intimacy until we've got to know each other for at least six or eight dates first so that I know they are into me for me and aren't just after one thing. To help me feel more confident about taking things slowly, I'm going to focus my mind in the direction I want to go in (exercise 6), towards my goal of dating slowly and thoughtfully. I'll also give myself a confidence and goal-clarifying pep talk (exercise 5) before I go on dates and during them (in the privacy of my mind) such as 'I am valuable; people have to get to know me before they can have all of me' or 'I am classy and respectable and have to be treated as such' or simply 'I am worth waiting for'. I may also need to practise responding differently to the usual triggers (exercise 3) that make me abandon my common sense and self-respect so that I instead respond with confidence and self-respecting behaviours. I will also boost my self-worth before dates by creating a positive mind–body connection (exercise 21) so that I find doing the above much easier.'

Calm Pillar 3: Take Thoughtful Action To Resolve the Issue
This is where you get proactive about completely resolving the problem, the threat.

Once you know the cause of your anxiety, whether real or imagined and whether self-generated or externally-generated, and you've identified solutions to solve it (Calm Pillars 1 and 2), all you then need to do is to take thoughtful action to resolve it (Calm Pillar 3).

Whilst Calm Pillars 1 and 2 get you out of the passenger seat or off auto-pilot and into the driving seat of your life, Calm Pillar 3 gets you pushing the actual accelerator pedal and steering towards calm. Calm Pillars 1 and 2 are where you become reflective about your anxiety rather than stuck like a rabbit caught in the headlights; Calm Pillar 3 is where you stop being reactive to anxiety and instead become proactive about resolving it.

In life, you have to take action on your problems, and you have to take action on your goals; anxiety is alerting you to a problem, and inner calm is the goal. Remember, in the modern day, most of us who are suffering from anxiety or one of the anxiety disorders are suffering from a threat to our mental or physical well-being rather than a threat to our survival. Of course, some people sadly are experiencing a threat to their survival, such as the homeless or those dying from a terminal illness, but most of us are way more fortunate than that. On most days we're also not likely to be mauled by a tiger or attacked by a murderer. We are, however, still likely to experience a threat to our mental or physical well-being at some point. Whether you have anxiety or an anxiety disorder, you can always resolve it if you truly want to; all you need is a little know-how which is exactly why you're here and that makes me proud of you and excited for you. Well done for deciding to take charge of your anxiety and your life; you'll be glad you did and I'm privileged to help you.

You Could Solve Your Anxiety Problem In The Next Few Minutes

So that you might be able to solve and resolve your anxiety within the next hour or within the next few days, before you've even finished reading this book, let's take a look at how you can quickly identify what the true cause of your anxiety is (Calm Pillar 1) and what solutions there are to overcome the threat (Calm Pillar 2) so that you can take thoughtful action to resolve your anxiety (Calm Pillar 3). Depending on your situation, you may still need to finish the book before you can fully resolve your current anxiety, because sometimes you need help from the upcoming Five Calm Strengthening Habits to help you honour Calm Pillars 1, 2 and 3 easily. Even if you do resolve your anxiety fully before finishing this book, you should still finish reading this book so that you are armed with all the knowledge and tools at your disposal for the next time anxiety pops into your life.

The following applies whether you have suddenly encountered a bout of anxiety or have generalised anxiety disorder, social anxiety, health anxiety, obsessive compulsive disorder, post-traumatic stress disorder, panic disorder, phobia or perinatal anxiety. Please remember that the word 'disorder' simply means a break down of order or a state of confusion. The word does not mean that you are doomed or that you have a massive, long-winded, uphill struggle ahead of you. Quite the contrary in my experience. The word disorder also isn't an invitation for a pity party unless the person wants it to be. Given you have proactively picked up this book to resolve your anxiety in four weeks or four minutes, you are clearly not looking to play the victim.

The thing with **mental and physical health** labels is that they can invoke a victim mentality. Sure, labels can sometimes be useful because they can help us to work out solutions, but it's better to prevent a victim mentality by saying 'I have symptoms of...' rather than 'I have...'. That one tiny tweak – adding in 'symptoms of' – in how you think and talk about any anxiety you experience will make a significant difference to how you feel about your predicament and how quickly and well you problem-solve as we will see in the thoughts chapter, because words are powerful.

Now, when I work with coaching clients, a few questions is usually all it takes for them to identify the true cause of their anxiety. We're going to make sure the same is possible for you. The sooner you know the true cause of your anxiety (Calm Pillar 1), the sooner you can work out what will solve the underlying issue that is threatening your mental or physical well-being or safety (Calm Pillar 2), and the sooner you can plan what actions you're going to take and then take them (Calm Pillar 3), whether the threat is:

a. real or imagined,

b. major or minor,

c. self-generated or externally-generated.

What you have to do is ask yourself some questions with the aim of drilling down to the possible root causes of your anxiety until you arrive at the correct answer by a process of elimination. You will usually notice the tension within your body dissipates somewhat once you've identified the true cause of your anxiety or certainly once you've decided on a (possible) solution because of the relief your mind will experience. You may not be able to take immediate action, but if you know what action you will need to take and plan how and when you will take that action (Calm Pillar 2), you will quell your anxiety, at least to some degree, as your brain will be reassured that you know what you need to do and will do something proactive about the threat it is alerting you to. You basically want to tell your brain, 'Thanks for the warning! I'm on it!'

Here's a little table to show you how this process will work in real life, bearing in mind that Calm Pillars 1, 2 and 3 are...

1. **Identify the cause** of your anxiety.

2. **Identify solutions** to overcome the threat.

3. **Take thoughtful action** to resolve the issue.

Can you identify Calm Pillar 1 immediately?	Can you identify Calm Pillar 2 immediately?	Can you implement Calm Pillar 3 immediately?
No	No	No
Yes	No	No
Yes	Yes	No
Yes	Yes	Yes

You need to progress from the first row above to the fourth row above, from all 'no's to all 'yes's.

You'll find you either start on row one or row two, because sometimes you instantly know the cause of your anxiety and other times you just know you're feeling anxious about something but not what it is.

You'll find that progress from rows one or two to row four is usually quick and easy when you ask yourself good questions and use the other problem-solving techniques in the problem-solving chapter (p.213). Often, though, a few good questions in the space of a few minutes is all it takes.

You may find it helpful to visualise this as a staircase leading you down, step by step, to the cause of your anxiety, its solutions, and taking necessary action (Calm Pillars 1, 2 and 3), and that when you have fully resolved the threat, you can then climb down off that last step and walk on towards the rest of your life. Until you do, you'll be stuck on that staircase.

Sometimes you will think you have identified Calm Pillars 1 and 2 correctly, only to find upon implementing Calm Pillar 3, that you haven't (and you'll know because your anxiety will still be present, even if it has reduced). At that point you need to look once again at whether you have correctly identified Calm Pillars 1 and 2, using the same process of asking yourself good questions and the other upcoming problem-solving techniques.

Ask yourself questions that begin with who, what, where, when, why, how, etc. For example:

◊ Who or what makes me feel apprehensive/nervous/worried/anxious?
◊ What changed in my life around the same time this started?
◊ Where can I get help with this type of threat to my well-being/safety?
◊ When else do I normally feel anxious like this?
◊ Why does this type of event or situation make me feel anxious?
◊ How can I prevent this type of situation from arising?

As you ask yourself questions in your mind or on paper, pay attention to your emotions and bodily sensations as you ask and answer; those emotions and sensations are a source of knowledge and are there to guide you. What do sudden changes in emotion and bodily sensations convey to you? Do you get a change in physical sensation when you think of one thing in particular? When you think of one aspect of your life, do you sense relief of some weird unknown sort, as though you've hit upon something significant, a sort of 'aha' moment? Do your mind and body feel more relaxed?

As a reminder, the cause of your anxiety will fall into one or more of these categories:

Self-Generated Threat	Externally-Generated Threat
Repetitive negative thinking (e.g. self-criticism, worry and rumination)	People (e.g. negative relationships)
Self-image (i.e. how you view yourself)	Objects (e.g. clown dolls)
Authenticity (i.e. whether you behave in line with your true inner self)	Situations (e.g. life goals seeming out of reach, living conditions, dark alleyways)
Overload (i.e. taking on too many tasks or mentally processing too much information)	Events (e.g. a presentation, job interview, social occasion, your own impending wedding that you're having second thoughts about)

Sometimes a few fairly broad questions will be enough to pinpoint the exact cause of, and solutions for, your anxiety, and to plan thoughtful actions that will resolve it:

◊ What might my mind be worrying about?
◊ What can I do about it?
◊ How and when can I take the necessary action to resolve it?

Other times, you will need to ask yourself more specific questions and remember that sometimes there can be more than one cause of your anxiety. For any threat, use the following sequence of four questions:

a. **Who or what is the source of the threat**?
b. **How are they threatening** my mental and/or physical well-being or survival?
c. **Who or what would help** me to prevent or completely eliminate the threat(s)?
d. **How can I make these changes** so that I can prevent or eliminate the threat(s)?

Below I have posed these questions more specifically for each possible cause of your anxiety. If you answer 'Yes' to any of these eight leading category questions (the first question for each category), also answer the four sub-questions within that category. If you answer 'No' to any of these leading category questions, move on to the next category.

Repetitive negative thinking

1) Are the majority of my **thoughts**, in general, making me feel worried, nervous, uneasy, overwhelmed, pessimistic, a sense of dread or lacking in self-confidence or self-esteem?

◊ What do my negative thoughts tend to be focused on the most?
◊ How do these negative thoughts sabotage my mental or physical well-being or survival?
◊ Who or what would help me to prevent or completely eliminate negative thinking?
◊ How can I make these changes or invite any help I need with it?

Self-image

2) Is my **self-image**, how I view myself (my capabilities, appearance, and personality), making me feel lacking in

self-confidence or self-esteem, uneasy about the future, or unsure about decisions I'm making?

⋄ What negative thoughts do I tend to have about myself?
⋄ How do these negative thoughts sabotage my mental or physical well-being or survival?
⋄ Who or what would help me to improve my self-image or completely eliminate anything that undermines it?
⋄ How can I make these changes or invite any help I need with them?

Authenticity

3) Is living **inauthentically**, i.e. not living my life in accordance with who I am at my core, making me feel worried, nervous, uneasy, overwhelmed, pessimistic, a sense of dread or lacking in self-confidence or self-esteem?

⋄ What aspect of my life am I living inauthentically?
⋄ How does this inauthenticity sabotage my mental or physical well-being or survival?
⋄ Who or what would help me to live authentically?
⋄ How can I make these changes or invite any help I need with them?

Overload

4) Are the amount of **duties** I need to achieve each day or the amount of **information I process** (seen or heard) making me feel overwhelmed, overworked, worried, nervous, uneasy, or lacking in confidence, self-esteem or inner peace?

⋄ What am I overextending myself on in terms of tasks to be completed or the volume of information I'm processing?
⋄ How does this duty and/or information overload sabotage my mental or physical well-being or survival?

◊ Who or what would help me to prevent or completely
   eliminate this threat?
◊ How can I make these changes or invite any help I need
   with them?

People

5) Are there any **people** who are making me feel worried, nervous,
uneasy, overwhelmed, lacking in confidence or self-esteem, or
that I dread encountering?

◊ Who is undermining my mental or physical well-being or
   survival?
◊ How do these people sabotage my mental or physical well-
   being or survival?
◊ Who or what would stop them from negatively affecting
   my life or help me to reduce or completely eliminate my
   contact with these people?
◊ How can I make these changes or invite any help I need
   with them?

Objects

6) Are there any **objects** that make me feel worried, nervous,
uneasy, overwhelmed, lacking in confidence or self-esteem, or
that I dread encountering?

◊ What triggers worry, nervousness or panic just by its sheer
   presence?
◊ How does this object sabotage my mental or physical well-
   being or survival?
◊ How can I positively change the association I have with this
   object to reflect objective reality rather than a feared or
   worrisome negative association?
◊ How can I make these changes or invite any help I need
   with them?

Situations

7) Are there any **situations** that are making me feel worried, nervous, uneasy, overwhelmed, lacking in confidence or self-esteem, or that I dread encountering?

◊ What situations make me feel worried, nervous, panicky or overwhelmed?
◊ How could these situations sabotage my mental or physical well-being or survival?
◊ How can I prevent or eliminate potential threats or minimise their impact if they do occur?
◊ How can I make these changes or invite any help I need with them?

Events

8) Are there any upcoming **events** that are making me feel worried, nervous, uneasy, overwhelmed, lacking in confidence or self-esteem, or that I am dreading?

◊ What upcoming event is making me feel worried, nervous, panicky or overwhelmed?
◊ How could this event sabotage my mental or physical well-being or survival?
◊ Who or what would help me to prevent or completely eliminate this threat or minimise its impact if it does occur?
◊ How can I make these changes or invite any help I need with them?

Once you've implemented your identified solutions, if a threat still exists, you simply repeat this process. A threat will still exist if there is more than one threat you need to identify, solve and resolve (Calm Pillars 1, 2, 3) and/or if you have not identified the cause/solution (Calm Pillars 1, 2) correctly yet.

Of course, at this stage in the book you may not have all the tools yet to be able to identify the cause, solve and resolve your anxiety (Calm Pillars 1, 2 and 3).

It's also helpful to remember that sometimes we can become stuck in the midst of anxiety because we don't want to acknowledge the thing it is alerting us to. Of course, only by confronting the threat and resolving it will we diminish the anxiety from our life, even if that means short-term pain for long-term gains.

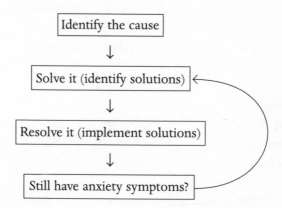

The Importance of Self-Assessment

'The mind's first step to self-awareness
must be through the body.'
George A. Sheehan

When you're feeling anxious, the sooner you identify its presence, the better, because then you can launch into using the Three Pillars of Calm instantly in order to overcome your anxiety quickly. Otherwise you can spend days feeling less than happy and not know why and this inevitably has an effect on the rest of your day-to-day life and future goals, whether you're aware of the ripple effect taking place or not. It's fascinating how tweaking just one thing can change a client's entire life. Sometimes that one thing can be holding my clients back from so many great things: inner peace, happiness, self-belief, achievement and more. Sometimes one change is all you need.

Once you've identified your tell-tale anxiety symptoms (see pp. 5–6) you can easily remind yourself, each time one of your anxiety symptoms arises, that '_____ is a sign that I need to address something my mind is concerned about' or better yet: '_____ is a sign that I need to immediately use the Three Pillars of Calm'. It can be helpful to say to yourself, 'My anxiety symptoms are alerting me to the fact that I need to resolve a threat my mind is concerned about, whether real or imagined, major or minor, self-generated or externally-generated.'

Even if you can't immediately take action to resolve the anxiety (Calm Pillar 3), you must still immediately identify the cause of your anxiety (Calm Pillar 1) and, if possible, immediately identify solutions to overcome the threat (Calm Pillar 2). This is important for two reasons. Firstly, because you want to resolve your anxiety-causing issue as quickly as possible. Secondly, because you want to train your brain (yourself) to experience anxiety as something helpful rather than harmful and as something that inspires action rather than inaction. Our life and our happiness are determined by our daily and weekly habits. You are going to create a habit of responding to anxiety with solution-focused action combined with a feeling of gratitude for the warning and empowerment (feeling in control) because you're taking charge of the situation upon receiving your brain's anxiety warning. You do not want your brain to create or maintain a habit of responding to anxiety with inaction, fear or panic because that will prolong the anxiety and its physical and psychological symptoms as the threat isn't being resolved. The brain does, after all, create a habit out of anything we do repeatedly and consistently so you want to foster a habit of calm by being thoughtful and proactive every time your brain sounds the warning system that is anxiety.

Some sports coaches will use biofeedback methods with world-class athletes to help the athletes see the impact of their thoughts and emotions on their internal physiology and neurology – for example, by measuring heart-rate variability (HRV) and brainwaves.[10] Such awareness inevitably changes how a person thinks and behaves when they want to improve their life because it raises their awareness of how their brain and body react to stress and stress-reduction exercises such as slower, steadier breathing. It also allows a person to see how different mental states affect their brainwaves, such as stress and lacking concentration versus feeling calm and focused.

Whilst you may not have easy access to biofeedback equipment to measure your HRV or brainwaves, you do still have your own in-built biofeedback monitors – your bodily sensations. When you turn your focus inwards towards your bodily sensations, you can notice instant changes that have taken place in terms of your heart rate, heartbeat strength, muscle tension or relaxation, breathing changes and sweating.

Importantly, research finds that if a person broodingly ruminates a lot but is not very good at noticing changes to their internal bodily sensations, they are likely to report higher levels of depression and anxiety-related distress.[11] Brooding rumination is when you repetitively think about a negative experience you've had that makes you sad, angry or worried. It is different from when you reflect on a negative experience you've had with the goal of learning from it and finding solutions to resolve it and/or achieve a certain goal and/or prevent the negative experience from occurring again. Brooding rumination is problem-focused thinking that simply keeps you stuck in the misery and makes you feel bad whilst reflective thinking helps you out of the misery and makes you feel good. Therefore, the less you ruminate/obsess over negative experiences and the better you can become at identifying changes to internal bodily sensations (greater mind–body awareness), the less anxiety you're likely to experience. Self-awareness is daily natural self-help.

What's more, in research on financial traders working the stock markets on a London trading floor, it was found that those working the stock markets were better able to detect their heartbeats than those who did not work in trading.[12] Furthermore, this interoceptive ability in traders predicted their profitability and even how long they survived in the financial markets. Such research further highlights the importance of using gut feelings, or intuition, for real-world decisions and successful living, since interoceptive ability helps you to tune into your intuition (see intuition research on p.238).

The thing about internal bodily sensations is, they help you to know (a) what your mind is thinking, (b) how you feel about what your mind is thinking, (c) help you to identify feelings of anxiety and (d) help you to know whether the calming solutions you are using are working or not. Your body's internal sensations are thus a channel of communication that let you know, for example, who or what:

◊ makes you feel more anxious or calm;
◊ makes you feel helpless (disempowered) or in control (empowered);
◊ makes you feel sad or happy;
◊ gives you energy or drains your energy;
◊ gives you clarity or distracts you.

Overall, bodily sensations help you to:

◊ work out the effects your thoughts have on your emotions and behaviours;
◊ understand the effects your emotions have on your behaviours and your life;
◊ recognise how your behaviours affect your thoughts and emotions;
◊ learn about yourself;
◊ learn about other people;
◊ learn about situations you encounter;
◊ figure out the answers to life's many puzzles, including the cause of your anxiety, its solutions and the necessary actions to resolve it (Calm Pillars 1, 2 and 3);
◊ and work out which decisions are right for you.

From this point on, tune in to all the information your brain is communicating to you by using your body as a channel of communication. It's there to serve you, your goals and your mental and physical health. To use your body as a source of information, tune in to it. If you first need help tuning in, close your eyes and take three or more deep breaths to help relax you. Breathe in, hold your breath for four to five seconds and then breathe out. By slowing your heart rate, you relax your mind. Now turn your mental attention away from your breathing or the outer world and inwards to your body's inner world. Focus your mind deep inside your body, where all the blood, water, muscles and organs move or twitch. Simply tune in to your bodily sensations and listen to what they are telling you. Especially communicative can be the area around your heart. Pay attention to signs of tension or relaxation to guide you, like antennas from the heart, towards what feels relaxed or good and away from tense or bad. Trust the feeling. Learn from the feeling. Use the feeling to your advantage.

It can help to ask yourself questions whilst focusing your mind on your heart area, or your gut, back, or entire body, and feel for changing bodily sensations and listen for the instinctive answers that come back. This is often a key way to tune in to your intuition. Intuition is when you access information that your brain has stored, that it is receiving through the senses and that it is processing, both consciously and subconsciously. Your changing internal bodily sensations can often be a response to those evaluations and calculations your brain is making; so when you get a distinct feeling, for example, that something is the right anxiety threat solution for you (Calm Pillar 2), you may not know why yet, you just know it *feels* right because it helps you to feel relaxed or calm. Sometimes moments, hours or even weeks later, your conscious mind catches up by being able to tell you, in words, all the reasons why that answer or decision was the right one for you and it feels good to back up that feeling, that hunch, with logical reasoning. You'll usually find yourself saying, 'I knew it!' And you did know it, you just didn't know why. I'll cover intuition in more detail in the problem-solving chapter so for now just remember, focus your mind on your body and trust yourself. To solve and resolve your anxiety completely, listen to:

◊ the thoughts you're consciously processing,

◊ what your body is telling you about your conscious and subconscious thoughts,

◊ and that inner voice in your head that answers effortlessly and rapidly.

Whenever you experience anxiety, you will now instantly seek to identify the cause, identify solutions and take action to resolve your anxiety (Calm Pillars 1, 2 and 3) and use the above three forms of communication to help you. Here is how you tune in to your body.

⊨ OVER TO YOU ⊨

Tune into Your Body's Communication of Your Subconscious Thoughts

Use your body as a communication device. Check in with it any time you need to, to help you (a) easily identify that you are feeling anxious, (b) work out the answers to Calm Pillars 1, 2 and 3, and (c) know when something has reduced or completely resolved your anxiety. All you need to do is:

1. TUNE IN to what your bodily sensations are telling you about your emotional state, e.g. anxious, calm, panicky, confident, tense, relaxed, sad, happy.

2. PINPOINT where you're experiencing your bodily sensations of anxiety and/or other thoughts and emotions, e.g. is it around your heart, the pit of your stomach, in your throat, around your upper back and shoulder blades, or somewhere else?

3. PROBLEM-SOLVE what needs to happen in order for that feeling to dissipate; more on how to problem-solve your anxiety in the problem-solving chapter (p.213).

Your bodily sensations will tell you when you have reduced or resolved your anxiety. Your body will often tell you quicker than your mind will, when something needs addressing in your life and when a solution you have applied has worked. When you're feeling any negative emotion, it's helpful to ask yourself, 'What would help me to feel calm, confident, relaxed, happy?' Use all of the information at your disposal that comes from the workings of your brain and body; reflect, introspect, become a great student of your life, and keep a note pad for writing down epiphanies.

SUMMARY

You can become anxiety-free and achieve a calm state of mind by honouring the Three Pillars of Calm. There are eight types of threats that can cause your anxiety; four are self-generated – repetitive negative thinking, self-image, authenticity, overload – and four are externally-generated – people, objects, situations, events.

Your anxiety will always stem from one of, or a combination of, those eight sources and you can often identify the solution/s for resolving the issue pretty quickly once you've identified the cause. You can solve your anxiety pretty quickly when you give it some thought – even if you can't immediately resolve it. You can usually solve and resolve your anxiety within a few hours or a few weeks when you approach your anxiety with the Three Pillars of Calm.

You will often notice anxiety symptoms dissipate even before you have fully resolved the threat, if you have at least identified the cause of the threat (Calm Pillar 1) or identified the cause and solutions for resolving it (Calm Pillars 1 and 2).

Tune in to your body and become familiar with your telltale symptoms of anxiety and calm as well as how your body feels when it is tense and how it feels when it is relaxed as this will help you as you honour the Three Pillars of Calm and employ the upcoming Five Calm Strengthening Habits to help you.

PART 2:
The Five Calm Strengthening Habits

The Five Calm Strengthening Habits we shall now cover in Part 2 are:

1. Create self-serving, positive thoughts
   ◊ that soothe, prevent or completely eliminate anxiety in the moment and long term, and help you to honour the Three Pillars of Calm
2. Regulate your emotions with intention
   ◊ with simple, fun strategies that soothe your anxiety symptoms, and consequently better enable you to honour the Three Pillars of Calm
3. Build positive relationships, prune away negative ones
   ◊ with yourself and others so that you soothe, prevent or completely eliminate anxiety, and help you to honour the Three Pillars of Calm
4. Indulge in proper self-care
   ◊ to soothe, prevent or completely eliminate anxiety in the moment and long term, and help you to honour the Three Pillars of Calm
5. Use problem-solving thoughts and behaviours
   ◊ to help you quickly and easily honour the Three Pillars of Calm

In a nutshell, the Five Calm Strengthening Habits enable you to soothe your anxiety in the short term, build resilience in the long term, utilise your mind–body connection to your advantage, and better problem-solve and resolve your anxiety, i.e. honour the Three Pillars of Calm.

It's also important to remember that sometimes we might have more than one cause of our anxiety, as Maria did (as we'll see on pp.81–2), and so the chapters in Part 2 will provide solutions to 'clear the path' so that we're able to fully solve and resolve all threats causing our anxiety. As we have direct control over our own thoughts and behaviours, but more indirect control over others' thoughts and behaviours, you'll find that first resolving self-generated anxiety with the Three Pillars of Calm helps bring clarity and energy for resolving externally-generated anxiety with the Three Pillars of Calm. If you have two forms of self-generated anxiety, it is usually better to first address anxiety that stems from your thoughts to help you more easily resolve self-generated anxiety that stems from your behaviours, because your thoughts can immediately influence your behaviours, as we'll see shortly.

The sooner you notice how everything has a consequence, whether seen, heard, felt, or none of these three, the sooner you'll treat yourself, and other people, with much more care and by doing so live a much more harmonious life.

Create Self-Serving, Positive Thoughts

*'The mind moves in the direction of
our currently dominant thoughts.'*
Earl Nightingale

Thoughts are powerful, they influence the things you notice, what you remember, how you behave, the emotions you feel, and the sensations within your body. Your thoughts steer the direction your life is going in, in each moment of each day. Your thoughts can also be at least partially responsible for creating your anxiety and for maintaining long-term, pervasive anxiety such as generalised anxiety disorder, social anxiety disorder and obsessive compulsive disorder.

In this chapter we'll look at how powerful thoughts are, what happens when you let negative thoughts govern your life and how you can take charge of your thoughts so that you can easily honour the Three Pillars of Calm: identify the cause of your anxiety, identify solutions to overcome the threat, take thoughtful action to resolve the issue (identify, solve and resolve). Thoughts can help you to feel anxious by focusing your mind on problems that don't exist. Thoughts can keep you focused on problems that do exist that you can't do anything about right now, creating unnecessary stress for you in the present moment. Thoughts can also make your anxiety worse than it need be because you can perpetuate it with your thoughts. On the flip side, thoughts can help you to feel calm by focusing your mind on solutions that could or will help eliminate anxiety. Thoughts also have the power to create inner calm, confidence, clarity, self-belief, optimism, motivation and more. As we'll see, thoughts steer your life.

Two forms of repetitive negative thinking that are frequently researched are worry and rumination. Rumination is when you think deeply about your distress and its possible causes and consequences rather than its solutions. Both types of negative thinking have been repeatedly linked to anxiety and depression.[13] When looking at a sample of 2,143 adults clinically diagnosed with either anxiety disorder or a mood disorder such as major depressive disorder, or a combination, researchers found that rumination was most strongly associated with major depressive disorder whilst worry was most strongly associated with anxiety disorder.[14] However, both types of repetitive negative thinking, worry and rumination, are found in both disorders, and anxiety and depression often develop in the same person. Research also suggests that when a person develops both depression and anxiety symptoms, it may well be connected to repetitive negative thinking and that a tendency to think repetitive negative thoughts is positively correlated/linked with experiencing unwanted intrusive thoughts and negatively correlated/linked to low levels of mindfulness.[15] So be careful what you think about and for how long because the mere way you use your thoughts can result in, or at least maintain, anxiety and/or depression.

It's also been found that after a stressful life event, people who have generalised anxiety disorder or major depressive disorder or both conditions, ruminate more than people who are not suffering from any mental disorders,[16] demonstrating that people with anxiety or depression (or both) develop a negative thinking habit for stressful situations. According to this study, rumination immediately after a stressful event led to more maladaptive behaviours (or we might say, self-sabotaging and goal-sabotaging behaviours) and more symptoms of the disorder itself. I've definitely found that as well. When clients have been ruminating when they come to me for coaching, they report what I can only describe as getting sucked into focusing on the problem and carrying out behaviours that are only ever going to perpetuate their anxiety. No matter how intelligent they are, and they usually are, they just can't see how they are sabotaging themselves. That's the power of negative thoughts, though; they suck us into stupidity. The funny thing is, the moment I highlight the obvious, clients also realise how obvious and common sense my observations are of how they are sabotaging themselves, because I've given them a different way to look at their situation. Sometimes you just need to angle the lens of your mind differently in order to see answers and solutions you may have cut your mind off from, sometimes for months, as we'll see in a moment with the thought–feedback cycle.

I remember my client, Robert, a corporate man who was suffering from anxiety. His anxiety reared its ugly head particularly when he was around a certain group of business associates. With them, he felt insecure. His insecurity stemmed from two things and both were self-generated anxieties. One was how he thought about himself (his self-image) and the other was his behaviours. He was viewing himself as less intelligent than he actually was, because he had been unable to pursue his career of choice due to a medical issue that had nothing to do with his intelligence. He was also *allowing himself* to have lots of worrisome thoughts about the social gatherings with that group of people, worrisome thoughts that were shaping his behaviours when with them. As conversation would flow, he would spend so much of his time in his own head that he would lose track of the conversation and then fumble to add something meaningful. His negative thoughts left him so preoccupied that he would lose the thread of the conversation and so there was no way he could ever contribute something valuable. He sabotaged his own ability to add his intelligent input because of his repetitive negative thoughts. This is just one example of one way in which he sabotaged himself. He also spent a lot of time feeling tense and worried because he spent so much time thinking about his predicament, i.e. ruminating. When he came for his first session his shoulders were raised and tense and his head slightly down. By the time he somewhat bounced into the therapy room for his third session, his shoulders were relaxed and hanging downwards, he looked straight ahead, his eyes sparkled a little and his face looked much more peaceful and happy. He was a different man from the one I had first met two sessions ago. This was the real him, the one that had been pushed down below the anxiety. It was great to meet the real him; still sweet, lovely and intelligent, but now calm and quietly confident, too.

Thoughts are powerful and when you have anxiety, it might be because your thoughts are wholly or partially sabotaging you.

Positive Thoughts Serve You, Negative Thoughts Sabotage You

So that you can instantly understand first-hand how your thoughts are steering your life, check out what happens when you have positive thoughts and what happens when you have negative thoughts. In coaching I use this alternate version of Cognitive Behavioural Therapy's Hot Cross Bun (5 Areas) Model called the Thought-Feedback Cycle (see diagrams). This helps clients to understand exactly how their thoughts/outlook affect their life.

Hot Cross Bun Model (CBT)

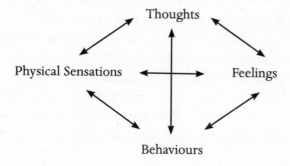

Thought–Feedback Cycle

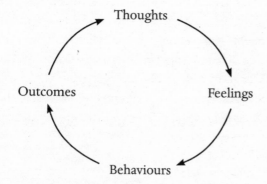

When you choose a frequently recurring negative thought and take it through the cycle, listing the resulting emotions, behaviours, outcomes and subsequent thoughts, you'll notice a pattern of self-sabotage. When you then run through the exercise again, this time replacing the negative thought with a realistic, positive one, you'll notice a self-serving pattern emerge. The only difference is the thoughts you choose to attach to your self, situations, events and people.

Now try this with a frequent negative thought you currently have. I do this with clients and it instantly changes how they view the power of their thoughts, and the need to take responsibility for them. It will take you about 60 seconds to run a negative thought and then an alternative positive thought through the cycle. You must do this right now before you continue reading this book.

⊨ OVER TO YOU ⊨

The Effects Thoughts Have On My Life

A) Run one of your frequently occurring negative thoughts through the thought-feedback cycle by completing the statements on the left:

A frequently occurring negative thought I have is…	e.g. I am not smart enough for this role at work, I am going to fail and feel so embarrassed.
The emotions/feelings I subsequently experience as a result of those negative thoughts are…	e.g. Anxious, panicky, and unhappy.
The behaviours I subsequently indulge as a result of those negative emotions/ feelings are…	e.g. I tend to make more mistakes than usual and end up disturbing my colleagues with unnecessary questions just because I'm panicking.
The outcomes I subsequently achieve as a result of such behaviours are…	e.g. I perform worse at my job than I know I am capable of and I am damaging the relationship between myself and my colleagues.
The subsequent thoughts I then have that feed back in turn into my emotions as the cycle continues are…	e.g. I'm not going to succeed and I'm going to feel deeply embarrassed.

B) Now repeat this same exercise but this time start with a positive alternative thought you could have about that same topic.

Notice what a difference thoughts make through how they change your emotions, behaviours and the outcomes you achieve? They will affect your entire life. You are in control of your thoughts just as your parents, children, friends and colleagues, neighbours are all in control of their thoughts. And it doesn't even matter if your thoughts are realistic or not, they will still shape your life! Allow me to share a silly example to drive this point home so that you will always take responsibility for your thoughts because you'll see the power they have over your life. This isn't motivational fluff; this is common sense.

Imagine for a moment that you think all cats are highly dangerous animals:

◊ Would you avoid domesticated cats in close proximity to you?
◊ Would you experience anxiety and/or fear when you were near domesticated cats?
◊ If you were dining outdoors in the summer, would you struggle to enjoy your meal if a neighbour's cat kept wandering about by your table?

Of course you will have answered yes, yes, and yes because you intuitively know that these would be natural reactions if you viewed all cats as highly dangerous animals. In your mind, your safety is being threatened even if in reality it isn't.

Is the reality shaping your reaction in this scenario or your thoughts? Your thoughts: because the reality is that all cats are not highly dangerous animals but if your thoughts state that they are, you will respond accordingly, regardless of the reality.

So if your thoughts are shaping your reality and it doesn't matter whether they are based on reality or not, what happens when we use positive thoughts and what happens when we use negative thoughts in a potentially anxiety-provoking situation? Let's have a look.

Scenario: imagine for a moment that June has started a new job and her goal is to be happy, stay there for the long-haul and make some work friends at the very least. Unbeknown to June, the Friday before her arrival, her colleagues were told they need to work harder at hitting their targets or risk losing their bonuses. Morale in the office is low come the following Monday morning, when June starts work.

Negative Thought:
◇ June thinks: 'My colleagues aren't being very friendly; I don't think they like me.'
◇ Consequently, June **feels**: sad and anxious and low in confidence.
◇ June's subsequent **behaviour** is to: lower her gaze at work and avoid having conversations with colleagues.
◇ The **results** June achieves: difficulty engaging in conversations and building relationships with colleagues.
◇ These results feed back into June's **thoughts**, reinforcing them: 'See, they rarely make an effort to talk to me. They don't like me. I knew it.'

Positive Thought:
◇ June thinks, 'As I'm new here it might take a little while to get to know my colleagues but I'm looking forward to making some new (work) friends.'
◇ Consequently, June **feels**: patient, optimistic and excited.
◇ June's subsequent **behaviour** is to: make good eye-contact with and smile at other colleagues and to engage them in conversations when she can.
◇ The **results** June then achieves: making some new (work) friends and enjoying work more as a result.
◇ These results feed back into June's **thoughts**, reinforcing them: 'See, now we've got to know each other more, they make an effort to talk to me and I think they like me. I knew we'd eventually get on well.'

Notice how, although the scenario is exactly the same, the thoughts we attach make the reality appear and feel different. Notice also how:

◊ Negative thoughts lead to self-sabotaging and goal-sabotaging emotions and behaviours and thus sabotage your wellbeing and your life.
◊ Positive thoughts lead to self-serving and goal-serving emotions and behaviours and thus serve your well-being and your life.

We attach thoughts to things every day, throughout the day. We don't often think about how our thoughts are shaping how the present moment is unfolding, but they do. Thoughts shape your life. They influence what you notice, how you feel, how you behave and your future thoughts.

Here's the thing: two things can be occurring in your immediate environment but which one do you think your brain hones in on if you've been thinking much more about one over the other? The one you've been thinking about, of course. It's natural! Just like when you buy a certain car all you then see everywhere is that same model or colour. Just like if you keep telling yourself your partner is always in a mood, you'll keep finding examples to 'confirm' your hypothesis. What you repeatedly think to yourself becomes a self-fulfilling prophecy and as you start to take note of your thoughts from now on, you'll notice this. You'll notice how you'll find 'proof' of what you're thinking about repeatedly. This can work against you or with you, depending on the nature of your thoughts. For example, it works in your favour when you focus on your desires and goals because whatever you think about repeatedly, determines the opportunities you spot, grasp and create that make those thoughts a reality.

Your Habits Change Your Brain's Structure and Function

Thoughts also change your brain. Neuroimaging research of mental disorders, including anxiety disorders, studies structural and functional changes that occur in the brain, which gives us huge insights into how mental disorders change the brain, to 'malfunctioning' and how we can change those brains back to healthy. Structural changes relate to how much grey or white matter there is in certain brain regions of mentally healthy vs. unhealthy individuals. Functional alterations relate to how different brain regions function and the difference in brain function between mentally healthy vs. unhealthy individuals. In some cases, the research extends to how talking therapies can help 'repair' the brain's structure as well as how it reacts to tasks and stimuli, for example giving a presentation to a group of people or looking at an unpleasant image. We can change the structure and function of our brain by how we habitually use it, which is how people end up with things like generalised anxiety disorder, phobias, obsessive compulsive disorder and social anxiety disorder. Over time they worsen their condition by allowing negative thoughts to control them and their life and stop checking whether those thoughts are helpful or even necessary.

It's funny how we can think of ourselves as at the mercy of our thoughts but in reality we're usually just at the mercy of the thinking habits that we've created, albeit unintentionally. The good news is, we can change our thinking habits and the structure of our brain by changing how we frequently use it. Just like you change your body with physical training, you can change your brain with mental training. Interestingly, talking therapies have been show to be effective in treating most mental disorders including anxiety disorders, likely because it results in new learning and new habits and, therefore, changes the brain's structure and functioning.[17] One area of research that brilliantly demonstrates how easily we can change our brain by changing how we use it frequently is mindfulness research. Mindfulness is about being present and consciously aware, focusing only on what you're absorbing through your senses, right here, right now, in the present moment, whether making a cup of tea, eating a biscuit, driving somewhere, sitting on a sofa, or whatever. Your worries and stresses slip away and relaxation and peace take over, even if just for those few moments.

When I have anxious or depressed clients who use mindfulness or mindfulness mediation, they report back how it's transformed their inner peace. They begin to feel in control of their thoughts and their life rather than feeling at the mercy of their mind, their brain, and their thoughts. They go from experiencing frequent inner chaos to experiencing frequent inner calm, despite what else is still going on in their life. And it's not just a temporary state. How we frequently use our brain remoulds it *and* how it functions. This is why you'll no longer use your brain with the sort of slapdash manner you might have used until now!

To demonstrate how your thoughts change the structure of your brain, in one study, meditation novices were asked to use a basic mindfulness meditation practice for eight weeks. After eight weeks, the participants' brains had physically changed. Compared with their own pre-meditation brain scans and participants who didn't meditate, the meditating participants had increased the concentration of (the amount of grey matter in) the parts of the brain involved in learning, memory, emotion regulation, perspective taking, and processing information in relation to ourselves.[18]

What's more, in a previous study led by the same leading researcher, a positive correlation was discovered between a reduction in stress and a decrease in grey matter density in the amygdala, the brain region that plays an important role in stress and anxiety.[19]

Therefore, not thinking negative thoughts is good for your brain, helps build your resilience to daily stresses and feel more calm overall. Feeling anxious all the time? It might be because you've trained your brain to become anxious by default, so to speak. This is how you take it from 'malfunctioning' back to healthy.

⊨ OVER TO YOU ⊨

Train Your Brain to Become Calm
with Mindfulness Meditation

If you have a tendency to worry all the time or a lot of the time, then get serious about retraining your brain with a simple mindfulness meditation exercise. You can use a mini version of this day to day, too.

The 'long meditation':

- Sit or lie somewhere warm and relaxing.
- Set an alarm for ten to thirty minutes and close your eyes.
- Take three to seven deep breaths, inhaling slowly, holding for a few seconds and then exhaling slowly.
- Mentally scan your body for any tense muscles and relax each one by just letting go.
- For the remaining time simply focus your mind on your breathing.
- Each time a thought pops into your mind, observe it without analysis or judgement and then imagine it floating away with clouds or getting washed away in a river or via a powerful waterfall and then refocus on your breathing.

The 'mini meditation' is the same as above but you:

- Set an alarm for one to five minutes.
- Use the breathing exercise to relax: inhale slowly, hold

breath for a few seconds, and exhale slowly (three to seven times).

- Sit, lie or stand for the meditation.

These practices calm the mind and help generate inner peace as we learn how to live in the moment: not in our heads, not in the past and not thinking about something in the future; just right here in the present moment, just being.

Do the meditations as often as you can and work them into your lifestyle. If you find mini meditations effective and more achievable, do them daily as and when you can and when you feel you need help relaxing. If you need to make more drastic changes to your mental well-being because of how you've been moulding your brain for a while, do the long meditations three to seven times a week. Remember, the more you train it, the more you will change it.

———

Maria is highly intelligent and successful. She had started creating a lot of anxiety in her life by obsessing over negative thoughts so much that she got into a downward spiral that meant she now spent about 70 per cent of her time worrying. Whilst staying with a partner that wouldn't provide the sort of long-term relationship she was looking for was causing her anxiety to some extent, she was also gaining benefits from that relationship and so the decision to stay with him whilst still keeping her options open felt desirable to her. However, staying in that relationship was also causing her to think negative, worrisome thoughts every time he wouldn't reply to her emails promptly or call to confirm meet-ups he thought were already confirmed. Over time, however, her ongoing worrisome thoughts became more frequent, making her feel anxious, distracted and unhappy, and no doubt made making confident decisions for the sake of her important relationship and life goals more difficult. Maria found that mindfulness meditation helped her to rewire her brain for calm, and once again she was able to feel much more at peace within her own mind and body. When our anxiety is externally-generated by a person or situation, for example, it can lead to a secondary well-being threat such as self-generated anxiety stemming from our thoughts. When there are two different causes of your anxiety, sometimes you need to resolve the self-generated anxiety with Calm Pillars 1, 2 and 3 (identify cause, identify solutions, take thoughtful action) to clear the path ahead of you enough to be able fully resolve that other cause of your anxiety, too, which also requires you to again identify and implement Calm Pillars 1, 2 and 3.

How You Think Can Become A Habit

So habits change the brain and the brain creates habits out of anything it experiences repeatedly and then carries out those habits somewhat automatically without you really having to think about it. Automating things your brain knows how to do is your brain's way of conserving energy but it doesn't take into account whether it is a good habit or a bad habit; whether it is serving you or sabotaging you, your brain is simply trying to work efficiently. Over time, habits start governing your life because your subconscious mind begins to execute them automatically without really consulting with your conscious mind. Repetitively doing something is in fact so powerful that we sometimes form habits without any intention, like when someone takes on the messy or cleanliness habits of their spouse. Other times, of course, we form habits with intention because we believe they will serve us, like eating nutritional foods every day.

Think of the person who can't start their day without a coffee or the person who has to drink a glass of wine or beer every evening. Their brain has come to expect that specific behaviour at a specific time of day. These people weren't born with these requirements; heck, they may not have even done this four months ago, but now they are compelled to do these things and it feels strange for them if they don't do them because their brain is now wired that way. This is how addictions are created *and* take over a person's life and it's also how we create our simple daily habits, good or bad, whether brushing our teeth, arguing with our children or worrying about how the guy we're dating feels about us. Something will trigger the response as if it's an automatic reflex; for example, the fact that a person has just washed their face first thing in the morning, or that they can hear the children playing when they should be in bed, or that they haven't yet received a response to the text they sent twenty minutes ago.

Habits can be hypnotising! Think about habits you've formed just because you've become used to doing them and which have now become your default way of doing things even when you're not really thinking about them. For example, if you usually vacuum your home in a certain order and whilst vacuuming you are at the same time thinking about the food shopping you need to do afterwards, chances are you'll still vacuum your home in that same order you normally do it in, even if your conscious thoughts have been focused on your supermarket shop rather than the vacuuming task in hand. Similarly, if you are driving a car from your home to the supermarket and you usually drive a certain route to get there, if you're chatting with your passenger and your conscious thoughts are focused on the conversation you're having with them, chances are you'll still subconsciously drive to the supermarket using the route you usually use.

We do things we're not even thinking about and because we're now so distracted by all the information we consume, it's easy to sabotage ourselves for a while with our thoughts and behaviours before we even realise what we're doing – what we're doing to our mental health and our life.

When anxiety turns up in your life, take stock to check if you're indulging habits that are sabotaging you. Consciously ridding your life of bad habits (habits of thought and behaviour) that aren't serving you and simultaneously creating good habits that do serve you and your mental and physical well-being, are necessary for overcoming incessant anxiety and becoming calm in general. Replacing bad thinking habits and bad behaviour habits with good ones will also help you to become calmer in the face of future anxiety-triggering issues.

Now, we'll look at how you can easily change your habits by retraining your brain to rewire it for different habits. It's super simple and this is how you change any thinking or behaviour habits that you indulge that are inviting, creating or maintaining anxiety, into habits that protect and calm you instead.

Just Retrain Your Brain

Anything we do repeatedly becomes a habit. A habit remains a habit until we break that habit. To break old habits and create new habits you simply have to change what you are doing, with **focus**, **consistency** and **repetition**.[20] Just as you can train your physical body to improve its fitness, flexibility, stamina and muscularity, you can train your brain to improve its fitness and performance.

So how does the brain actually create habits that can become automatic behaviours we carry out over and over again? Remember that classic dog experiment from the early 1900s? Physiologist Ivan Pavlov consistently and repeatedly presented dogs with a plate of food whilst at the same time sounding a metronome. Each time, the dogs would salivate when the food appeared. Pavlov went on to discover that when he later sounded the metronome on its own, *without* presenting any food, the dogs still salivated at the mere sound of the metronome. As Pavlov had **consistently and repeatedly** paired the sound of the metronome with the food, the dogs' brains had eventually come to associate the sound of the metronome with the presence of food and so produced extra saliva at the mere sound of the metronome regardless of whether any food was actually present. Pavlov and his dogs demonstrated almost a century ago how we physically 'wire' habits into our brain.

The brain contains individual neurons which process and transmit information through electrical and chemical signals. When we do even the simplest tasks, the brain requires a large number of interconnected neurons to work together like a team in order to process and transmit all the necessary information in order to accomplish the task, including walking and brushing your teeth.

Now, a change of habit (breaking the old habit and replacing it with a new one) requires us to make a conscious choice to change existing neural networks and create new ones.

There are three useful terms from the world of neuroplasticity research that will help you remember how you are rewiring your brain all the time: 'neurons that fire together wire together', 'neurons that fire apart wire apart', and the 'use it or lose it' brain.[21]

In simple terms, when two things repeatedly and consistently occur simultaneously or near simultaneously, the brain begins to associate one with the other. Consequently, the occurrence of one (the trigger) prompts the occurrence of the other (the response) without much thought, if any, because 'neurons that fire together wire together'. When you want to break a habit, you have to stop indulging it, forcing the neurons to consistently fire at different times and thereby breaking the brain's association of one with the other because 'neurons that fire apart wire apart'. The brain comes to treat them as separate 'events' rather than intertwined 'events' so that eventually one will no longer trigger the other as the brain will no longer expect them to occur simultaneously or near simultaneously.

The third term, the 'use it or lose it' brain, refers to how the brain 'prunes away' any neural connections that are not being used. This is why it's so important to repeatedly use skills we have honed so we don't lose them. This is also partially why the brain declines into old age; the brain responds to how we are exercising it. Therefore, we can lose an old skill through lack of use because we either 'use it or lose it' and in the exact same way we can lose (eliminate) self-sabotaging habits to the point where we have no desire to repeat them.

Training the brain to change any habit requires a simple three-step process. You have to do this with conscious attention because you need to record the new learning in your brain for it to work, and consistently so that the brain doesn't receive mixed messages and instead knows which one you want it to do, keep the habit or lose the habit:

1. Identify the trigger, e.g. hearing about someone getting married (**trigger**).
2. Consciously and consistently abandon the old response every time the trigger occurs, e.g. thinking, 'I'm never going to get married' and doing nothing productive to help you find your life partner (**habitual undesirable response**).
3. Consciously and consistently use the new response you want to reinforce, every time the trigger occurs, e.g. taking self-serving action on your goal* (**new, desirable response you want to make habitual**).

*That self-serving action could be, for example, affirming positive statements instead of negative statements about yourself or your situation, arranging a first date with someone, connecting with two potential new dates on an internet dating site, and/or finally seeking out a counsellor or coach to assist with deeper psychological barriers to finding lasting love.

Your brain training will start taking effect pretty quickly too! When you indulge a consistent pattern for about two to three hours a day, the brain can start to make visible changes within just forty-eight hours.[22] I've found with clients that old habits die easy when you consciously and consistently abandon them and instead respond to your usual triggers with your new, desirable thoughts and behaviours.

So, when your anxiety is purely self-generated by repetitive negative thinking, use frequent mindfulness and mindfulness meditations (see p.80) to rewire your brain for calm in four weeks.

Equally, when your anxiety is purely self-generated by your behaviours (e.g. subjecting yourself to information overload), or by your thoughts and behaviours (e.g. you're really worried about hitting a deadline but are stuck in avoidance or inaction and so aren't doing the work required to hit that deadline), you can break those anxiety-creating habits by rewiring your brain for better habits that delete the anxiety from your life and create calm instead (use the exercise on p.89).

Similarly, even when the threat is externally-generated, there are often habits that you can create or change in order to eliminate that anxiety from your life (e.g. changing how you interact with a significant other who is causing you ongoing distress, in order to influence a change in their behaviour towards you).

Plus, regardless of the cause(s) of your anxiety, you want to train your brain into a habit of immediately responding to anxiety in a calm, thoughtful, proactive way, rather than with panic, fear, avoidance or inaction, and you do that by immediately implementing Calm Pillars 1, 2 and 3 (identify, solve, resolve), or whichever still need action. When you do, the Three Pillars of Calm help you to feel calmer because you're reassuring your brain you're taking proactive steps towards resolving the threat(s) it's warning you about *and* you also resolve the anxiety by honouring those Three Pillars of Calm. Making progress is a wonderful anti-anxiety drug.

Sometimes you'll be able to execute all Three Pillars of Calm immediately and in quick succession in response to an anxiety trigger, which is brilliant for calming your brain because you're instantly reassuring it with your thoughts (Calm Pillars 1 and 2) and actions (Calm Pillar 3) and resolving the threat that your brain is alerting you to.

For example, you feel anxious because you're worrying about something that may never happen that you also have zero control over and so you decide to distract yourself from the worrisome thoughts (see exercise on p.93) so that you don't waste hours of your life for nothing.

On other occasions, completely resolving the anxiety-causing issue may take time but you'll find that even just immediately executing Calm Pillars 1 and 2 (identify the cause of your anxiety and solutions for overcoming the threat) in response to an anxiety trigger, will still make you feel calm because you're instantly reassuring your brain with your solution-focused thoughts (Calm Pillars 1 and 2). Often, we don't need to fully resolve a threat to feel calm; just knowing we've thought of the solution brings that calm even when we can't necessarily implement it straight away. When you do something about the cause of your anxiety, even if you've only planned the resolution in your brain at the present moment, you feel better because the worry has been (somewhat) extinguished even if the problem hasn't yet.

For example, you realise your sudden onset of anxiety stems from the presentation you have in a week's time but you've rehearsed it pretty well already and know you still have time to rehearse. Then finally, after mulling it over for a bit you realise that what's worrying you is the realisation that you may have made a big error in one of the calculations you've included in your presentation. You know you can only check your maths and correct any errors when you're back at work tomorrow; you know what the source of the anxiety is and you know the solution is (Calm Pillars 1 and 2) but can't immediately do anything to resolve it (Calm Pillar 3). You now know what your brain was concerned about, what you need to do and have ample time to do it; the threat to your well-being has thus been averted.

Every time you notice your anxiety levels rise, psychologically or physically, consciously train your brain to remain calm by making progress on resolving the issue with Calm Pillars 1, 2 and 3 (identify, solve, resolve), or whichever still require effort if you can't execute all three pillars together. For example, you may have already correctly identified the cause of your anxiety and the solutions for resolving it (Calm Pillars 1 and 2) and you may now just need to keep taking thoughtful action in a timely manner in order to fully resolve the threat (Calm Pillar 3). Remember, progress always makes you feel calmer and happier, and inaction makes you feel panicked and more anxious.

⊨ OVER TO YOU ⊨

Rewire Your Brain for Calm and Any Good Habits

Train your brain to face anxiety in a calm, thoughtful, proactive way, rather than with panic, fear, avoidance or inaction. Use it as the alerting system it is and immediately respond to your anxiety with:

- Calm Pillar 1 – **identify the cause** of your anxiety
- Calm Pillar 2 – **identify solutions** to overcome the threat
- Calm Pillar 3 – **take thoughtful action** to resolve the issue

or whichever still require action, starting with Calm Pillar 1 and ending with Calm Pillar 3.

Every time you experience anxiety, make progress on identifying, solving and resolving it. When you do, your brain will thank you and become calmer or completely calm. Once you've finished honouring Calm Pillars 1, 2 and 3, you will be anxiety free.

To rewire your brain for any habit you want to change, whether to eliminate a bad habit (including a habit that is causing your anxiety) or create a good habit (including a habit that will make you calm again), use this simple three-step process:

1. Identify the trigger, e.g. hearing about someone getting married (**trigger**).
2. Consciously and consistently abandon the old response every time the trigger occurs, e.g. thinking, 'I'm never going to get married' and not doing anything productive to help you find your life partner (**habitual undesirable response**).
3. Consciously and consistently use the new response you want to reinforce, every time the trigger occurs, e.g. thinking, 'I am in the process of finding my future spouse' and proactively arranging a new first date and making acquaintance with two new potential dates (**new, desirable response you want to make habitual**).

You may find it helpful to create three columns like so:

What are the triggers? (e.g. things that trigger my anxiety or things that trigger my bad habits)	What thoughts and behaviours do I currently respond to those triggers with?	What thoughts and behaviours would I rather respond to those triggers with?

The triggers could be your thoughts about yourself, your thoughts about someone or something else, your self-sabotaging behaviours, a particular person or situation, someone's behaviour, a place you visit, and so on. Each time you encounter one of your triggers, consistently stop the old thoughts and behaviours you currently tend to use and simultaneously use the new thoughts and behaviours you want to create a habit of.

Here are some examples:

- Replacing repetitive negative thoughts with mindfulness and positive thoughts (see p.97).
- Replacing constantly comparing yourself to others with focusing only on what you are doing and achieving (which can mean not looking into other people's online profiles).
- Replacing staying isolated at home with going out into the world, bit by bit increasing how many people you see and interact with calmly and confidently. For example, using more realistic, positive thoughts about yourself and the situation, knowing how you will respond to any conversations you're likely to encounter that might make you feel anxious, and taking time to get dressed so you feel relaxed and confident before leaving home.
- Replacing an open door policy to negative relationships with saying no to the negative relationships more often and yes to the positive relationships more often.

Remember also that negative thoughts result in negative emotions and when we experience negative emotions or stress the body can go into fight-or-flight mode, and when it does, the thinking part of the brain stops working at its optimum level.[23] Although this is meant to protect you in times of danger so that you can act instinctively and thus quickly rather than thoughtfully and thus more slowly, which in times of grave danger can get you hurt or killed, this disruption of your 'logical brain' makes it difficult for you to think clearly and rationally when you actually need to. So thinking positive thoughts helps prevent fight-or-flight mode and thus ensures you can use your brain well to think clearly, problem-solve and make great decisions.

Positive Thoughts and Images Reduce Anxiety

In one study, researchers tested over 100 people to see if people with **generalised** anxiety disorder (where the anxiety is pervasive) could reduce their anxiety by replacing their negative thoughts about a future outcome with either (a) images of possible positive outcomes, (b) verbally represented possible positive outcomes or (c) positive images unrelated to the original worries.[24] All three methods of thinking positively about outcomes rather than negatively, led to significant reductions in negative intrusive thoughts and reports of worry and anxiety. What's really interesting and enlightening about this study is the fact that there was no significant difference between thinking about possible alternative positive outcomes in word or image form and thinking about something positive that was completely unrelated to the cause of the worry! So merely forcing your mind to think positive thoughts instead of negative ones, provides instant relief from anxiety. That's pretty telling! Your minute-to-minute thoughts are shaping your mental health, including your anxiety levels.

When I have clients who are obsessing over thoughts that are making them miserable all the time – anxious or sad thoughts – they get trapped in a downward spiral of anxiety or sadness and that dark hole stops them from taking positive self-serving steps to resolve whatever is bothering them (e.g. the cause of their anxiety) or move on from whatever is bothering them (e.g. a mean ex-boyfriend).

Sometimes it is solely or mostly your thoughts that are causing your anxiety, like if you keep comparing yourself to your friends or colleagues on social media, or you keep worrying about something that may never happen, or you keep critiquing or bullying yourself in your mind. Firstly, retraining your brain to not check social media every ten minutes and instead do something calming, uplifting or exciting, may be all you need to do. However, sometimes you need help getting out of that mental ditch you're in, in the first place. When I have clients getting stuck in this mental rut, what helps is having a 'go-to distraction exercise' that instantly transforms their thoughts, and thus emotions and behaviours, from negative and self-sabotaging to positive and self-serving. Create yours now so that you always have it at your disposal whenever you need it so that you don't have to think about how you can distract your mind, you already know how and you instantly employ it.

⊨ OVER TO YOU ⊨

Create and Use Distraction Exercises

A 'go-to distraction exercise' is one of the quickest and easiest ways to successfully distract your mind from thinking, or obsessing, about something you are feeling anxious or sad about, and instead focus it on something that makes you feel calm or happy. This also enables you to quickly and easily identify and implement Calm Pillars 1, 2 and 3 (identify cause, identify solutions, take action). Remember, there is a difference between broodingly ruminating over negative thoughts and reflecting on and introspecting about an issue that needs resolving in your life. The former is self-sabotaging and doesn't offer you solutions to get out of the misery, the latter is self-serving and allows you to identify solutions to propel you away from the misery towards happiness and inner peace.

Your go-to distraction exercise needs to be something accessible that you can use anywhere at any time. Here are some examples:

- A feel-good playlist saved onto your mobile phone of two or three songs that always make you feel happy whenever you listen to them. You can use these at home, go for a walk and listen to them, put your earphones in and lock yourself in a bathroom at work or home, or listen to them at your desk, in your car, or at the gym.

- Recall a certain memory that always makes you feel happy whenever you think about it, such as from your wedding day, a family holiday, your childhood, a funny incident with a friend, and so on.
- Look at images of cute baby animals, for example, on a social media account you like.
- Read funny quotes from a TV show you love, either online or saved on your phone to access when needed.
- Look at photographs of good times you've had in your life that you're grateful for and make you feel happy.

Create your distraction exercise now so that you can instantly use it the moment you realise you're driving yourself crazy with your thoughts.

Positive Self-Talk Is Vital No Matter What Is Going On

Whilst it's helpful to distract yourself from negative self-sabotaging thoughts, it's even better for resolving your anxiety and your mental health if you get yourself in the habit of thinking positive thoughts most of the time. Plus, getting into a positive thinking state is also vital for you to be able to properly use the reasoning, problem-solving, decision-making part of your brain in order to honour the Three Pillars of Calm (identify, solve and resolve your anxiety).

Positive self-talk – or how we talk to our selves – is a research-backed method for helping us to achieve what we want, and is perhaps most notably embraced by world-class athletes and entrepreneurs. From the very early days of my coaching practice I witnessed first-hand with clients who were anxious, depressed, frustrated or confused, how changing that internal dialogue changed their emotions, energy levels, behaviours and daily outcomes. Sometimes, in as little as two weeks of intentionally positive self-talk my sweet clients had started to transform their mental well-being, relationships and life. I was astounded. I already believed in the power of positive self-talk but to see it work the way it did and as quickly as it did, surprised me and reinforced my belief in its power.

Research finds that positive self-talk moves us in the direction of our goals when it is focused on desired emotions, behaviours and outcomes/goals.

An analysis of thirty-two sports psychology studies revealed that 'Instructional' self-talk helps a person execute a task with more precision (e.g. 'arm straight').[25] 'Motivational' self-talk, on the other hand, helps a person to boost their overall confidence and self-belief that they're capable of acting in accordance with, and achieving, their goals (e.g. 'I can do this').[26] As an example then, to help you deliver a great speech you might use the instructional self-talk, 'Breathe calmly' and 'Make good eye contact throughout', coupled with motivational self-talk, 'I feel confident talking about this topic'.

In other self-talk research, a large-scale study of over 44,000 people playing an online game demonstrated that self-talk focused on improving results (e.g. 'I can beat my best score') as well as on the methods employed (e.g. 'I can react quicker this time'), both improved the gamers' achievements.[27]

Anxiety research also suggests that self-critical self-talk actually makes you more anxious. For example, in a study looking at communication apprehension in public speaking anxiety, researchers found a positive correlation between a person's anxiety levels and their self-critical self-talk, whereas self-reinforcing self-talk was associated with a lack of anxiety.[28] In other words, criticising yourself, however subtlety or subconsciously, makes you feel more anxious whilst reinforcing your worth and capabilities makes you feel less anxious or feel calm.

So, all you need to do is (a) identify your frequently occurring negative thoughts, (b) consciously stop using them until you lose that bad habit, and (c) instead use positive statements (affirmations) at will to focus your mind on instructional, motivational and goal-focused thoughts that are going to help you to feel positive emotions (e.g. calm and in control), and employ behaviours that help you to become anxiety free (e.g. 'I will speak succinctly and confidently when broaching that issue with my friend'), and help you to focus your mind on your goals and desires rather than your fears and dislikes. As you start taking note of how your thoughts play out, you'll notice your thoughts become a self-fulfilling prophecy, regardless of whether they are positive or negative, what you desire or what you fear, so focus your thoughts on what you want, not on what you don't want. I understand that sometimes you might feel that talking positively to yourself is difficult because those positive statements feel unbelievable to you and so that internal conflict makes you want to reject that statement and so not act upon it. For this reason, one study suggests that you may find it helpful to talk to yourself in positive terms in the third person much like how another person would talk to you or how you would talk to someone else, e.g. 'you can find a solution' or 'you deserve to be treated well by him' rather than 'I can find a solution' or 'I deserve to be treated well by him'.[29]

Your body also feels it when you're talking negatively to yourself. Our physiology highlights the difference our thoughts make to how our bodies react to our negative thoughts. For example, in one study, after being faced with a speech task designed to induce stress around being evaluated by others, participants were later fed messages to evoke feelings of hope or rumination, or altogether distract them from thinking about the speech task.[30] Rumination led to a higher heart rate (a sign of increased stress) than did hope and rumination also led to more guilt and anger and less happiness than did hopefulness about the task or being distracted from the stress of the task. So, whenever you're feeling anxious, psychologically or physically, the first thing you must do is check in with your thoughts to ensure they are not contributing partially or wholly to your anxiety.

⊨ OVER TO YOU ⊨
Create a Habit of Talking Positively to Yourself

Whether your anxiety is being wholly or partially caused or maintained by your negative thinking or whether your negative thoughts are simply sabotaging your ability to identify, solve and resolve your anxiety-triggering threat (Three Pillars of Calm), ensure you talk to yourself as you would want a best friend to talk to you. As a simple rule:

- if it's negative, deflates you, knocks your self-belief, knocks your self-worth, knocks your confidence, and/or sounds like something a non-well-wisher would say, don't say it;
- if it's positive, helps you to believe in yourself, helps you to feel confident, helps you to focus on your goals, and/or sounds like something a well-wisher would say, say it.

Use the following steps to help:

1. List any negative statements you frequently say to yourself that sabotage your well-being and your goals, and stop saying them. As you identify more, ban them too.
2. Make a habit of talking positively to yourself ALL the time. Remember, do something often enough and it becomes a habit.
3. Use affirmations to help you. Affirmations are positive statements spoken in the present tense that help you to

focus your mind on the necessary thoughts, qualities and behaviours for you to have good mental health and achieve your goals including successfully resolving the cause of your anxiety.

a. Affirmations should create inner ease rather than inner uneasiness. So if you are affirming, 'I feel calm' and this is creating inner uneasiness, temporarily affirm, 'I am becoming increasingly calm every day' and then once your inner peace has grown, with thanks to your self-talk and ensuing emotions and behaviours, then you can affirm, 'I feel calm'. Your bodily sensations and inner critic will instantly tell you if something feels comfortable or not, so use those to inform your affirmation creation process.

b. Create your affirmations in the present tense to reflect that you already think a certain way and/or already possess certain qualities, for example:

- 'I have mental clarity.' (Or 'I have increasing mental clarity.')
- 'I am capable of achieving anything I set my mind to.'
- 'I am compassionate and patient with myself.'
- 'I am skilled at resolving my anxiety.'
- 'I always find solutions, quickly.'
- 'I look after my mind and body.'
- 'I communicate well with my loved ones.'

c. You want to make a habit of talking to yourself in a self-serving way so that positive statements about yourself, your capabilities and the world at large, become part of your routine. Therefore, affirm these statements as often as you can but at least first thing in the morning and last thing at night, repeating each one a few times, as desired. The former will help set your day up with a self-serving focus. The latter will help you to absorb it in your relaxed state, and the statements will also be fresh in your mind so that whilst you sleep, your brain can consolidate them as memories and aim to problem-solve how you can become or achieve those things, too. More on this later.

The Power of Your Thoughts May Surprise You

To finish off, so that you see just how integral to anxiety levels thoughts are, allow me to share some really fascinating experiments with you. We saw earlier with the help of the thought-feedback cycle that your thoughts steer your life. Negatively or positively, your thoughts steer your life. Thoughts also help you to achieve things you may not think possible. Thoughts are incredibly powerful. Think of placebos, for example. Placebos work because we expect them to work – we **think** they are going to work. Like a sugar pill you've swallowed or the surgical procedure you believe you've had, placebos aren't really the substance itself rather; the placebo is the mind's expectation that something is going to work. In recent years placebo research has gained popularity again to help us understand how our thoughts can physically impact our brain and body.

The placebo effect occurs because of a psychosocial context effect, i.e. different social stimuli such as words (e.g. false suggestions) and rituals (e.g. a fake 'surgery') can actually change how the brain works.[31] Placebo effects have been noted in research even after accounting for other plausible causes for their positive effects, e.g. a client's disease naturally going into remission. The processes that take place within the brain and body after a placebo has been administered have been found to be the same as the processes that take place when the actual drugs take effect, which fascinatingly demonstrates that our thoughts alone can make tangible changes to our brain and body; **we can *actually make things happen* inside our brain and body with just our thoughts**. Also, if the prefrontal cortex is damaged in some way, as happens in people with Alzheimer's type dementia, placebo effects either don't work as well or do not work at all. Therefore, the reasoning, problem-solving, decision-making part of the brain needs to work for us to make actual physical changes within, purely with the use of our thoughts...which makes sense, further confirming the power of our thoughts.

It has also been found that anxiety can be reduced by the mere suggestion that a drug has been swallowed that will reduce anxiety when in reality no such drug has been given. In one experiment, over two thirds of the participants in the study reported decreases in how unpleasant they perceived unpleasant images shown to be, purely because they believed they had swallowed an anti-anxiety drug that would produce this effect.[32] In reality, the effect was produced by their mind only, their beliefs and expectations, and yet fMRI scans demonstrated that brain regions involved in pain control also became activated, regions that become active when people take an actual opioid pain relief drug (e.g. codeine, tramadol, morphine) or think they have when they've been given a placebo instead. So your mind can alter your emotional experience by changing how your brain works purely with your thoughts. In other words, expectation leads to reality, or we might say, your thoughts become your reality.

Whilst that was a positive effect on a person's anxiety using a placebo, the same trick can be played on humans to have the opposite effect, a negative effect produced by mere suggestion called a nocebo effect. In one experiment, verbal suggestion that participants would feel pain during a procedure produced pain in the participant.[33] When an area on their body was merely stimulated to produce the sensation of being touched but not actual pain, participants felt pain and when their skin was stimulated to produce low-intensity pain, they reported high-intensity pain.

In another experiment, eighty-four female room attendants from seven different hotels were experimented on to test the difference a thought can make on their physical health. Researchers found that the mere suggestion that the physical job they were employed to do was enough physical exercise for an active lifestyle as recommend by a highly-qualified health professional, with examples to justify how this was so, resulted in a decrease in weight, blood pressure, body fat, waist-to-hip ratio, and body mass index.[34] How cool is that! Talk about influencing your physical health with the power of your mind! The participants reported that they had not changed their diet, nor their exercise habits out of work, nor the workload taken on. Sure they may be lying or deceiving themselves but either way, whether they made changes to their lifestyle or not, the mere suggestion still resulted in the outcome. In other words, a positive thought they believed in resulted in positive tangible effects on the person's life, regardless of whether that positive thought was based on reality or merely an illusion.

Our mindset, our outlook, clearly makes a difference to what we achieve, even in ways we would deem impossible. Check this out. In an experiment that demonstrates the sheer power of the placebo effect in such unimaginable ways, participants were asked to answer general knowledge questions and were told that the answer to those questions would be flashed on a computer screen – slow enough for the subconscious brain to notice it but too quick for the conscious brain to perceive it.[35] In reality, only scrambled letters were flashed onto the screen rather than the answers themselves and yet those who were told the answers would be flashed on-screen, actually performed better than those who were not primed to believe the answers would be flashed on-screen for their mind to subconsciously perceive them. In other words, your belief about the amount of knowledge you have can be influenced by the suggestion that you have that knowledge somewhere in your subconscious brain. In that case, we can say our thoughts about what we know can shape what we know, which would suggest we know more than we think we do, and when someone or something helps us to believe that, we are able to access knowledge either within ourselves or within the universe somewhere outside of ourselves. That may sound a little 'out there' but that is exactly what this placebo research demonstrated, that things that seem impossible are possible and that the mind is incredibly powerful and so our thoughts create our reality in more ways than one. Our thoughts create our reality by (a) changing how our brain and body physically function and (b) changing how we behave, all of which then influences what happens in our lives, or what we make happen. Remember, anxiety can be triggered by our thoughts and anxiety can be maintained or perpetuated by our thoughts even when its cause is self-generated (stemming from the our own thoughts or behaviours) or externally-generated (stemming from people, objects, situations or events).

So we see that placebos – which can be made of words, rituals or symbols – can produce positive or negative effects on us purely with the power of our thoughts and whilst this research is fascinating, it is at the same time unsurprising because we do know that humans still have so much to learn about human abilities. The aforementioned research demonstrates that we limit what we can do by *thinking* that those limits exist but some of those limits are illusions we've created with our thoughts. **Our thoughts, whether based on reality or illusion, steer our life regardless**, so you must choose thoughts that steer you along a smooth road towards your desired destinations rather than thoughts that steer you into pot-holes, ditches, lampposts and other vehicles.

Now that you can see how powerfully your thoughts influence the direction you are steering your life in, sometimes in seemingly impossible ways as we have just learned, even though outside influences will have an effect on which route you travel, you must always make sure you are steering around any obstacles and dangers by using your thoughts in a self-serving and goal-serving way. Remember, as we saw in the example where June started a new job (see p.76), it didn't matter what the reality of the situation was, but it did matter how she thought about everything. How June used her thoughts determined her emotions and the direction she steered her life in.

Focus Your Mind in the Direction You Want to Go

I see clients who have got into the habit of thinking and talking negatively, worrying about every little thing, things that don't really warrant any worry or at least not that level of anxiety. It becomes a bad record that just keeps playing, making them unhappy and sometimes making their loved ones unhappy, too. The reality is they don't even want to be playing that record (or MP3), but they do. It's like they're stuck in a negative loop. Their brain isn't engaging, they are really just on auto-pilot, saying and thinking anxious, worrisome thoughts. Panicking. Shaking even. Even when the cause of your anxiety is something other than your repetitive negative thoughts, sometimes those ongoing negative thoughts can massively inflame the situation, taking you to increasingly 'crazy' levels as the days and weeks go by. Plus, ongoing negative thoughts can make it impossible for you to focus on identifying, solving and resolving (Clam Pillars 1, 2 and 3) any other threats your anxiety is also stemming from.

⊨ OVER TO YOU ⊨
Focus Your Mind in the Direction You Want to Go

When you find yourself feeling like you're 'going crazy' and getting worse over time, that record or MP3 of repetitive negative thinking is usually playing on and on. Take stock of your predominant thoughts, stop using the negative ones that focus your mind, and thus your behaviours, on your fears or dislikes and instead focus your mind on your goals and desires. In life, always focus your mind on the thing you want to work towards because your brain will work towards anything you focus it on repeatedly. Make sure you focus on what you want, not on what you don't want. For example, instead of focusing on 'not worrying every day' which focuses your brain on 'worrying every day' and what that looks, sounds and feels like, flip it to its polar opposite which is 'feeling calm every day', which focuses your brain on 'feeling calm every day' (and what that looks, sounds and feels like). When you think of something you don't want, you still build up a mental picture of the thing you don't want which then means you are still focused on it. Make sure the focus is on the direction you want to travel in and that way your thoughts will steer you towards your desires and goals rather than your dislikes and fears.

a. Write down all the negative statements you repeatedly say to yourself so you know which statements you need to eliminate from your life. It may take a few days to list them all. Then consistently stop using them as they are sabotaging you and your life.

b. Be clear on what you want to be working towards. Write down the goals – emotions, behaviours and achievements – you want to work towards (not away from) e.g. feeling calm, feeling confident about an upcoming interview, executing a groom's speech effortlessly, running a 10-minute mile, meeting potential future friends at a party, people avidly enjoying your presentation, and so on. Review your list frequently, daily if you can, so that your brain is constantly reminded of what it needs to work out and what it needs to do to make your desire or goal a reality. Anything you keep thinking, negative or positive, you keep reminding your brain to work towards. Focus your mind in the right direction.

Using your thoughts to your advantage, rather than disadvantage, is vital for resolving anxiety that stems solely from your thought processes and vital for helping to resolve anxiety that stems partially from your thoughts or anxiety which is being perpetuated by your thoughts. It's really just a matter of taking control, in the moment, of your thoughts and self-talk. Changing the negative words you're thinking or saying that are deflating you and making you anxious and foggy-headed, into positive words that elevate you and make you feel calm, clear-headed, confident and capable.

SUMMARY

Thoughts are powerful! They change what you notice, how you feel, what you do, what you're capable of and what happens to you!

Repetitive negative thinking can create and maintain anxiety. Repetitive positive thinking, on the other hand, can soothe, prevent or completely eliminate anxiety in the moment and long term, and help you to honour the Three Pillars of Calm (identify the cause of your anxiety, identify solutions to overcome the threat, take thoughtful action to resolve the issue).

How you frequently use your thoughts becomes a habit, including a habit of worrying, ruminating, or being self-critical. To break a habit you also have to use your thoughts to commit a new habit to memory until it becomes your new natural way of being.

Simply train your brain into habits that help you to feel calm, in control and resolve your anxiety, even when you're not actively thinking about it, with: mindfulness, mindfulness meditation, positive self-talk, and self-serving thoughts and behaviours.

Whatever you frequently focus your mind on, you work towards, consciously and subconsciously, so focus in the direction you want to go in, towards your goals and desires and away from your fears and dislikes.

Remember, sometimes you can fully resolve your anxiety with your thoughts. For example, you can retrain your brain to become calm again with mindfulness meditation if you've accidentally wired it to be habitually anxious. Another example is when you distract yourself from worrying incessantly about something that may never happen and which you can't do anything to prevent, anyway.

Regulate Your Emotions
With Intention

'Human behaviour flows from three main sources:
desire, emotion and knowledge.'
Plato

Emotions can have such a powerful hold over our lives even though, as we saw in the last chapter, we can change our thoughts to change our emotions. When your emotions feel really good, you can feel like you're floating and when they feel really bad, you can feel like you're sinking or even being magnetised into the ground. The positive tend to give you energy, the negative tend to sap your energy.

So even though thoughts produce emotions, and we can change our emotions by changing our thoughts, sometimes those thoughts aren't as easy to purge from the mind as we might hope they'd be. Why is that? One possible reason is brain circuitry having been wired over time to reflect how we've habitually used our thoughts and behaviours, making it easy to become entrenched in thinking habits good and bad. Also, though, when your brain is sounding its alarm to tell you there is something that needs your attention, something that threatens your emotional or physical well-being or safety, until it is fully acknowledged, the emotion of anxiety will remain. Think of it like that niggling feeling where you know you've forgotten something but can't yet pinpoint what.

All emotions can be seen as our mental health feedback loop, much like your physical health feedback loop. Just as you feel pain when you burn or cut your skin, which tells your brain you need to move away from the source of the danger to keep safe and alive, your emotions tell your brain you need to pay attention to something that is sabotaging your mental well-being or outright safety. With physical pain we quickly learn what to avoid and pay attention to the lesson, yet with emotional pain we often endure it and don't even realise we need to pay attention to the lesson it's trying to teach us. We've been acting like emotions are just a part of life but now, with technology-enhanced research and our evolving self-awareness as a civilisation, we are able to embrace what is really common sense – that within our emotions lie answers, truths and instructions. Your emotions are always a source of invaluable information. They tell you what makes you feel good and should be pursued or maintained and what makes you feel bad and should be avoided or eliminated. What are your emotions telling you? To answer this question, work backwards on the thought-feedback cycle on page 73 to suss out which thoughts are shaping your emotions, even if those thoughts have until now been subconscious. You can then also work out what the implications of your new found awareness are and what the solutions are to change your emotions from negative to positive:

1. What's the emotion I'm experiencing?
2. What's the thought that this emotion is stemming from?
3. What does this mean for me and my life?
4. What do I need to do about it?

You will usually find your bodily tension eases when you correctly identify your negative emotion (question 1 above) because identifying a negative emotion with the correct word label has been shown to diminish the brain's fight-or-flight response and simultaneously engages the problem-solving region, helping the body to feel more relaxed again.[36] A decrease in tension is a good way for you to know if you have answered question 1 above correctly, which then means you're on the right track for identifying what is bothering you and what needs to be done about it, including what is causing your anxiety and how you can resolve it (Calm Pillars 1 and 2).

A simple way to get into the habit of tuning into your mental health feedback loop is to look at it this way:

◊ negative emotions tell you 'something doesn't feel good' and needs addressing;
◊ positive emotions tell you 'things feel good' and can or should continue.

Annabelle noticed that something didn't feel good and needed addressing, and because she had been made redundant and this had made her question her abilities, she came to me thinking she needed a career change. What transpired through exploring career options was that it was not her redundancy and career that were making her feel anxious but the fact that she still hadn't put major life goals in place with her husband, such as deciding where to live and when to start a family. The anxiety actually stemming from the career change was highlighting to her subconscious mind that there were some big life goals she wanted to achieve that she needed to start making plans towards and had not yet paid attention to. As she worked towards those goals, the anxiety dissipated progressively and so she decided to stick with the career path she was on, though she had initially come to me 'not feeling good' about her work life. Sometimes events happen in life that give rise to anxiety but we can incorrectly identify the cause of the anxiety (Calm Pillar 1) as being associated with something seemingly obvious, when in reality that event just highlighted an underlying threat to our well-being or safety. Just as smart communications with others are reflective rather than reactive and require us to work out the underlying intention, not just the face value of what the other person said, so too do you have to drill down to understand where your anxiety is actually stemming from (Calm Pillar 1). You may think, for example, that your anxiety is to do with the new person or situation that has just turned up in your life but it may be that this new person or situation only led your mind towards an underlying issue that you had not previously attended to, or even noticed.

Regulating Your Emotions When You Have Anxiety

So emotions can be a source of invaluable information that can move you towards your goals, mental health and happiness. However, when you have still to identify the cause of and solution to your anxiety and resolve it (Calm Pillars 1, 2 and 3), if you are in such a negative emotional state that your brain won't permit you to think clearly and problem-solve well, then you must do something to help regulate your emotions, even if just for long enough for you to make progress on whichever stage of the Three Pillars of Calm you're working on. Plus, in periods of time where you can't do anything proactive about your anxiety, you still want to be able to get on with life with relative inner peace. So, sometimes you'll want fast-acting emotion-regulation strategies and you always need emotion-regulation strategies that are going to have a long-term effect on your mental well-being and so most of these upcoming tools will serve you in both ways, immediately and over the long term.

Looking at Things Through a Different Lens

Changing thoughts about a specific memory or situation or person in order to change our emotions about them can work miracles in terms of your mental health and your relationships and your life goals, whereas suppressing the actual thoughts we're having about them doesn't work.[37] Realistically reappraising a memory or thoughts about something or someone means you are able to take a file from the 'library' in your brain, edit and re-record your views and then re-file those edited views back in your brain's library as less negative and more positive. That way, when you re-access that file – the memory or the thoughts you have attached to a particular person or situation – you experience a different effect from those thoughts. For example, your previous thoughts were, 'My father wasn't very warm and attentive in my childhood and that makes me question my worth and how loveable I am.' In hindsight, when you actually think about your father and look at him through the eyes of a more objective adult, rather than through the eyes of the hurt child who has recorded and relived this negative memory over and over, you might reappraise this as, 'My father wasn't very warm and attentive in my childhood and that probably stemmed from his upbringing with his cold mother. I will try to get to know him now, adult-to-adult and aim to create a better relationship now because I am loveable and I want him to know that he is, too.'

I've seen this one quick strategy work miracles on clients' well-being, relationships, self-esteem and life goals. Sometimes we really do just need to get a different perspective by looking at things through a different lens from the scratched one we've been looking through, over and over and over again, without questioning it.

⊨ OVER TO YOU ⊨

Reappraise a Memory or Situation to Release Its Hold Over Your Life

If there are difficult memories or situations, old or new, that are weighing you down or outright holding you back, identify them and then reappraise them. It can be useful to take a step back and look for alternative ways to view them, or to think of the advice you would give a close friend if it was their experience you were trying to help them to view from a different realistic perspective.

Use the following steps to do this and then repeat for each painful experience or memory:

1. Recall a painful memory/experience.
2. Tune in to your bodily sensations to rate the tension it creates on a scale of 1–10 where 10 is 'very tense'.
3. Reappraise the memory/experience in a less negative and more positive way that still feels realistic.
4. As you reflect wholeheartedly on the new appraisal, take another reading of your bodily sensations on that same scale of 1–10 where 10 is 'very tense'.

Your body will tell you if the reappraisal has helped. If not, try a different realistic appraisal that is more positive or at least more neutral than the original one.

You may not feel a massive positive difference immediately but rather after some days have gone by, as you notice the difference the new appraisal makes to your self-worth, confidence, resilience and relationships.

Music for Relieving Anxiety

There has been an increase in recent years in the amount of research being conducted on the effects of music on health and well-being, looking at music as therapy and as self-care in everyday life.[38] Neuroimaging studies show that listening to music can induce positive feelings and functional changes in brain regions implicated in depression and emotion dysregulation.[39] A review of research looking at the effects of music on anxiety in healthy individuals, i.e. non-clinically anxious people, revealed that listening to music can affect our blood pressure, cortisol level and heart rate.[40] In one study, it was found that listening to relaxing music prior to a stressful event resulted in faster autonomic recovery after the stress compared to not listening to any music.[41] The autonomic nervous system is centrally implicated in the fight-or-flight response and is responsible for regulating bodily functions, mostly without conscious thought, such as your heart rate, digestion, breathing rate and the response of your pupils. Therefore, music can directly 'calm' your brain and body down and help you to feel calmer, quicker. However, the tempo of the music may be important when choosing music for calming anxiety.

In one study, researchers tested the effects of fast tempo music, slow tempo classical music and no music on a person's behaviour when faced with having to make price comparison calculations in a store, just as we might compare the price of six cans of 330ml of a cola drink with a litre bottle of it.[42] Results from three separate experiments showed that when either fast tempo classical music was played or no background music was played, people with high math anxiety displayed heightened avoidance behaviours when required to make price calculations and comparisons and buying decisions. However, slow classical music in the background did not produce such an effect so it seems slow tempo classical music can have a calming effect, producing relief from anxiety and as such, also prevent avoidance behaviours.

Always remember that avoidance reinforces anxiety because it tells your brain there must indeed be something to worry about, and because you're not resolving the threat, the anxiety remains. So if you're getting anxious about something impending you have to do and are tempted to avoid doing it, like going to a party or signing up for a course or approaching your boss about a pay rise, slow tempo classical music may help diffuse your anxiety and boost your inner calm. Doing so could help you to instead resolve your social anxiety and make new friends, sign up for that course that is going to help you to pursue a fulfilling career, or get that well-deserved pay rise.

When using music for anxiety-symptom relief, it's important to think about how different types of music *feel* for you. If you tune into your bodily sensations, you will know which type of music makes your body feel more relaxed or makes you 'feel good' and which makes your body feel more tense or makes you 'feel bad'.

How you use music is also just as important as the type of music being listened to. If you want to reduce anxiety, it may be better to listen to music to **distract** yourself from negative emotions, for example, than listening to music for **discharge** (to express negative emotions like sadness or anger) which may actually increase anxiety, particularly in males.[43] It was also found that listening to music for **solace** (to feel comforted) when you're in a negative emotional state, is also better for emotion regulation than using music for discharge. Perhaps this research highlights how the focus of the mind when listening to music is integral to the effects listening to music produces; if we are listening to music whilst feeling anxious but are still focused on negative thoughts throughout the music, then we are still ruminating on self-sabotaging thoughts, which is not going to help with emotion regulation. Again, you can use your body in the moment to know if the manner in which you are using music is helping you to feel good or feel bad, feel calmer or feel tense or…anxious.

Other research highlights the beneficial effects of music practice and participation on a person's general well-being,[44] so using music for dancing, singing or listening can be a long-term emotion regulation strategy, too.

Another field in which research has repeatedly demonstrated the positive effects of music on anxiety is in people facing anxiety around surgical procedures. In a review of fifteen studies that employed music before or during a surgical procedure to reduce anxiety in patients undergoing cardiac catheterisation (the inserting of a catheter into the heart), two thirds of the studies produced evidence supporting the anxiolytic (anxiety-reducing) effects of listening to music.[45] The researchers explain that they believe the magnitude of the positive effects of music are also understated in their review, given that other studies which were not included in their research showed even more pronounced effects of music on anxiety reduction.

These findings are echoed in other reviews looking at music interventions for preoperative anxiety[46] and in studies using music interventions to calm pre-operative anxiety in patients who may, for example, be anxious about surgical complications or death or of being aware of medical professionals during the procedure.[47] In many of these studies, people's heart-rate variability and blood pressure have provided useful, tangible independent measures of the effects of music on anxiety reduction, rather than the results being merely down to subjective experience. That's also useful to know because they are measures you can tune in to yourself, such as your heart-rate pattern becoming more steady and any tell-tale signs you get when your blood pressure is rising or falling, such as a headache or difficulty breathing.

In another study looking at the beneficial effects of music on preoperative anxiety but this time before dental surgery, researchers compared people with dental fear who listened to music from the moment they entered the waiting room until they departed from it with fearful patients who didn't hear any music in the waiting room whatsoever.[48] Researchers found fearful patients who listened to music in the waiting room until surgery reported less anxiety and their heart-rate variability reflected this too. Other studies have also found music to be effective in reducing anxiety and pain to the point where patients are more compliant during procedures and likely to require less painkilling medication.[49] In newly diagnosed head and neck or breast cancer patients, who are undergoing a simulation of radiation therapy, music has again been shown to reduce anxiety.[50] Remember, staying calm instead of becoming anxious and triggering the fight-or-flight response, which suppresses the immune system, is so important during illness and surgery and their recovery periods. You don't want to be in fight-or-flight unnecessarily, ever, but especially when you need your immune system to fight off illness and protect against infection.

Another time in life where staying calm is so important is when a woman is pregnant and when people become parents, lest you create an anxious atmosphere for yourself and your developing child. Research suggests that relaxing music can help pregnant women to get a better quality of sleep at night[51] and can reduce anxiety and promote greater satisfaction in first-time fathers.[52] And making music has also been found to help promote health and well-being in older citizens[53] and can feel like a nice stress release for musicians old and new.

The message is clear, if you want to calm your mind and body, relaxing music is a great and easily accessible tool. Use it to distract yourself temporarily from your worries, like when relentless rumination is making you oh so miserable, or use it to physiologically calm your mind and body down so that you can feel better immediately and problem-solve and resolve your anxiety more quickly and easily.

⊨ OVER TO YOU ⊨

Use Music to Soothe

Music makes a great distraction tool and a great soothing tool to help quell our anxiety symptoms.

The music should feel calming rather than stimulating, so tune into your body and see which songs hinder and which help, which stimulate and which calm.

Good options are music with a steady, gentle tempo like slow tempo classical music or steady instrumental music. You also want to ensure you are using the music for distraction rather than discharge (to express negative emotions like sadness or anger).

It's best to have a go-to playlist saved on your phone or laptop or saved as a 'calming playlist' in your Youtube or Spotify account, so that when the moment arises it's easy for you to instantly employ this soothing tool.

Dancing to Relieve Anxiety

Dancing is an important part of some cultures and even forms part of their good health and well-being strategy. For example, in African culture dance can be used as a form of individual healing and community healing when someone is going through psychological trauma. Also, some African societies tend to emphasise the social causes and impact of one person's illness in terms of the individual's relationship to the community and the spiritual world.[54] It's a wonderfully holistic view, one that encompasses society and quite rightly acknowledges the effect an individual has on society and vice versa.

In other cultures, dance is used for celebration or entertainment. For many, however, dance is something that is either performed professionally or not at all. Whether performed recreationally or professionally, dance is a fantastic way for people to regulate their emotions and maintain resilience for brain, body and mental health. Dancing is therapeutic. In a study of 474 non-professional adult dancers, participants completed a survey about their perceptions of the well-being effects they experience as a result of dancing recreationally.[55] Numerous beneficial effects on their emotional, physical, social and spiritual well-being were mentioned, including benefiting their self-esteem and their ability to cope with stress and challenges, helping them to stay in physical shape, reducing pain and improving posture. Other benefits that really excite me are these I want to share with you. People reported that dancing:

◊ makes them feel happy / elated / pleased / euphoric;

◊ helps them to feel released / relaxed / balanced;

◊ makes them feel energetic / alert / strong;

◊ helps them to express emotions;

◊ reduces negative feelings;

◊ help them to feel positive;

◊ improves their self-confidence;

◊ helps them to be in harmony with themselves;

◊ makes them more receptive / highly productive / focused;

◊ gives them a feeling of togetherness / affiliation;

◊ helps them to relax / rest the mind;

◊ helps them to forget worries / problems / negative thoughts;

◊ helps them to get rid of everyday hassles / get away from the everyday;

◊ helps them to nourish the soul.

What incredible benefits for emotion regulation and mental well-being in general! Whether you dance socially when out, in a dance studio at a fitness class, professionally on a stage or at home in the privacy of your bedroom, the benefits of dancing can again be tested by using your body as a device for measuring tension or anxiety, relaxation or inner calm. There is certainly something incredible that happens when you allow your mind to focus on the music and the movement and when you allow yourself to express and/or release emotion. Sometimes it is as though you have shaken or even flung those emotions from your body. It's interesting how the shaking of anxiety from your body can be all you need sometimes to shake it from your mind; for example, when we're having relentless negative thoughts, the distraction and movement that the music provides helps us to dispel the anxiety, even if just for a while.

Plus, like all physical exercise, because dancing creates movement in your body and puts your focus on the music and the movement rather than your problems, it can be fantastically transformative when you feel stuck in your mind, stuck in life and are searching for solutions to problems. When you read the chapter on problem-solving (p.213) you'll notice two very specific research-based reasons why dancing can help you to gain answers and epiphanies. You may well find yourself stopping every so often to jot down answers and solutions that have 'magically' revealed themselves to you mid-dance, answers and solutions that will help you to solve and resolve your current anxiety completely (Calm Pillars 1 and 2).

Dancing also helps the brain to reap benefits similar to those we reap from physical exercise, such as a release of pain-reducing endorphins which make us feel happier, memory improvement and strengthened neuronal connections in the brain, which help us to learn and retain skills, as well as exercising several brain regions at once.[56] Included are the motor cortex (involved in the planning, control, and execution of voluntary movement), the somatosensory cortex (responsible for motor control and plays a role in eye-hand coordination), the basal ganglia (work with brain regions to smoothly coordinate movement), and the cerebellum (coordinates and regulates fine and complex body movements). So dance is good for mental health and mental agility, skills you want to retain for overcoming anxiety throughout your life and for general health and happiness; and remember, you have a 'use it or lose it brain' so dancing is a way to ensure you retain good physical and mental health throughout your life.

In a study looking at the effects of cognitive- and physical-leisure activities on the risk of developing dementia in the elderly, researchers found that of eleven different types of physical activity, including swimming, cycling, tennis and golf, only one of the activities studied lowered participants' risk of dementia – and that physical leisure activity was dance![57] It is possible that this is due to so many brain regions being employed and exercised and integrated.

In a study looking at the effects of dance on well-being in young women, researchers noted that young women who practised dance regularly (in one of three dance schools) were more mindful and expressed greater life satisfaction than those who did not practise any kind of dancing or sport.[59]

In another study on even younger females, adolescents between age 13 and 18 years who struggled with stress, a depressed mood and/or low self-worth, attended 75-minute dance classes twice a week for eight months with a focus on joy of the movement, not on performance.[60] After the eight months, the girls in the dance group reported improved self-rated health and this improvement remained a year after the intervention.

In another study, researchers studied the effect of ballroom dancing on those dancing recreationally, on competitive dancers doing ordinary training, and on competitive dancers taking part in a dance competition.[61] The study looked at the effect of dancing on tense arousal (tension and nervousness vs. relaxation and calmness), energetic arousal (vigour and energy vs. fatigue and tiredness) and hedonic tone (pleasantness vs. unpleasantness). Results found that the group of recreational dancers had significantly higher hedonic tone after dancing, reflecting their being pleased, optimistic and happy, whilst competitive dancing resulted in low hedonic tone, associated with being sad, depressed and dissatisfied. Amateur dancers felt generally positive after dancing, echoing results from other studies which have demonstrated that well-being increases and depression and psychological distress decrease as a consequence of recreational dancing. All dancers experienced a reduction in tension and nervousness and an increase in relaxation and calmness, perhaps because it is an energetic physical activity. Lastly, whilst taking part in competition reduced energy levels for the competitive dancers, the recreational dancers reported an increase in energy after dancing. So recreational dancing clearly benefits us at any age and may produce lasting mental and physical health benefits that are going to contribute to great brain, body and mental health as we age. Wow, all that from a little boogie in the privacy of your own home, or out partying with friends or during a fun dance class!

⊨ OVER TO YOU ⊨

Use Dancing to Soothe and Problem-Solve

Use dancing as and when required to help soothe anxiety symptoms and find inspiration for problem-solving your anxiety as you work out and apply Calm Pillars 1, 2 and 3 (identify the cause of your anxiety, find solutions, take thoughtful action to resolve it).

Use dancing regularly to help keep the mind fit, e.g. three to five times a week.

You can dance: (a) in the privacy of your own home, (b) out partying with friends, or (c) during a fun dance class.

Decide on your best option, something accessible, fun and sustainable long term.

It can help to have a 'feel-good' playlist of music saved on your phone, or in a music account such as YouTube or Spotify so that when the moment arises, it's easy for you to instantly employ this anxiety-soothing tool.

⊨⊨

Art for Regulating Emotions and Problem-Solving

Art can be another way to regulate your emotions, whether in the moment for calm or to help you overcome the anxiety altogether.

It's as though we somehow purge negative emotions from the mind and body by artistically expressing ourselves. Whilst the cause of your anxiety may remain, distracting yourself from it when you cannot do anything about it or when you're too mentally exhausted to work on it, can provide much needed relief for your mental and physical well-being. Art, however, can also help you to resolve the anxiety-causing issue itself, either directly or indirectly, as we'll see in a moment. Indirectly, art can help because regulating your emotions from anxious to calm or calmer, even if just temporarily, helps you to think and problem-solve better again, so that you can easily indulge all three pillars of calm: identify the cause of your anxiety (Calm Pillar 1), identify solutions to overcome the threat (Calm Pillar 2) and take thoughtful action to resolve the issue (Calm Pillar 3). Directly, you can use art to help you to work out what Calm Pillars 1, 2 and 3 actually are.

There is something about creativity that helps us to relax, and not just because it distracts our brain from the thing we are worrying about. For example, in one study, participants were either assigned to participate in (a) an individual art project, (b) a group art project, or (c) given a puzzle to play with or paper to read without any requirements to finish either.[62] Those who participated in either the individual or group art project significantly reduced their anxiety levels, whereas those in the puzzle-solving-or-newspaper-reading group did not. Other studies have similarly found that a short period of making art can result in signifiant decreases in anxiety.[63] Feel like you're wasting time by painting or drawing when you've got so many other chores or a family to take care of? Think again. That art session may be exactly what you need to help you be there for your family and get your life in order. Never feel guilty about taking a little time out to regulate your emotions and/or reenergise; it's the only way you can be there for others, be happy within yourself and achieve your goals to the best of your ability.

Similar positive results have been found for victims of bullying whereby an art-therapy intervention reduced anxiety levels in bullied anxious people.[64] In this study, researchers used art therapy to help bullied participants express the source of their anxiety or express their traumatic experiences through the medium of drawing, as well as identify 'a safe place' and solutions to the problem. So art was partially used to identify the cause of the anxiety and solutions to resolve the threat (Calm Pillars 1 and 2). In this study, art was used to help directly resolve the anxiety but the art therapy probably also helped indirectly with the expression of emotions that words might not facilitate in a person at the time, helping them to dispel tension from the body. Art, whether as a way to regulate your emotions in the moment for calm or to help you overcome the anxiety altogether through problem-solving, is well worth considering as part of your arsenal, whether you are good at art or not. Nobody has to see what you create, you are simply using it for your personal power. Give yourself permission to do what feels like a bit of fun-time because it's actually self-care time and self-care is crucial for your mental well-being.

⊱ OVER TO YOU ⊰

Use Art to Soothe and Problem-Solve

If art relaxes you, consider it an important part of your emotion regulation arsenal. Use art as and when required to help soothe anxiety symptoms and find inspiration for problem-solving your anxiety as you apply Calm Pillars 1, 2 and 3 (identify the cause of your anxiety, identify solutions, take thoughtful action to resolve it).

You can do art at home or at a local class. Find what soothes you and helps you to feel inspired, e.g.: (a) painting, (b) pottery, (c) drawing or sketching, (d) colouring in.

Decide on your best option, something accessible, fun and sustainable long term. Mix up the medium or the setting from time to time when it starts to feel boring or uninspiring, e.g. paint in a different room in the house, attend a class you don't usually go to, etc.

It can help to have all that you need for your art therapy organised and easily accessible, so that when the moment arises, it's easy for you to instantly employ this anxiety soothing tool.

Happiness-Inducing Activities

There are four happiness-inducing activities that have been highlighted through research that are fantastic immediate, short-term and long-term emotion regulation activities because the more we do them, the happier we feel. Those four types of happiness-creating behaviours you need to stock up on are:

◊ **social activities** such as spending time with friends and family;
◊ **recreational activities** such as hobbies or interests;
◊ **achievement-oriented behaviours** such as working on a goal that will create a sense of achievement;
◊ **spiritual activities** such as praying, meditating and worshipping.[65]

Notice how these four activities are things we consider a 'normal' part of everyday life? Next time you feel guilty about indulging a hobby or hanging out with friends, remember that those activities are important for your mental health. Same goes for if people criticise you for being spiritual or dedicating your time to important goals.

There are also a number of simple, quick, cost-effective activities for improving well-being that have been empirically tested many times over which you can use when you want to quickly achieve a positive frame of mind and emotional state. Notice how most of the suggestions in the exercise opposite are quick and easy and can be done anywhere such as counting one's blessing and visualising one's ideal future self.[66]

⊨ OVER TO YOU ⊨

Use Happiness-Building Activities to Soothe and Build Resilience

Use happiness-building activities as and when required to help soothe anxiety symptoms and also every week to help maintain positive emotions and resilience, long term.

When you maintain habits that help you to feel happy, calm, confident and resilient day to day, it's much easier for you to resolve your anxiety, completely and quickly, as you apply Calm Pillars 1, 2 and 3 (identify the cause of your anxiety, identify solutions, take thoughtful action to resolve it).

Schedule the following into your diary using these frequencies to guide you:

a. socialising one to two times a week;
b. indulging interests or hobbies two to seven times a week;
c. being spiritual weekly or daily;
d. striving for and achieving goals daily or near daily.

Examples of activities for each category:

a. socialising – seeing family/friends at home, going for a meal with your partner, going out on the town, attending a meet-up or interest group;
b. indulging interests or hobbies – arts and crafts, computer games, hiking, dancing, reading, playing a musical instrument;
c. being spiritual – praying, meditating, attending places of worship, reading religious books;
d. striving for and achieving goals – learning a new skill, creating something valuable out of a hobby (like an

album or a career), earning a university degree, getting married, creating a pension or investing money.

When it comes to quick-fixes for in-the-moment happiness, calm and resilience, use these as and when required:

a. writing letters expressing gratitude, e.g. giving written thanks to a partner, family member or friend, in the form of a letter or greetings card;

b. counting one's blessings, e.g. anything you're grateful for: your family, your health, your home, your good looks, success at work, loving friends, a goal you recently achieved, a holiday you've been on, your upbringing, your income;

c. performing acts of kindness, e.g. giving your time to an elderly neighbour, helping out at a food kitchen, helping a friend in need, supporting a colleague;

d. cultivating one's strengths, e.g. spending time refining your skills for a hobby or your career;

e. visualising one's ideal future self, e.g. as someone happy, successful, peaceful or self-sufficient, as a leader who's created a positive change in society, as a person who's achieved a major goal-related feat of some sort;

f. meditating, e.g. meditation or prayer, spiritual or mindful.

Sensory Changes Help or Hinder

In one study on 988 people, it was found that if lighting in a workplace was too bright or too dark, it lowered employees' moods but when the lighting was just right, people's moods were at their highest.[67] Have you ever noticed how easily your emotional state can change from one minute to the next because of some small change in your environment? For example, when you've gone from tense to calm because you've walked into a massage therapy room and you can hear the relaxing music playing and see the soft lighting. Or perhaps you can remember a time when you've felt soothed and calmer as you drank a hot drink. Or maybe you can recall feeling instantly more relaxed after lighting some candles. The tiniest bit of information absorbed through our senses can trigger a rapid change in our emotional state. And even though we are absorbing a lot of that information subconsciously, we can consciously make tiny tweaks to our environment that will help us to propel our emotions in a positive direction either in general or as and when we need. So, for example, a permanent tweak to your environment to enhance your emotions in general might be the dressing up of your living room or office with pleasant paintings on the wall or a couple of plants. On the other hand, a quick 'pick-me-up' as and when you need it might be a hot drink, a hot water bottle behind your back or on your thighs, listening to relaxing classical music or looking at images that always put a smile on your face, such as photos of cute baby animals. Anything that quickly (a) shifts your mind to positive thoughts or (b) relaxes your body, is a great way to instantly change your mood. Once you've changed your mood from negative to positive, you've either resolved the anxiety by taking thoughtful action (Calm Pillar 3) because, for example, maybe the anxiety was lingering from something earlier but your mind had forgotten the threat had been resolved, or you're now in a positive emotional state so you can then better honour Calm Pillars 1, 2 and 3 – identify the cause of your anxiety, identify solutions, take thoughtful action to resolve the issue.

⊱ OVER TO YOU ⊰
Use Sensory Changes

What can you use to help you to feel calmer or happier or energised or whatever emotion you want to evoke? Is it a warm mug
in your hands when you're feeling nervous or a soft jumper when
you're feeling fragile? Would you feel calmer with a more pleasant painting hanging in your office or would brighter cushions in
your living room uplift you? Could you save images of cute pup-
pies or pandas on your mobile phone if they always trigger an
instant happy feeling when viewed, or should you create a playlist
of songs that always make you feel upbeat and ready to take on
any challenge?

Whilst this is fresh in your mind, create a quick 'go-to' list now
of the things that, when absorbed through your senses, would
help transform your emotional state within moments. Finish the
sentences below. They might be permanent changes like a picture
by your desk or furnishings in your home, or they might be
momentary changes like a warm cup in your hand:

- 'The following things always help me to feel relaxed: . . .'
- 'The following things always help me to feel happy: . . .'
- 'The following things always help me to feel
  confident: . . .'
- 'The following things always help me to feel
  energised: . . .'
- 'The following things always help me to feel empowered
  (in control): . . .'

Now you have them listed, set about making the sensory
changes that are permanent and ensure the other in-the-moment
sensory changes are accessible, e.g.:

- saving a playlist of music that always makes you feel happy in your phone, so that when the time comes you can simply press play;
- saving images of adorable baby animals, or happy memories, in your phone;
- holding a hot drink in your hands to relax you;
- having a hot water bottle to warm you up and relax you;
- having any candles that help you relax at the smell or sight of them lit.

Importantly, it is easier for us to maintain resilience in the face of life's challenges when we are already low in negative emotion or high in positive emotion before an obstacle/challenge hits.[68] Therefore, make a habit of indulging daily and weekly habits that help you to maintain positive emotions such as happiness and calm, every single day. That way, when something does raise the anxiety alarm, you'll feel better equipped to handle it, whatever it is, rather than it knocking you sideways, disorienting you and making the road ahead look foggy. You'll also have the resources for applying Calm Pillars 1, 2 and 3 immediately (identify the cause, identify solutions, take thoughtful action).

SUMMARY

Negative emotions hinder your ability to think clearly and intelligently and problem-solve well. Regulating your emotions at will is one of the most important life skills you can hone because it allows you to maintain resilience and take charge of your life, immediately and in the long term.

When you regulate your emotions with intention, you can soothe your anxiety symptoms so that you feel immediately calm or calmer. By becoming calm(er), you can better honour the

Three Pillars of Calm (identify the cause of your anxiety, identify solutions, take thoughtful action).

You also can't always solve and resolve your anxiety within a few minutes and when you can't do anything proactive about it, you still want to be able to get on with life with relative calm and ease.

Music, dancing, art, happiness-inducing activities, and tweaks to sensory information you're absorbing, all help you to regulate your emotions and most are easily accessible.

Build Positive Relationships, Prune Away Negative Ones

'Be yourself, but always your better self.'
Karl G. Maeser

Our minute-to-minute thoughts and behaviours shape our relationship with ourselves and our relationships with others. On the one hand anxiety can be caused by how we think about and behave towards ourselves, how we think about and behave towards others, and by how we let others treat us. On the flip side, we can soothe or completely alleviate anxiety by again addressing how we think about and behave towards ourselves and others and how we let others treat us.

Our descent into anxiety isn't always obvious at first because we ourselves, and the other people in our life, can cause our anxiety in subtle and insidious ways. Because relationships can cause anxiety in such a slow, subtle and pervasive way, you may not notice it until that anxiety punches you in the chest or just will not go away, finally grabbing your attention. So, let's have a look at these everyday threats.

One type of self-generated anxiety can stem from **our thoughts about ourselves** e.g.:

◊ our self-identity (how we think about ourselves),
◊ our self-worth (how we value ourselves),
◊ our self-esteem (how confident we are of our worth and abilities).

Another type of self-generated anxiety can stem from **our thoughts about others**, thoughts that deflate or disempower us, e.g.:

◊ when we compare ourselves to others (our looks, intelligence, achievements, etc.),

◊ when we obsessively ruminate over others' treatment of us.

Yet another type of self-generated anxiety can stem from **our behaviours,** e.g.:

◊ how authentically we are behaving (how much we live life in accordance with our true inner being rather than in line with how others have raised us to be or how society expects us to be),

◊ how proud we are of how we behave or perform (how happy we are with how we conduct ourselves, including how we treat others, and how we carry out important life tasks).

Then there is the externally-generated anxiety which can stem from **other people,** e.g.:

◊ how they behave in close proximity to us and how they treat us (how they threaten our physical safety or destabilise our mental well-being).

Now here's the thing. We live in a society where we are almost constantly connected to other people digitally, watching them, learning about them, learning about mankind and sort of forced into comparing ourselves with others whether we care to or not. Sometimes that ongoing comparison can knock our **self-esteem**, negatively impact our **self-image**, mentally exhaust us, and make us question our worth and our intuition. Sometimes because of all of that noise and outward focus on what the world is telling us about who is good and who is bad and how we should think, feel and behave, we can be persuaded into behaving inauthentically and thus, over time, lose our true sense of **identity** or struggle to embrace the one we have (e.g. racial or religious identity). For example, as that noise feeds into our insecurities, particularly as we make comparisons with others or second-guess who we want to be and how we should behave, it results in some of us stage-managing our image on social media and presenting an idealised version of ourselves to the world.[69] Such behaviour can keep our true idea of who we are, blurry, and keep our self-esteem low. After, all time and focus you spend thinking about what will look good in other people's eyes are time and focus you are not spending on (a) doing things that will truly raise your self-esteem and (b) creating a life that feels good on the inside because it's aligned with who you are at your core. There is so much noise, and a lot of it can cause anxiety, sometimes daily, purely because we are so hyperconnected now.

Self-Worth and Self-Esteem

Self-esteem has been found to fluctuate and significantly change during our lifetimes,[70] which is wonderful news if you're currently suffering from low self-esteem. People with historically low self-esteem can at later life stages have healthy self-esteem and vice versa. I've worked with clients who have dramatically improved their self-esteem through changes in how they think, how they live, who they build relationships with and how they interact with them. There are two ways anxiety and self-esteem are connected: through avoidance of anything that causes anxiety and through repeat exposure to anxiety-provoking people or situations. Both have a negative impact on self-esteem.

Low self-esteem can reduce your desire to interact with the world and achieve your goals, even simple goals, because of the fear that doing so may threaten your self-esteem. If you feel something could risk your self-esteem, you can feel anxious and consequently avoid putting yourself in that situation. When you avoid something due to anxiety about it, you only reinforce the anxiety as you then tell your brain that the situation is indeed something you should be anxious about and as you don't provide your brain with any opportunity to learn otherwise, your brain is forced into accepting that the situation is a threatening one. However, when you get up close and personal with the situation that you are avoiding, you can realise that you had been worrying unduly and the anxiety dissipates. You'll find this is the case most of the time; we usually anticipate things are going to be more stressful or painful or scary than we later find them to be.

On the other hand, if you repeatedly expose yourself to people or situations that sabotage your self-esteem and self-worth, you will maintain anxiety in your life. People can do this in various ways by, for example, disrespecting you, knocking your confidence, emotionally abusing you, or bullying you. Some of these people do this to you intentionally to gain something for themselves, others do it unintentionally. Situations can also sabotage your self-esteem and self-worth if you are, for example, subjecting yourself to situations in which you are blatantly going to fail at something, maybe just because you need some more skills before you can succeed at that thing, or because it's not a place where you feel you can be yourself, or you're in a situation that just doesn't suit your integrity or your self-respect.

How you use your thoughts in relation to yourself also impacts on how other people and situations affect your level of anxiety and self-esteem. For example, maybe you make excuses for those who frequently treat you badly at the cost of your self-esteem or maybe you've been telling yourself you're not good enough for this new job role or your new partner. You can talk and think yourself into more anxiety and less solution-finding or you can talk and think your way into less anxiety with (a) reassuring, positive self-talk and (b) more solution-finding and by being proactive about resolving your anxiety (i.e. honouring Calm Pillars 1, 2 and 3 – identify the cause, identify solutions, take thoughtful action). After all, your thoughts steer your life. You steer your life. Challenging events happen but how we use our thoughts in relation to them determines the paths we go down.

Self-Image and Identity

Your self-image is how you perceive yourself (your capabilities, appearance, and personality) and it influences your thoughts and behaviours with yourself and others. When we have a positive self-image (i.e. we're happy with and even humbly proud of who we are) and when we live authentically, we maintain mental well-being because we feel good about ourselves, know our likes and dislikes, know what we stand for, and know what we are striving for. This creates inner calm. We feel at ease within our own skin because we feel comfortable being ourselves and we make the right decisions quickly and easily over and over again, which creates happiness and calm immediately and in the long term. Consequently, we are also able to face life more confidently. 'Just being you' is easy; it takes less effort and energy than presenting a false version of yourself whether by hiding elements of your inner being or adding elements for appearance that aren't a part of the real you deep inside.

Your self-image, because it's how you view yourself, can either serve you or sabotage you. It impacts what happens in your life because it determines what you are willing to try, what you think is possible, what you actually do and how all of that makes you feel about you. Research, too, demonstrates that holding a negative self-image can help people to create and maintain social anxiety disorder by knocking their self-esteem and that holding a positive self-image can help people to raise their self-esteem.[71]

⊨ OVER TO YOU ⊨

Ways to Raise Your Self-Image

Here are six ways to raise your self-image:

1. Indulge in proper, regular self-care (see self-care chapter), including talking kindly to yourself (p.97) and being self-compassionate (p.205).
2. Be kind to others as you go about your day-to-day life, show others appreciation for how they add positively to your life, pay someone a compliment, etc.
3. Give your time or money to others; do something for someone like giving an elderly neighbour some company; help your parents with chores around their home; give money to a charity.
4. Increase your confidence in small increments by striving to achieve new goals that progressively make you stretch slightly further than the last goal you hit.
5. Surround yourself with people who uplift you and reinforce you.
6. Eliminate, or minimise, time around people who sabotage your self-image and who, despite your best efforts to form a healthy relationship with them, refuse to treat you well, e.g. people who criticise or bully you, online or offline, and partners who cheat on you or flirt with others more than you can condone or handle.

⊨ ⊨

As for identity, when you embrace your identity you tell yourself you are good enough, yet in this hyperconnected world we live in, embracing your identity can sometimes feel difficult. For example,

if the media or people on social media are fuelling dislike towards
a group of people with whom you identify, it can make you feel
anxious about being a group member and may even cause you to
behave inauthentically because you are trying to dissociate from
that group, at least publicly anyway. That's so sad and messed up
and yet it's an understandable response to the peer pressure we
now receive from all over the world because of how hyperconnected
we are. People we don't know let loose with their opinions online,
sometimes in an aggressive, ignorant, hurtful way. Even that
behaviour in itself is a recipe for anxiety as it threatens our
well-being because it can make us feel bad about ourselves by
sheer association with a group being vilified.

Also challenging our self-image, our ability to embrace our
identity and how easy it feels to be our authentic (real) selves, is
how we constantly **compare** ourselves with others. We're pretty
much forced to. Other people's lives are stuffed down our throat.
Social media says, 'Here – eat a load of that, digest it and then tell
us how it tastes.'

For many of us the response is, 'It tastes like self-disappointment,
disempowerment, stress, sadness, a few giggles, a little happiness,
feeling noticed, overwhelm, self-doubt, frustration, anger, anxiety.'

Social media responds with, 'Here, have some more.'

All this comparison can be debilitating and cause so much
anxiety and bring your life to a standstill no matter how ridiculous
you know it is to compare yourself to something incomparable:
another person's life and one being portrayed online in curated
snapshots. You are also forced into comparing your 'popularity'
and 'success' with other people's 'popularity' and 'success' based
on follower counts, comments, 'likes' and 'shares', and yet this is
a false economy – and here's why. Social media networks like
Facebook and Instagram use algorithms to manipulate who is
seen more and who is seen less, thus falsely orchestrating who
receives those followers, likes and shares and thus who is deemed
to be 'popular' or 'successful' and who is not. Whether you use

social media for personal or business reasons, such purposeful manipulation mixed with comparison can knock your self-esteem, make you feel anxious, unhappy and even depressed, and distract you from what's really important in life: your happiness, your mental health, your relationships and your important goals. Then add into the mix the fact that this type of human manipulation results in people resorting to their own manipulation tactics on these social networks and others like them, to prove to the world that they are 'successful' and 'popular', such as using software to gain fake followers or following and then unfollowing people once they have followed back in an attempt to boost their own 'follower to following' ratio...and self-esteem. What a way for us to live and think! Social media has the power to destroy your inner calm, and that of others, by distracting you from what's real and important in your life and focusing your mind instead on mentally unhealthy processes such as comparison, inauthenticity, insincere relationship building, manipulative behaviours and self-doubt.

Another challenge when it comes to identity is feeling conflicted about how we should behave. If you belong to many social groups (online and offline) and in such a public way as we now do, you may experience anxiety in situations where you're not sure how to behave. We can worry about the backlash we may receive for how we conducted ourselves in a meeting, worded an email, the comment we posted online, or even just the post we 'liked' or shared...or didn't 'like' whilst visibly online. Research suggests that when the brain is conflicted about which behaviour is appropriate in a given situation, e.g. 'Do I respond as the professor I am in my professional life or as the athlete or mother I am in my personal life?', the fight-or-flight response becomes activated.[72] We can feel anxious because of the negative repercussions that could ensue as a result of our chosen behaviour, which could threaten our mental or physical well-being; once a single solution that satisfies all identities is uncovered, the anxiety can be extinguished.[73]

Sometimes, though, we end up at a standstill, feeling anxious but without knowing why. Other times we make behaviour choices that invite threats to our well-being and then feel anxious about those threats we have invited. This way we now live where we feel on display for judgement all the time – our own and others' – is such a subtle yet powerful threat to our daily well-being that we now suffer from mini or major bouts of anxiety all the time much more easily. Sometimes, you've got to unplug from this ridiculousness (use exercise on p.149) and your brain and body will thank you for it.

Identity Loss

Sometimes people lose touch with who they are; for example, because they unexpectedly lost their career, because they accidentally lost their identity when they became a parent, because they have been living their life for how it will look online, or because they've had a prolonged period of mental illness. If you feel like you have lost your sense of self, your self-identity, it can be very helpful to learn about yourself – whether rediscovering old aspects of yourself or uncovering new ones – and a great way to do that is by interacting with other human beings.

One study found that people who had been hospitalised in a Norwegian mental health hospital and had immersed themselves in music or theatre work with others, reported being able to develop their identity again by being able to hold multiple identities and explore different perspectives as they collaborated in creative teamwork.[74] All action is useful though, even if it is on our own, because we can sometimes learn more about ourselves and others and how to resolve problems in five minutes of action than we might with five months of thinking.

When we are interacting with others, it's important that we use those interactions for the good of ourselves and for the good of others. So much of the world we now live in is about superficiality in terms of keeping up appearances in comparison with others that some people can let this become the focus of their mind and thus their moment-to-moment behaviours. When we are thinking so strategically about every bit of our interactions with a focus on how others are seeing us (something we can never know for sure) we will inevitably be more likely to feel anxious or unhappy and fatigued. It also means we are sidelining authenticity and embracing inauthenticity which in itself is stressful because we are not truly just being ourselves, being comfortable in our own skin. And being you is effortless and so just takes so much less energy. It also helps you to form and nurture positive relationships in your life because authenticity tells others who you are and it tells you who you are and that helps you and others to find who you connect with and who you don't connect with. Never be anything but yourself, whether on a first date or with your family or with a prospective employer, people you meet in the gym, wherever, and life will be much easier. Obviously you still have to tailor your approach to each situation but it should always still be part of the real you that you show the world. When you don't, anxiety is likely.

Research also demonstrates that when anxious or depressed individuals strive to maintain a particular self-image in front of others ('self-image goals'), they actually make their anxiety or depression worse and experience higher levels of conflict; and yet when they strive to support others ('compassion goals'), they experience relief from their symptoms and higher perceived support from others.[75] That's a good way to look at things, supporting others, having a focus on others. We humans do, after all, gain from giving to others; for example, it can make us feel happier[76] and lower our blood pressure[77] and when we focus on others we forget about the things we are worrying about or upset about. Positive distractions are always a great way to stop your mind obsessing over repetitive negative thoughts and help wire it for calm rather than anxiety because 'we are what we repeatedly do' and what you focus your mind on determines how you feel, too.

Just Be You

When you create a life to fit who you are deep inside, your relationships, career, hobbies, etc., you make the right decisions for you and life feels good. Introspect so that you get to know yourself, your likes, dislikes, values, motivations, goals, strengths, and so on, as well as the different identities you hold like nurse, father, divorcee, friend. Think about how the different people in your life complement or frustrate the different facets of your inner self, that is all you, just different parts of you. For example, you may be calm and subdued in the presence of one friend and an adventuress with another, or you may have parents who still treat you like a child in your personal life but have employees who admire and respect you and hang on your every word.

Research on African Americans suggests that higher ethnic identity is correlated with reduced anxiety and depression, though this effect may only exist when the person is an ethnic minority in the country of residence rather than an ethnic majority.[78] It seems identifying with an ethnic group we belong to can help buffer us from the negativity of being discriminated against, thus promoting psychological well-being, highlighting the power of the human connection.[79] Humans can help us to feel accepted or rejected and by doing so can help us to accept ourselves or reject ourselves. They can also help us to build pride around our identity. Gaining benefits from mixing with members of a group you identify with also tends to extend to other groups you may identify with as well, such as being a 'hippy', 'goth', 'nerd' and so on.

Once you have self-awareness about who you are at your core, you can identify ways to satisfy each element that makes you, you, both in general and during specific situations. You can then also identify any areas you want to work on so that your mental well-being does not feel under threat, thereby preventing/ eliminating anxiety.

Examples of how you might satisfy the different elements of your inner self:

◊ You might work full-time in a science laboratory and then attend a weekly art class to satisfy your otherwise relatively untapped creative side.

◊ You might seek out people who match one half of your racial identity as a biracial person if so far you have only been able to connect with your other racial identity through family and friends.

Examples of ways to prevent/eliminate anxiety:

◊ You may decide that you want to increase your knowledge on a subject to help you feel more confident, and emotionally safer, at work in your new job role and eliminate the anxiety you have been experiencing of late.

◊ You might decide to surround yourself with people who reinforce a positive self-image in you, people who encourage and uplift you, and eliminate any people in your life who don't need to be there, who discourage and deflate you.

You deserve to be comfortable within your own skin and you must strive to be. Your happiness and mental health depend on it.

⊨ OVER TO YOU ⊨
Embrace Your Identity

Seek out others within any group you identify with, off-line and online e.g. artists, goths, geeks, Buddhists, activists, Scots, etc.). They could be someone you know through a mutual friend (and so come somewhat vetted) or someone you meet through an activity that interests you or you could seek out community/group leaders.

a. You can then explore what they, and you, like about belonging to your group, and learn more about the achievements of your group to bolster pride and reject harmful/negative stereotypes.
b. You can partake in traditional activities associated with that group to increase your sense of pride and belonging, whether you do them alone or in a group.
c. You can also learn about the achievements and contributions to mankind your group have made by reading books, particularly those written and published by credible sources so that the true history hasn't been concealed or distorted by another group.

Take On What You Can Handle

Social comparison, lack of self-care and low self-esteem can also make you indulge in self-sabotaging behaviours like overwhelming your life with too much, saying yes to too many things or planning your diary poorly. If given the choice you would rather excel at something than fail at it, then help yourself by not overloading your brain and your day with more than you can perform well at. If you underperform because you have too many tasks on your daily to-do list, you will knock your self-esteem with your underperformance and if you keep doing that, you will keep experiencing anxiety because you are threatening your own well-being. Repeatedly taking on too much and then making mistakes or underperforming can also make us repeatedly feel embarrassed in front of others, or worried about our future (career, finances, security, etc.), thus threatening our mental well-being, thereby also creating anxiety. On the other hand, if you mentally absorb too much information, for example, by being on social media for hours each day, you exhaust your limited energy and that can have a knock-on effect on your performance in your work, personal relationships, and your personal and professional goals. Plus, if you frequently subject yourself to online comparisons, you can feel deflated by your own progress or the quality of your life or relationships, even though we know comparisons with others are futile.

Interestingly, researchers at the University of Cambridge conducted a systematic review of forty-eight reviews of anxiety studies from around the globe and discovered that women are almost twice as likely to experience anxiety as men (female:male ratio of 1.9:1).[80] Furthermore, the prevalence of anxiety disorders was seen to be higher in young adults and people with chronic diseases, and for individuals from Euro/Anglo cultures when compared with individuals from Indo/Asian, African, Central/Eastern European, North African/Middle Eastern, and Ibero/Latin cultures. It appears there is something about our lifestyle and/or mentality in the Western world, e.g. the UK, Western Europe, North America, Australia and New Zealand, that lends itself to anxiety. For example, we have less focus on spirituality, more focus on materialism and consumerism, less focus on the group (extended family, community), and more focus on the individual. Given about twice as many women suffer from anxiety as men, I wonder whether this is partially because women feel they have more to prove in society than men and are still suffering from the dual burden.

Looking at the geographical (or cultural) differences, perhaps the higher prevalence of anxiety in countries such as the UK and USA is also about how much we feel forced to focus on presenting an inauthentic perfect-self to the world, with the sheer dominance of social media and vast consumption of digital media in our lives in general, and how that drives our daily thoughts and behaviours towards promoting an inauthentic persona to match what we are being told is important (e.g. beauty, money, power) which then causes an internal conflict and anxiety about living up to others' expectations. Plus, it also means we are comparing ourselves to others all the time, because it's in our face what others are doing and what we 'should' allegedly be achieving. It's nonsense. How can anyone else say what is right for you? Only you can know that.

Lack of Privacy Leads to Vulnerability

Sometimes we feel vulnerable to threats and dangers to our mental and physical well-being and survival because we are putting ourselves 'out there' in a big way through things like social media, websites, directories, online forums and so on. We are grossly lacking privacy whether we want to be or not, because so many people/companies have our information and because many of us frequently post information online about ourselves too, whether for business or pleasure. Every time you leave a digital footprint – any form of communication such as a 'like', 'share' or comment – you make yourself vulnerable to judgement or attack, in the short-term or in years to come. Even when you have very good mankind-serving reasons for doing so. Even when you say something positive or share something you deem to be positive, people can fly in with their abuse. It also seems the same rules of respect and goodwill don't apply in the same way online as they do offline, and when you put something online, the world is your potential audience. Common sense and research suggests that privacy is essential for human functions such as autonomy, development, and creativity[81] and having privacy is also a huge part of feeling physically and emotionally safe. **Notice how we can invite anxiety into our lives as a result of activities that we now consider 'normal' everyday activities**. It's so important to recognise that threats to our mental/physical well-being or safety that cause anxiety can come from the most seemingly inane day-to-day stuff, like posting on Instagram, scrolling through Facebook, sending important emails in a hurry, or reading an article online.

The thing you have to remember is that when you are done scrolling, reading or posting on social media, you will often continue to process what you have seen, read or done, albeit subconsciously. Maybe you are reminded of the things you feel you haven't achieved by comparison with someone on a social networking site or someone in a magazine. Maybe you're reminded of an ex-partner or ex-spouse and maybe that makes you feel bad about yourself or where you are in life. Maybe you've posted a 'like' or a comment and are now second-guessing how it may be misconstrued. Maybe someone is trying to flirt with your partner. Maybe someone is grooming you romantically like a sociopath might or outright stalking you. Maybe someone is grooming your child. There are so many opportunities for threats to our mental well-being when we connect with the world where people are either being paraded (media) or are parading themselves (social media) because we put ourselves in a vulnerable situation every time we do so, whether we are snooping privately or being active online. You never know what you are going to be confronted with so it's a bit of a mental-health gamble, especially when you're already feeling anxious or low on resilience (inner strength). This is why it's importatnt to use your body as a gauge to determine whether you want to be online right now, and to make your online world as safe as possible in terms of the people you surround yourself with.

Digital Ease Leads to Vulnerability

In a digital world, communication can take place in very little time and is usually free or included in our internet or phone tariff. As a result, we can sometimes take less care than we might if we were posting a handwritten letter and that can lead to problems, anxiety problems. When you are done emailing or texting, you will sometimes continue to ponder what you have written, worrying about whether you put your best foot forward, explained yourself well and that you haven't just invited a threat to your well-being such as an angry response from the receiver or the loss of a big business contract. How much time do we spend worrying about things we never used to spend that much time worrying about and how often do we do things in a rush, which could invite threats to our well-being? If you're in the habit of rushing around haphazardly in life, sending ill-thought-out emails and social media posts may also be a habit that causes you a lot of anxiety.

I remember one of my clients, Katherine, was a strong-minded business woman who would rush into responding to customer complaints emails. Even though she replied quickly to dissipate the anxiety and also sometimes the anger that the complaints triggered, because she was responding whilst in a state of fight-or-flight and, therefore, feeling defensive or combative and unable to think clearly and logically, her rushed emails opened her up to the risk of her mental well-being being threatened, and potentially a loss of income as a result, because she was more likely to write something she would regret. Sometimes, doing the thing you may be doing to alleviate the anxiety or anger can, ironically, be the very thing that opens you up to more threats to your well-being than already exist. It's amazing how our own simple, ill-thought-out, one-off behaviours and habits can result in so much self-generated anxiety in our lives that doesn't even need to be there.

Get a Balanced View

The hyperconnected way we live invites anxiety into our lives so easily, every time we log on to the online world, because of the way it threatens our mental, and sometimes physical, well-being. The digital world provides relentless instant opportunities for derailing our self-image, our self-esteem and our general well-being. For example, research suggests making social comparisons on Facebook can lower our self-esteem in the present moment if we feel inferior as we compare ourselves with the details we see in another person's social media profile.[82] In fact, because social comparison is such a major source of self-evaluation now, one study even found that over 50 per cent of Facebook users studied said they 'friend' people on Facebook that they actually dislike, with some of them stating they do so to engage in downward social comparison, comparing themselves to others whom they feel superior to.[83] It's a huge shame and worrying that we can now use a fake representation of people and their lives to judge our own life and ourselves and then feel down about ourselves as a result. Creating anxiety about where our own life is headed because of a false reality being portrayed by people and manipulated by networking sites' algorithms doesn't even make sense, yet it's become a norm.

Research suggests that frequent Facebook users tend to perceive others as being happier in their lives because they are more likely to be influenced, consciously or subconsciously, by information they remember seeing on Facebook, whereas spending more time socialising off-line results in less likelihood of people seeing others as having happier lives than them.[84] Presumably the off-line interactions allow for a more balanced dialogue of the positives and negatives in a friend's life and in our life and so we then recognise that perhaps we are as happy as one another. Imagine though how much anxiety that creates when, even if just subconsciously in the back of your mind as you go about your day-to-day life, you think most other people have a more exciting or glamorous life than you or are way happier or more successful than you. That's got to hurt because as happy as we are for others, we can then begin to feel sorry for ourselves or anxious about how our life is turning out. It's tough living in this hyperconnected modern world. We all deserve a pat on the back for the resilience with which we face it.

⊨ OVER TO YOU ⊨

Protect Your Vulnerability and Self-Esteem Online

To ensure you are not subjecting yourself to unnecessary vulner-ability by constantly comparing yourself to others and feeling you can't be yourself and feeling vulnerable to attack or negative judgement:

a. Use online communication and connection mediums when you are feeling resilient enough to handle whatever they may throw at you, i.e. when you're feeling internally strong and optimistic rather than pessimistic, over-whelmed, fatigued or fragile.

b. Practise self-awareness and others-awareness and self-compassion and empathy when you do expose yourself to such threats. (More on this in the next chapter.)

c. Be a great gatekeeper of who you allow into your online and offline social networks. (More on that, next.)

d. Have a social media detox as and when required, meaning don't access your social media accounts for forty-eight or seventy-two hours (e.g. Friday through to Sunday) or for a week or two or four. You can schedule updates for business social media accounts using sched-uling software whilst you personally unplug from it for a few days or weeks.

e. Be aware of the thoughts you are focusing on most when online. Try to avoid self-comparision, ignore updates from those whom you can't cull that bother you and instead focus on the people and accounts that uplift you.

⊨ ⊨

People Are Powerful

We've been looking at how we can use our own thoughts and behaviours in relation to ourselves, and how they can cause anxiety, and what we need to do to prevent and eliminate those threats. Then there are people and our actual relationships with other people rather than just our perception of them from afar or our social comparisons based on partial and often misleading information. People can be the source of our deepest pleasure and our greatest pain. As we'll see, our relationships with other human beings can provide actual health benefits or health deficits, depending on whether the relationship is a positive one that serves your well-being, helping create inner calm, or a negative one that sabotages your well-being, helping create inner turmoil or anxiety. People are an incredibly powerful force in our lives, incredibly powerful. One email, phone call or text message from someone can be all it takes to give you that power to lift yourself up when you feel weighed down by anxiety, and help spur you into action to resolve it. Equally, we must never underestimate the power of just one person to easily and massively sabotage our mental well-being with their words or behaviours, offline and online. Becoming anxiety free requires you to be a gatekeeper of the types of relationships you allow into your life.

The Good

Good people can help you in so many ways. They can be a listening ear and a shoulder to cry on. They can become bodyguards in your life protecting you from bad people trying to enter it or stick around. Their emotional support can buffer us from feeling the full extent of our emotional pain. Their physical touch can relax us, make us feel safe and buffer us from feeling the full extent of our physical pain. They can help stop the tears with their emotional, physical or practical support and instead make you laugh. They can help give you a clearer or more positive perspective on things. They can help you to come up with solutions for resolving your anxiety and help you to carry those solutions out. In fact, good people are one of the most important assets in your life. Don't let some people's blasé attitude towards human relationships in the modern world fool you into thinking that humans are dispensable, that family and friends are dispensable, that marriages are dispensable. They are not and they never will be. Good people are your key to sanity. Good people are your survival.

Feeling connected to other human beings is fundamentally important because we help each other. For example, when you hold a door open for someone, you help them, whether because they are physically weak, tired, burdened with what they are carrying or because you just allowed them to feel noticed and valued. We want to know that we are noticed and valued, by at least someone. Every time you do something kind for someone, however small, you demonstrate that you notice and value them, even if they are a stranger. When you show someone kindness, you help reinforce their worth as a human being. A smile, picking up something that someone has dropped, letting someone go ahead of you in a queue because they might otherwise miss their flight, giving the homeless money, food or your time, chatting with an elderly neighbour, the list is endless. Acknowledging someone's existence and value as a fellow human being is such an incredibly powerful gift to give and receive. Plus, every action has a consequence, a ripple effect on them and their social network offline and online, you and your social network, and mankind itself. And, as we'll see, our social networks influence our mental health.

Imagine, you have a conversation with someone whilst waiting to catch a train. Unbeknown to you, they were having a horrible day and on the verge of tears. A simple conversation with you put their mind's focus on something positive or they were simply uplifted by the human connection. They go home and instead of crying their eyes out, they decide to call upon a friend to have some much needed love and relaxation. It turns out their friend needed the same. The two friends meet up for a drink in a bar, have a laugh and a giggle, smile at the other customers, and with their positive energy, help create a better working day for the bar and waitressing staff. Some of the other customers go on to other bars and pass on that happy mood you have helped create to the others they meet and the staff then go to their respective homes, shower their loved ones with more attention and appreciation than they would have done had they had negative experiences during their work shift. Your kindness to just one other human being serves mankind. Never underestimate the power of you and never underestimate the power of just one other person to help you soothe or completely quash your anxiety and change your life for the better.

The Bad and the Ugly

Sometimes you find there are bad people in your life or people who are simply treating you badly, undermining your well-being or safety in some way. Sometimes you invite these people into your life as a new friend, lover or business associate. Sometimes they are in your life by default, such as a family member. Other times people try to enter your life through a third party, such as a friend or family member that you do have a good relationship with. With social media in our lives, it can now be so much easier for bad people or people with bad intentions to waltz into your life.

People can insidiously undermine our well-being and cause our anxiety both online and offline, for example, by knocking our self-esteem, cyberbullying us, sabotaging our self-image, insulting our identity or intelligence, undermining our authority, stifling our personal development, or sabotaging our treasured relationships, career, health, happiness or well-being.

Some people set out to intentionally sabotage you and your well-being, others do so by accident; some of these people are in your inner circle, some you only have occasional dalliances with, some you can cut out of your life completely, others you have to tolerate. If after serious attempts to resolve the issue of how they undermine your well-being, you feel nothing has improved nor will improve, you either have to minimise the time spent around those people if you must keep seeing them (e.g. family members) and make any changes you can that help protect your well-being, or you must prune them out of your life. A core mental well-being skill is to nourish positive relationships so that you maintain them and their health- and survival-serving effects and prune away negative relationships so that you eliminate them and their health and survival-sabotaging effects.

Quality Over Quantity

Research demonstrates that positive relationships are incredibly good for our health and negative relationships can damage our health! Back in 1938, The Harvard Study of Adult Development began and it is one of the world's longest long-term studies ever conducted. Between 1939 and 1944, 268 members were recruited from Harvard college classes into what is known as the Grant Study and then between 1940 and 1945, a second cohort of 456 underprivileged young men from Boston's inner-city neighbourhoods was recruited for the Glueck Study. Of the original Harvard cohort recruited, nineteen are still alive and all are in their mid-nineties, and forty of the Boston cohort are still alive at the time of writing.[85] Over the decades they had physical examinations and interviews addressing, amongst other things, psychological well-being, and triumphs and failures in careers and marriage. You can just imagine how many intriguing insights this data provides given the length of the study! The study revealed that our close relationships matter more to our happiness and longevity than money, fame, social class, IQ, or even genes.

Robert Waldinger, one of the Harvard researchers, found that three major themes showed up time and time again in the seventy-five years' worth of data he reviewed:[86]

◊ Relationships are a lifeline. People who have social networks (family, friends, community) are happier, physically healthier and live longer than less well-connected people, whilst people who feel lonely are less happy, tend to have declining health sooner (in midlife) and die younger than people who are not lonely.

◊ It's about quality, not quantity. The quality of our close relationships matters more than, say, whether we're in a committed romantic relationship or have lots of friends; and living in the midst of high-conflict relationships is very bad for our health.

◊ Good, secure relationships are good for the brain. They protect our brains from decline and we maintain sharper memories. Even if you're in late adulthood and bicker a lot with your significant loved ones, as long as you feel you can rely on them when you really need to, your bickering won't hinder your memories.

Another interesting finding from the Harvard study is that a healthy, stable marriage is important to our happiness in later life. When we're young and married, we can be learning how to navigate conflicts. When we're older and married, however, we're providing each other with support and buffering one another from life's negatives, helping each other to be less affected by things like illness, pain and disability. So, a happy marriage can be an investment in your immediate and long-term mental and physical well-being and safety because we have a built-in support network from that one person who fulfils various roles in our life: friend, lover, coach, assistant. In other words, even just one close relationship can be a source of calm. Equally, as 'living in the midst of high-conflict relationships is very bad for our health',[87] don't force yourself to remain in endlessly unhappy relationships.

The message is clear: positive relationships keep us happier and healthier and help us live longer. People are so powerful it blows – my – mind! Is it time you took stock of the people you spend your life around? Are they a source of corrosion or vitality, happiness or anxiety? Be honest with yourself, whoever they are, however much you wish they were a positive influence in your life and use these tips to help you.

⊨ OVER TO YOU ⊨

Nurture Positive Relationships, Prune Away Negative Ones

Only surround yourself with people who reinforce your well-being and sense of self-worth. If they frequently make you question your self-worth and/or they proactively knock your self-esteem, or otherwise threaten your well-being and your life, whether intentionally or not, you need to remove them from your life or minimise the time you spend under their influence (around them).

Trust the bodily sensations you feel and the emotions they conjure when you interact with them:

- people who are good for us make us 'feel good', emotionally and physically, in their presence, most of the time;
- people who are bad for us make us 'feel bad', emotionally and physically, in their presence, most of the time.

Actively learn from each relationship, tune into the bodily sensations you experience most frequently around each person, online and offline, trust yourself to know who is a threat to your well-being and who is a friend.

Identify the threats, improve the relationship or distance yourself from it if you can't. If you feel someone may be the (partial) cause of your anxiety because they are somehow sabotaging your well-being or safety, online or offline, ask yourself questions like:

- 'What is it about them that sabotages my physical or emotional safety and well-being?'
- 'What do they say and do that suggests they are more of an enemy than a friend?
- 'What are the characteristics of the relationships that truly make me feel happy, safe and valuable that I don't experience with this person?'
- 'Who can I explain my experience to who will understand and tell me if I am right in my suspicions that this person is a threat to my well-being or safety?'
- 'What can I do to help improve this relationship, if anything?'
- 'How can I ask/get them to start treating me with respect and compassion?
- 'What can I do to minimise time around negative relationships?'
- 'What can I do to maximise my time around positive relationships?'

Sometimes, solving anxiety requires changing relationship habits in yourself and/or others and though you can't force people to change, *you* can change how you behave and thus force them to respond differently. Retrain yourself into new habits and use the exercise on p.89 to help you.

Stock up on people power. To socialise with good people regularly, consider reconnecting with old friends or estranged family members with the intention of starting with a clean slate if you can, and/or go out and make new friends, or at the very least acquaintances, through local classes, meet-up groups, colleagues and existing friends (e.g. by attending parties). Just get around people, and only people who are good for you, and get away from bad people, or as the case sometimes is, especially in the online world, get bad people away from you and your loved ones. Remember that positive relationships are priceless for good health, happiness and longevity so you must invest your time and effort into them and when you do, your resilience and mental health will thank you. Spend time with the good people in your life when they need it as much as when you need it; give them your time, attention, respect and compassion. Be thoughtful and make sure you are there to support them in the bad times and there to celebrate with them in the good times.

Vet everyone, for your health, happiness and survival's sake. Regardless of whether you invited someone into your personal social network or someone else did, don't be afraid to cut people off from your social network just because they are already in it and/or have been in it for a while. Sometimes it takes time to vet people; simply tell yourself as you think about them, 'You have now been vetted. Your application has been denied. Goodbye!' and then hit delete, physically on your social media account or mentally.

Your Mind Can Send You to an Early Grave

In a review of seventy research studies conducted between 1980 and 2014, researchers concluded feelings of isolation and loneliness can reduce our lifespan as much as other well-researched mortality risks, like obesity.[88] They found that objective loneliness and isolation as well as subjective feelings of loneliness and isolation (even when the person is not objectively lonely and isolated) predicted a greater risk of death, at a rate similar to obesity. That's the power of your thoughts! Your mere perception of your life can kill you off younger, even if it is not based on objective reality. Remember we spoke before about improving your well-being and your life by replacing negative thoughts with positive thoughts and how, even when the thoughts may not reflect reality, they still shape your well-being and your life? This loneliness research highlights just how true this is and just how extremely your thoughts can affect you and your survival. So what might your anxious thoughts be doing to your health? Well, a statistical review of 203 studies from twenty-nine countries in six continents left researchers concluding that mental health disorders, including anxiety and depression, resulted in a lifespan that was ten years shorter on average compared with their mentally healthy counterparts.[89] Yikes!

So positive relationships and positive thoughts are crucial for a happy, healthy, long life and yet, when we need a good dose of positive people power, we can fool ourselves into thinking that we're getting it when we're not. It's so important to seek out quality interactions when you need a bigger dose of the drug that is human connection. Research suggests that social media can positively impact our well-being when we are seeking to feel connected to other human beings but face-to-face communication both enhances our well-being when we want to feel connected to other humans *and* helps when we want to avoid social isolation.[90] Social media, it seems, is limited in terms of the positive well-being effects it can give us, so be sure to seek out face-to-face interactions if you are feeling lonely or isolated and it will make a difference to your mental well-being and how long you live.

Whilst social media may be limited in its mental well-being and life satisfaction effects, it does sometimes serve a positive role as well as a negative role and that's what you need to remember – because social media is now a part of most peoples lives, even when we only join social networking sites to please a friend or family member. A review of how anxiety and depression relate to the use of social networking sites such as Facebook suggests that experiencing positive interactions and social support and feeling connected to others on social networking sites are consistently related to lower levels of anxiety and depression, whereas negative interactions and social comparisons on social networking sites are related to higher levels of anxiety and depression.[91]

People Communicate In An Unseen, Unheard Way

In this hyperconnected society, the focus of communication in relationships is nearly always on verbal communication and on non-verbal communication such as body language, tone of voice and facial expressions. However, there is another form of communication taking place that is unseen and unheard. That form of communication may be influencing how you feel around others and your well-being. Heck, I wonder whether this is one of the reasons poor mental health rates are so high these days, aside from, or in addition to, the fact that we're so excessively vulnerable to well-being threats because of this hyperconnected way we now live online.

The human heart is a source of intelligence with its own independent complex nervous system known as the 'heart–brain'.[92] The heart makes many of its own decisions independently of the brain, and is in a constant two-way dialogue with the brain. The heart beats because of an electrical signal generated from within your heart muscle.[93] Researchers have found that the electromagnetic field produced by the human heart can be detected up to several feet away and can actually register in the brain activity or body surfaces of people in close proximity or touching, such as their legs and forearms and scalp.[94] Given that information about our emotional state is also encoded in our heart's electromagnetic field[95] (because different emotions create different heart rhythm patterns), it's possible our heart communicates our emotions via the electromagnetic field it emits, to other people nearby or touching. This is interesting when you think about how we hear people say, 'I got a weird vibe from him' or 'I picked up on her energy'. Is it possible that you can pick up on messages that someone is a threat to your well-being, even though their words, body language and actions may not be obviously conveying this at first? Can other people's emotional state affect ours?

Our Body Communicates with Itself

Firstly, it's important to note that our heart rhythm patterns can affect our health and well-being. For example, when we first perceive a threat, the heart needs to decelerate initially in order to allow us to pay attention and regulate our emotional response and then accelerate to support us taking action. People with high HRV (more variance in beat-to-beat changes) have a better ability to switch between different responses (stay calm, take action) in stressful situations while research has shown a relationship between low HRV and worsening depression or anxiety.[96] Interestingly, soldiers with PTSD seem to experience a disruption in their ability to respond appropriately to a perceived threat and have been found to have reduced HRV. A small pilot study has found that those trained in generating a calm, positive state at will (or a 'coherent state') improved their ability to self-regulate their emotions and improved their cognitive functions such as information processing and learning.[97]

Below I share a quick breathing technique for achieving that calm, positive state at will. This will help you to deal with the ups and downs of life much more appropriately, giving you greater in-the-moment control over your self and (threatening) situations. Instantly need to calm down your physical and psychological anxiety symptoms? This quick breathing technique can be great because sometimes it's easier to calm the body down to calm your brain down. It will also help you to honour the Three Pillars of

Calm – identify cause, identify solutions, take action – so that you can eliminate your anxiety altogether; and it may also be a solution itself (Calm Pillar 2) if your anxiety is self-generated through your thoughts and behaviours such as in PTSD or OCD where no real threats are present.

⊨ OVER TO YOU ⊨

A Quick Breathing Technique for Achieving a Calm State

You can do this discreetly, anywhere, without others even realising what you are doing.

You will know when you feel calm as your body will feel calm and your heart area will feel relaxed.

When you feel yourself getting tense, you can calm yourself by repeating these steps about four to seven times (or about a minute), eyes open or closed:

a. Inhale deeply for about three to five seconds as you simultaneously focus your mind on your heart area and imagine yourself inhaling calm into the heart.[98]
b. Hold your breath for about three to five seconds.
c. Exhale deeply for about three to five seconds as you simultaneously focus your mind on your heart area and imagine yourself exhaling tension from the heart.

Instead of imagining breathing in calm and breathing out tension, you might find it helpful to focus on feeling the love or appreciation you have for someone or something.

⊨——⊨

This can be a great way to get yourself into a cool, calm, collected state rapidly (and secretly), even when mid-conversation with other humans, especially if they trigger anxiety. People can impact your emotions without even meaning to. Now, given your own heart rate affects your health and well-being, how do other people's heart-rates affect you? Let's see.

Our Body Communicates with Others' Bodies

The relationship we have with ourselves can influence others in unseen, unheard ways. When we induce a calm, positive ('coherent') state within ourselves, it's possible we can spookily influence others nearby to also achieve a calm, positive state. Results from 148 ten-minute trials involving six different experimental procedures with fifteen people trained in achieving a calm, positive state at will using that type of breathing technique above, and twenty-five untrained volunteers, demonstrated that when people collectively focused on achieving a calm, positive state themselves, they were able to influence the HRV of another person.[99] If the trained participant 'sending' the calm, positive state to the untrained 'receiver' focused on trying to change the other persons HRV, the results weren't so great, but when they focused on merely achieving that calm, positive state themselves, they were able to change the heart rhythms of another person as a by-product of their own internal state.

Your heart can also synchronise with a loved one's. In one experiment that made the headlines, twenty-eight people walked along seven metres of glowing red hot coals with a surface temperature of 677°C.[100] This is a ritual that takes place in the summer on one evening in a rural Spanish village. The ongoing heart rates of the 'fire-walkers' and twenty-nine spectators in the audience – twelve of which were friends or relatives and seventeen of which were not related to any of the locals attending the ritual – were recorded. Researchers found that the heart rates of the onlookers who were friends or relatives synchronised with the heart rates of the fire walker whose turn it was to walk along the coals. This effect only occurred with friends and family and did not occur with strangers. This physiological synchronisation between two different people who have a social bond demonstrates our emotional connectedness with others, deep inside, whether we are connected via an electromagnetic energy field or via some other means.

In another study that also made the headlines, researchers discovered that lovers' heart rates and respiration synced up when sat a few feet away from each other within a quiet, calm room, although they did not speak or touch.[101] The same effect, however, was not found when they mixed up the data to compare the heart rate and respiration of two different strangers in the experiment. Thirty-two heterosexual couples were tested and, interestingly, women tended to adjust their heart rates and respiration to their partners more than the other way around. When we consider our emotions are encoded within our HRV, this means our romantic partner may have an especially powerful ability to affect our emotions, positively or negatively.

In a study on twenty-two long-term heterosexual couples, researchers found that couples' heart rates and respiration would sync up when sat near each other but when the woman was subjected to pain, the synchronisation was disrupted, but if the man then proceeded to hold his partner's hand, their heart rates and respiration synced up once again and her pain decreased.[102] So pain can disrupt the internal bodily synchronisation between couples and touch can bring it back.

In an experiment examining how trust looks on the inside, one study revealed that when we build trust with another person, our heart rates synchronise.[103] Whilst the reason for this is unknown, it still demonstrates that a form of communication has taken place between people that isn't seen or heard. It also raises the question: do we experience a feeling of trust *because* our heart rates have first synchronised or do our heart rates synchronise after we experience trust through verbal and non-verbal communication? Either way, trust seems to lead to at least one type of physiological synchronicity, so when you feel anxious around someone, is it because your heart rate is not synchronising with theirs and that tells you they are a potential threat? In addition to using your bodily sensations to identify that your anxiety has been triggered by someone or something, it's important to pay attention to those sensations as a decision-maker, helping you to identify correctly and implement Calm Pillars 1, 2 and 3 (identify the cause of your anxiety, identify solutions, take thoughtful action to resolve the issue). For example, if you begin to notice you always feel uncomfortable in a certain person's presence, that can help you to identify them as the source of your anxiety (Calm Pillar 1) and then further reflection will help you work out how or why they threaten your well-being, thus allowing you to identify solutions for overcoming the threat (Calm Pillar 2).

When you think about how you feel better when you are around good people, is that purely a result of mental associations we have wired into our brains, whereby the presence of a certain person in your life instantly recalls the association of a good feeling, or is it because they have transferred their emotions of love and excitement to us? In talking therapies, how much of the client's progress is aided by the therapist's feelings of love and compassion for their client and the transference of this positive and calming energy enabling the client to feel calmer, more positive and thus think much more clearly and problem-solve their life more easily? The same might be true for supportive friendships, family relationships and workplace relationships. Given that our bodily functions such as our heart rhythm and respiration rates can sync up with others' and emotions influence our heart's rhythm, we need to think about how the people we come into contact with may be influencing our thoughts and emotions and thus behaviours, and vice versa. Looking at the research mentioned so far, this especially seems to apply to people we have close relationships with. 'You are who you associate with' suddenly has a very powerful meaning.

Who is in your sphere of emotional influence whether you invited them in or not? Some people waltz into or near your inner circle, online or offline, without being vetted and if they are not a necessary part of your life and are threatening your well-being or safety, you need to waltz them back out again or at least limit the time you spend around them and their damaging qualities. If we mould how others feel, and thus consequently behave, and others mould how we feel and end up behaving, then we cannot be blasé about who we allow into our social networks, online and offline. Those people could be influencing us into sabotaging our self-image, our self-esteem, our important relationships, and our efforts to be authentic. People who are not good for you and your life can both be an externally-generated cause of your anxiety and also influence you into creating self-generated anxiety. Be careful who you hang around with and who they hang around with, for they may be causing your anxiety. There are many unsavoury people around with bad intentions and easy access into your life.

Feeling Someone Staring at You

Many people from different walks of life say that they can often sense when someone is staring at them and various studies suggest we do sense when someone is looking at us when we can't even see or hear them or even know that they are present.[104] This research on the sense of being stared at has been popularised in *New Scientist* magazine, on BBC TV and on Discovery Channel TV, and one experiment was even conducted at the BBC Television Centre in London. Over the years, experiments have been conducted on humans in person and via CCTV; on animals to see if staring at them forces them to turn their attention to the person staring at them; experiments have been done in laboratory settings and in real life settings; and extensive interviews have been conducted with police officers, surveillance personnel and soldiers.[105] According to interviews, detectives are trained not to stare for any longer than necessary at the backs of a person they are following as the person may then turn around and see that they are being followed, even when being observed through binoculars. Celebrity photographers and army snipers have also stated that, through professional experience, they believe others can sense when they are being stared at. Photographers and hunters have reportedly said the reverse is also true, that they have sensed when a wild animal has been staring at them.

I bet you can think of incidences when this has happened to you; you've stared at the back of someone's head only to notice them turn around and look directly at you; and other times you've turned around suddenly to make eye contact with someone unexpectedly staring at you. What about when we think of someone and moments later they call, text or email – did we 'nudge' them with our thoughts which prompted them to get in touch or did we sense they had thought of us and then saw the proof of this via the received call, text or email? Just how much can and do we affect one another on an unseen, unheard level?

Emotions Are Contagious

Always guard your social networks, online and offline. People in the social networks of your social networks influence them and they then influence you, whether through their verbal communication, their non-verbal communication, or their actions, or via the communication exchange happening inside our human bodies. Be careful of where the people in your life are taking you and your mental well-being. Think about how many social networks we are now in and how many members there are in each of those networks, whether your family, friendships, local community, business colleagues and associates, a meet-up group you attend, your personal social media accounts, your business social media accounts, parent–teacher associations, and so on. How many people threaten your well-being, intentionally or unintentionally? Let's have a look.

Research into offline social networks using data from an ongoing long-term study called the Framingham Heart Study, a study started in 1948 to look at the common factors that contribute to cardiovascular disease,[108] highlights that emotions are contagious and spread through social networks.[109] When researchers looked at twenty years' worth of data of 4,739 individuals followed from 1983 to 2003, they discovered that happy and unhappy people tend to be surrounded by other people who are happy or unhappy, respectively and that those surrounded by many happy people are more likely to become happy in the future. They found that the happiness of one person was influenced by the happiness of others up to three degrees of separation, i.e. the happiness of one person was linked to the happiness of their friends, their friends' friends, and their friends' friends' friends – people well beyond their own immediate social network! Wow. That really makes you think about the people you surround yourselves with...and the people they surround themselves with and so on. The research highlights that if we have a friend living within a mile who becomes happy, that increases the probability that we will be happy by about 25 per cent. That's a huge effect and has far-reaching implications for you and mankind. Your happiness is affected by who you know and who they know and who they all know and vice versa. Similarly, spouses who live together, siblings who live within a mile, and next door neighbours, all have a significant effect on one another's happiness. Other research also demonstrates that the happiness of one spouse waxes and wanes in accordance with the happiness of the other spouse.[110] Never again can we think that other people's emotions are not affecting us and mankind itself. People are powerful and we are connected so make sure you surround yourself with people who serve your mental well-being, and therefore, your health and life achievements.

Are other emotions also contagious? Research into depression using data from the Framingham Heart Study of a densely interconnected social network of 12,067 people assessed repeatedly over thirty-two years found that depression was contagious and affected by those in one's social network up to three degrees of separation (one's friends, one's friends' friends and one's friends' friends' friends).[111]

Research into loneliness using data from the Framingham Heart Study found that loneliness also appears in clusters in social networks and also extends up to three degrees of separation, spreading via a contagious process.[112] The spread of loneliness was found to be stronger for friends than family members, and stronger for women than for men.

Now, of course, we have online social networking as part of our daily lives, so are emotions contagious in the same way online? Apparently so. Researchers looked at how rainfall directly influenced the emotional content of people's Facebook statuses, and found that their status updates also affected the status updates of friends in other cities who were not experiencing rainfall.[113] For every one person directly affected by the rainfall, that rainfall altered the emotional expression of about one to two other people, suggesting that online social networks can effect the emotions of others on a global scale at around the same time. What people feel and say in one part of the world may spread to many parts of the globe on the very same day. Is it any wonder that social media can have such a profound effect on our mental health, then, given how many social media updates we process on a daily basis? Which begs the question: how is your mood being affected by the people you've just come into contact with a few minutes before or by the people you are in regular contact with, online or offline? This is why it's important to pay attention to how each person in your life makes you feel most of the time; nurture relationships with those who mostly uplift and protect you (mentally/physically), and distance or eliminate those who, despite your best efforts to make the relationship healthy, mostly deflate or harm you (mentally/physically). If someone seriously needs cutting out of your life, do it, and get your loved ones to help if need be, e.g. asking a family member to delete your ex-boyfriend as a Facebook friend because you don't want to continue seeing into his life. When you do go online, if there are people you can't get away from, get your 'blinkers' on and just scroll past their comments and images instead of honing in on them. Similarly, in person, just because you might have to spend time around someone doesn't mean you have to converse with them at length or challenge every comment they make, when it's just going to be futile and leave you feeling eroded. When you're lacking resilience for connecting with people online or offline, because people require attention and energy, it's okay to first have some time out from people whilst you recharge yourself with self-care and the happiness-building activities in the last two chapters. Ultimately, become a steadfast gatekeeper of the relationships you maintain in your life, online and offline, because people have the power to influence your mental well-being, sometimes within seconds.

SUMMARY

We have to protect our mental well-being from threats to our self-image and self-esteem sometimes on an hourly basis now that we are so hyperconnected with other people. These threats that cause anxiety can stem from how we think about ourselves, how we think about others, how we behave with others and how others behave with us.

Our relationships with others can lift us up or drag us down, and people can be the source of our greatest pleasure or our deepest pain. People's emotions can also be contagious, both offline through syncing physiology like heart rates and online through social networks. People are powerful. They influence you, sometimes insidiously, so you must be a steadfast gatekeeper of who you let into your social networks and your inner circles… online and offline.

Some people intentionally threaten your well-being and safety, causing you anxiety, some people unintentionally. Build positive relationships and prune away negative ones, both with yourself and others, so that you soothe, prevent or completely eliminate anxiety.

Aside from people being a possible cause of anxiety (Calm Pillar 1) from whom we need to guard the gates to our mind and life; online and offline, people can also be a big part of the solution, from providing emotional support, to allowing you to run your questions and ideas by them, to practically helping you to resolve the anxiety itself. When we spend time with the good people in our life, they elevate our self-worth, reinforce our resilience, and help us to gain mental clarity, all of which help us to regulate our emotions and more quickly and easily problem-solve and resolve our anxiety with the Three Pillars of Calm (identify the cause, identify solutions, resolve with action).

Indulge in Proper Self-Care

Self-care is mental health care.

Think about the instructions we receive before a flight takes off. They are always the same: oxygen masks and inflatable jackets must first be applied to yourself, then to any child you have with you. We know the reasoning: you cannot help someone else if you have not first helped yourself. And so it is with day-to-day life. Self-care comes first. Only after we have performed self-care can we help others, experience emotional well-being, and achieve goals, big and small, whether that goal is having a good conversation with someone, being kind to a loved one, achieving success in the workplace, or whatever.

You have to treat yourself right because it influences:

◊ how you feel about you,
◊ how much good fortune you think you deserve (your self-worth),
◊ your behaviours day-to-day,
◊ and what you achieve.

Your brain is paying attention to how you treat yourself. Self-care is vital whether your anxiety is stemming from a lack of self-care or whether you need self-care to enable you to honour the Three Pillars of Calm (identify the cause of your anxiety, identify solutions to overcome the threat, take thoughtful action to resolve the issue).

Lifestyle Habits

There are some lifestyle factors that may be outright causing, or at least contributing to, your anxiety. Keep them in mind as you go about your day-to-day life so that you know what to say 'yes' to, what to say 'no' to, and which elements of your life need tweaking. The best thing you can do is to pay attention to your anxiety levels, use your body as a gauge and determine which lifestyle habits affect your anxiety.

Remember that sometimes your anxiety can be wholly or partially self-generated anxiety which stems from your behaviours. For example, do you rush around all the time from one task to the next? Or do you rarely leave yourself enough time to get ready to go somewhere? Are you often late for important things? How do you feel when you eventually sit down to do that task or when you eventually arrive at your intended destination? You can feel anxious, can't you? You feel that tension within your body and you feel panicked in your mind and that anxiety can then lead to difficulty in thinking clearly and a poor performance all round. Why do it to yourself? Learn from your past, add on an extra fifteen or thirty minutes or however long you need, prepare for things properly in plenty of time and by doing so, you'll stop creating unnecessary anxiety and sabotaging yourself unnecessarily.

Living Conditions

Another factor to consider is the environment in which you are living now or where you were brought up, and how that impacts your mental well-being and what you can do about it. Research shows that city dwellers are more likely to suffer from mood and anxiety disorders than those living in rural areas[114] and that current city living is associated with increased amygdala activity,[115] a brain region implicated in emotion regulation and mood. Interestingly, being raised in an urban environment also increases the chances of a person developing schizophrenia but due to a different brain region, the cingulate cortex, a region involved in the regulation of negative affect and stress. If you spend most of your time in built-up environments, how might all the bricks, concrete, greyness and sharp edges be making you feel tense or anxious? Does this type of research also suggest that nature is crucial for good mental health, then? If you live and work in an urban area, you may find it helpful to get a regular dose of nature and you'll see why, shortly.

Drug Habits

When you get used to taking a certain drug, daily, for example, cigarettes or alcohol, over time you tend to become more anxious in general and have less tolerance for anxiety-producing situations, also referred to in research as anxiety sensitivity. That baseline calm is gone, you now have this other version of you that is easier to tip over the edge or generally feels closer to the edge at most times. That inner peace you had before taking that drug frequently is now replaced with restlessness or nervousness or something else that doesn't feel altogether calm. As an example, smoking cessation research demonstrates that people experience significant reductions in anxious arousal when they abstain from smoking, both a month later and three months later, when compared with those who do not abstain from smoking.[116] In other words, you feel much more calm overall when you free yourself of the cigarette addiction and that means life's niggles won't stress you out as easily.

One might say that all drugs used frequently alter your baseline state from balanced and calm to unbalanced and anxious, unsettled or nervous.

Research on mice shows heavy drinking can rewire the brain to the point where it creates changes in the prefrontal cortex, the region involved in complex thoughts and behaviours.[117] This is the region you use after something threatening has happened where you then have to think about how to deal with the threat beyond your initial, instinctive fight-or-flight response.

In the experiment, some mice were given the equivalent of double the human drink drive alcohol limit and some were given zero alcohol over the course of a month. The researchers administered a mild electric shock along with sounding a brief tone. Over time the mice would associate the tone with the electric shock and the researchers would then be able to elicit the same fear response from the mice from playing the tone on its own, without the electric shock being administered. The 'non-alcoholic mice' eventually learned to stop fearing the tone because they learned that it no longer came with an electric shock, yet the 'alcoholic mice' remained in a frozen position, stuck in inaction, after hearing the 'threatening' tone, long after the electric shocks had stopped. This is similar to when people have experienced traumatic events and then suffer from post-traumatic stress disorder (an anxiety disorder) and then struggle to overcome anxiety when triggered again by something similar, even when they are no longer in a dangerous situation.

In research on humans it has been demonstrated that whilst excessive alcohol consumption may not lead to anxiety itself, abstaining from it is associated with a lower risk of developing anxiety,[118] and this research on mice highlights that it is how the brain is changed that may make someone more susceptible to anxiety and anxiety disorders. At the end of the day, with an excessive consumption of anything, you are messing about with the make-up of your internal design, chemicals, neurons, and so on. Moderation in everything is key. Abstinence, though, is even better because it is likely that most drugs, legal or illegal, have effects on your brain's chemistry and or structure. Plus, if you are self-medicating your anxiety with alcohol, just like the use of many prescribed drugs for various illnesses, you are only covering up the symptoms of an underlying problem that needs addressing, psychological or physical, or you are getting a chemical to do the work your brain or body needs to relearn how to do itself. You're not helping your brain if you stick to those drugs long term, you are only distracting yourself or allowing something else to take over its job roles.

I've had clients report how easily they've changed their alcohol habits by simply retraining their brain because they have been motivated for some reason to reduce or eliminate their alcohol intake. You can do the same to help improve your daily emotions and resilience to life's stresses by using the habit-changing 'Over To You' on p.89. Whenever clients go from drinking daily to drinking occasionally or not at all, they report back how they can feel the difference it has made to their emotions, energy, focus and outlook after just a week or a few weeks. It can help to replace a drinking habit with a healthy habit such as exercising, an enjoyable new hobby, mindfulness meditation or cooking nutritious meals. You see, when you feel on edge because your brain is used to something you're no longer giving it, it can help to tell your brain, I'm giving you something else fun or fulfilling instead. Soon enough, as the old neurons begin to fire apart and so the desire to indulge that drinking habit diminishes, you begin to realise you could have done this so much sooner. If you are an alcoholic, seek professional medical advice before attempting this, but otherwise, consider cutting out alcohol completely so that you quickly experience how that one change transforms your daily well-being and resilience. Another option is to immediately set yourself a goal to only drink, for example, a maximum of two glasses on a Friday night and two on a Saturday night, instead. Alternatively, set yourself a goal to reduce your alcohol intake down by 25 per cent or 50 per cent every day until you get down to zero glasses or an amount you feel serves your well-being and life goals.

Similarly, it can help to reduce or eliminate your caffeine

intake, especially if you tend to experience anxiety symptoms such as heart palpitations, a faster heart rate, nausea or shaking because caffeine, being a stimulant, has a tendency to exacerbate anxiety symptoms, making you feel even more tense or anxious.

Sleeping Habits

Sleep is vital for resilience and mental health as it helps you to regulate your emotions and recharge your body and brain, whilst chronic sleep problems increase the likelihood of negative thinking and emotional vulnerability. Anxiety sufferers will often experience sleep problems as well, although whether sleep problems stem from the anxiety or whether the sleep problems contribute to the onset of anxiety is as yet unclear.[119]

You know how some days you can agonise and worry over an issue for hours and yet after a good night's sleep you wake up feeling calm and self-assured? Well, there's a reason for that. Just one night's sleep deprivation impairs the functioning of the amygdala, which results in poorer memory consolidation the next day and a continuing negative reaction to a stressful situation (e.g. an ongoing worry).[120] Research into the effects of sleep disturbance in people with anxiety and depressive disorders also suggests sleep disturbance may play a role in emotion dysregulation (problems regulating emotions back to neutral or positive).[121]

On the other hand, getting a good night's sleep where the brain enters the dreaming phase (REM sleep) helps your creative problem-solving abilities as the brain seems able to make connections between previously unassociated information already stored.[122] So sometimes it really is a good idea to trust that 'you'll feel better after a good night's sleep' because it puts you in the driving seat of managing your emotions the following day, helps calm your anxiety and helps you to problem-solve, which is vital for good mental health and for your ability to identify, solve and resolve your anxiety, i.e. Calm Pillars 1, 2 and 3 – identify the cause of your anxiety, identify solutions to overcome the threat, take thoughtful action to resolve the issue.

Given that sleep helps us to consolidate memories, it makes sense that cognitive-behaviour therapy (CBT) has been found to be less effective for treating social anxiety disorder when the person has either had poor sleep quality at the time of starting treatment or when the person has experienced a lack of sleep during the night following a treatment session.[123] Similarly, CBT has been found to be less effective for treating panic disorder and generalised anxiety disorder when people have been experiencing poor sleep quality when treatment begins.[124] If you can't consolidate memories about techniques you've learned to help you overcome your anxiety, you can't implement those self-serving changes, after all. Therefore, for this book to work for you, you may want to consider re-reading any pages you read the day before a poor night's sleep! But don't worry, I'll shortly provide tips to help you get a good night's sleep, anyway.

Research into 4,181 people between the ages of eighteen and sixty-five years highlighted that people who have both an anxiety disorder and problems sleeping well, have significantly worse mental health-related quality of life compared to those who solely suffer from an anxiety disorder.[125] Quality of life was determined by assessing the past month with the use of scales for eight categories – physical functioning, role limitations due to physical problems, social functioning, bodily pain, mental health, role limitations due to emotional problems, general health, and vitality. Also, one-third of those with both an anxiety disorder and poor sleep indicated that they had experienced at least one day during the past month when they were completely unable to function due to emotional or substance-use problems compared with one-quarter of those who solely had anxiety disorders.

In fact, sleep is such a common co-occurring factor in cases of anxiety disorder, in children, teens, young adults and older adults, that it is important to both address sleep problems and to use sleep problems as a sign that you or your loved one may be struggling with anxiety. The thing is, many of us, old and young, don't really think about the habits we have that make it difficult for us to get a good night's sleep and how that in itself may be contributing to anxiety symptoms. To address this, a pilot study was conducted on college students who were split into two groups, one that attended a semester-long sleep course and one that attended a course on a different topic.[126] The results demonstrated that when students were educated about sleep topics, e.g. insomnia and better sleep hygiene practices, they improved their sleep hygiene and reported finding it easier to fall asleep more quickly. Two months after the course had ended, most of these positive changes had been maintained, plus the participants reported significantly lower symptoms of anxiety and depression. So getting a good night's sleep requires effort on your part – it doesn't just happen.

Also, you know how we've been speaking about using your body as a source of information about what your thoughts, emotions and your behaviours are doing to you? Well, that's a really useful tool at your disposal and yet when you suffer from anxiety and don't get quality sleep, it makes you more sensitive to internal bodily changes but more likely to interpret those bodily sensations incorrectly.[127] Research highlights that our ability to have interoceptive awareness (sense visceral signals from our inner body) and interoceptive accuracy is intimately linked with our physiological and psychological states, such as the quality of our sleep and our mental health.

Given the sheer prevalence now of anxiety and co-occurring sleep disorders and anxiety and depression occurring on their own and together, it is vitally important that sleep habits be given the attention they deserve. It's no longer okay to say, 'I have trouble sleeping.' You must do something about it or you are sabotaging your own mental health and achievements.

Research also demonstrates that when we lack sleep, we can

make riskier decisions because sleep deprivation can mess with our perspective even when we think we're being vigilant.[128] Of course, to be able to honour Calm Pillars 2 and 3 (identify solutions to overcome the threat and take thoughtful action to resolve the issue), you want to make sure you are not making bad decisions that will only exacerbate the problem. And, if you need to gain cooperation and help from the people in your life whilst solving and resolving your anxiety, sleep will also help because sleep deprivation can affect our emotional expressiveness, hindering our non-verbal communication, potentially causing misunderstandings with others.[129]

Aside from the usual relaxation ideas you might consider to help you get a good night's sleep such as hot shower or soak in the bath, for example, listening to soft and sedative music with stable melodies at a tempo of sixty to eighty beats per minute, for thirty to forty-five minutes per night has been shown to help people with poor sleep quality get to sleep quicker and have a better quality of sleep.[130] Similar results have been found with the use of forty-five minutes of relaxing music during pregnancy where good sleep quality may be particularly difficult.[131]

Aromatherapy may also help you as one study on patients in a coronary intensive care unit found.[132] Sixty heart attack patients took part and results demonstrated that inhaling pure lavender exact for twenty to thirty minutes, three times a day, morning, afternoon and night, for three days, significantly reduced state and trait anxiety levels (moment-specific and general anxiety levels) and significantly reduced blood pressure. Those who were not treated in this way were found to have increased state and trait anxiety levels, as one might expect of someone who has had a heart attack and now must reconsider their lifestyle, life goals, and will likely be concerned about their future. In other studies in coronary intensive care units, inhaling lavender oil has been shown to reduce anxiety and increase quality of sleep.[133]

⊨ OVER TO YOU ⊨
Get a Good Night's Sleep

A good eight hours' sleep, give or take, depending on your personal needs, is important. If you suffer from insomnia, try:

- working through your mental concerns with a solution focus, in a notepad, before you go to bed;
- not looking at emails or social media close to bedtime (for at least an hour before, preferably two);
- not having lots of light in the room when trying to fall asleep; consider an eye mask or even black-out curtains if your room isn't completely dark.
- reducing exposure to circadian rhythm-disrupting blue light from electronic devices before bed; try not watch a TV show or film on your phone or tablet or TV (again, at least an hour before bed, preferably two hours);
- listening to sedative music before bedtime;
- inhaling lavender oil before and/or at bedtime, e.g. by dabbing some on cotton wool and placing near your head or placing some lavender oil in an oil burner.
- physically exercising more in the day to help tire you out and expel tension from your body, e.g. brisk walking for thirty minutes or resistance training for an hour and a half;
- having a hot shower or soak in the bath before bedtime to relax you;
- a hot foot-soak in the evening;
- a meditation exercise (like the one on p.80);
- yoga or some other relaxing activity for the last hour or so before going to sleep;
- a cup of hot milk in bed to relax you;
- avoiding stimulants like coffee before bedtime;

- avoiding eating foods late at night that make you uncomfortable in bed;
- focusing the mind on positive, relaxing thoughts, like good memories;
- focusing the mind on subjects that completely distract the mind from worrying about the challenge you are working to overcome, e.g. something immersive like a book.

Nature Effects

Most of us know instinctively that we feel good when immersed in nature. We can feel calm, relaxed, happy, and even thoughtful; and research into the reasons behind this demonstrate that nature doesn't just have some sort of placebo effect because we've been told it will make us feel good, it actually changes how our brain and body function.

Sounds of nature calm us. Researchers compared participants' responses to exposure to naturalistic sounds and artificial sounds and found that familiar natural sounds increase parasympathetic activity ('rest and digest') whilst artificial sounds increase sympathetic activity ('fight or flight').[134] The parasympathetic system is like the brake pedal in a car whereas the sympathetic system is like the accelerator: both regulate processes beyond our consciousness that help the body to regulate functions such as heart rate, digestion and breathing. So even though we are not always thinking about how our environment is influencing our brain, body and mind's activity, our environment does play an important role in regulating our neural, physiological and psychological processes. Sounds of nature, when played to patients on mechanical ventilator support via headphones for ninety minutes over an eight-month period, have also been found to significantly reduce blood pressure, anxiety and agitation and these effects increased throughout the sound-playing period and after.[135]

Scenes of nature change how we react to stress. Viewing scenes of nature *before* a stressful event has been found to help the body to calm down and relax quicker *after* a stressful event as noted by changes in heart-rate variability (beat-to-beat time changes).[136] Researchers tested this by comparing recovery periods of participants who viewed nature scenes composed of trees, grass and fields with participants who viewed built-up scenes composed of man-made, urban scenes lacking natural characteristics. Therefore, frequently being around nature may reduce the extent to which a future stressful event affects you. Being able to recover quickly from a stressful event is indeed very important because of the spillover effects that ongoing stress and anxiety can have on your mental and physical health, your loved ones, your relationships, your mental clarity and focus, your motivation and what you achieve. Of course, it would also mean you'd be better able to quickly and easily honour the Three Pillars of Calm (identify the cause of your anxiety, identify solutions, take action) the moment something triggers anxiety.

Nature helps prevent both mental and physical health problems. In a study on 1,538 people, those who made long visits to green spaces had lower rates of depression and high blood pressure compared with those that didn't, and felt a greater sense of belonging (within society).[137] The data suggested that a dose of at least thirty minutes of green space immersion can result in up to a seven per cent decrease in the prevalence of depression and up to nine per cent for high blood pressure. Research on men aged between forty and seventy-two years found that 'forest bathing' or 'forest therapy' – time spent walking and relaxing in a forest environment – reduced their blood pressure[138] and brought about a reduction in negative emotions such as anxiety and anger. Forest bathing research on women aged between forty and seventy-three years resulted in a reduction in heart rate and negative emotions and an increase in positive emotions.[139]

Ninety minutes of walking in nature has also been shown to reduce rumination and reduce brain activity in a region associated with depression, whereas walking in an urban area for the same time period does not produce these effects at all.[140] It's unsurprising then that city dwellers are 20 per cent more likely to develop anxiety disorders and a whopping 40 per cent more likely to develop a mood disorder compared with people who live in rural areas.[141]

So whether sounds and scenes of nature simply calm us or calm and distract us from repetitive negative thinking, nature is clearly a quick and easy way to help ourselves to feel calmer and happier, now and in the long term, helping us also to better implement and identify Calm Pillars 1, 2 and 3 (identify cause, identify solutions and take action).

What's great about all this research is that it means that whether you are blind or deaf, live in built-up areas or green areas, there are ways to get a dose of nature that have tangible, testable benefits on your mental and physical health, including your anxiety.

Actual nature is better for your health than images of nature. Whilst both photos of nature and actual natural environments have a more calming effect on us making us less impulsive, when compared with photos of urban environments or actual urban environments,[142] there is an internal difference in the brain when you look at actual plants compared with mere images of plants, even if both make you subjectively feel relaxed.[143] Viewing actual plants significantly increased concentrations of oxyhaemoglobin (the protein in red blood cells) in the prefrontal cortex, whilst images of plants did not. As the prefrontal cortex is involved in emotion regulation, actual plants may be better for your mental health in general and when you're suffering from anxiety, more so than mere images of plants. Getting a few plants for the office or home could have very real, very meaningful effects on reducing anxiety, increasing calm, and thus increasing your ability to knock anxiety on the head by honouring Calm Pillars 1, 2 and 3 (identify cause, identify solutions, take action).

Interestingly, a study on hospital patients recovering from abdominal surgery found that patients in a room with plants and flowers, needed significantly **fewer pain relief drugs**, had **lower blood pressure and heart rate**, reported **less pain and fatigue and anxiety**, and reported more **positive emotions** and **satisfaction**.[144] Other research highlights other cognitive brain benefits, too, such as **increased attention** when viewing scenes of actual nature, such as through a window,[145] and **improved working memory** when you've been walking in nature compared with walking in urban areas.[146] I can't help but feel we humans are supposed to be frequently immersed in nature, and that by abandoning a core part of our humanity – our connection to nature – we have invited health and well-being problems at a rate that is not necessary. Your daily habits shape your long-term health and well-being, after all.

⊨ OVER TO YOU ⊨
Use Nature to Soothe

Sounds and scenes of nature can help you to lower your heart rate and blood pressure, feel less pain and require fewer pain relief drugs, give you more energy, positive emotions and satisfaction, and increase your attention and improve your working memory. Use these tips to help you get the most of this natural source of improved well-being:

1. Ensure you can view actual nature through a window as often as possible if you can't be immersed in it.

2. Get some easy maintenance plants for the office or home, especially if your time in or around nature is highly limited.

3. Regularly open the window at home, in your office or in your car so that you can hear sounds of nature when you can't get out into it. Wrap up or grab a hot water bottle if you need to in order to keep warm at the same time.

4. Regularly immerse yourself in nature with walks, picnics, yoga or whatever you fancy doing in nature.

5. Also immerse yourself in nature as and when required to help soothe anxiety. Consider unplugging your earphones whilst doing this so that you can hear the sounds of nature as well as see it and feel it. If it's cold, wrap up. If it's very hot, protect yourself from sunburn or heart stroke. Just know which walking shoes and clothing you'll use for your preferred forms of 'nature therapy' so that you can throw those clothes on and go, the moment you need to or want to.

6. Get recordings of the sounds of nature on a CD or MP3 and/or scenes of nature on a DVD of computer file or saved images or videos on your phone if you can't get out into nature, and have a listen or watch, as and when required.

7. Decide on your best options, something accessible, fun and sustainable long-term. Mix things up from time to time when it starts to feel boring, e.g. walk in a different (part of the) park.

Time to Relax and Switch Off

Sensory overload can be hugely impactful on your ability to relax and thus your mental well-being and yet we rarely talk about its importance. When your resilience is running very low, every little thing counts, every conversation, every electrical buzz in your home, every notification going off on your phone.

Even **too many relaxation techniques can lead to overload**, as strange as that sounds. You know how earlier we looked at the benefits of relaxing, sedative music, and the benefits of lavender oil, for anxiety and sleep? Well, one study suggests that using both techniques at once may become counter-productive. Researchers tested the effects of ambient scent and music, both separately and together, as a way of calming pre-operative anxiety which can lead to increased blood pressure, heart rate, and respiratory rate.[147] The scent and music used were chosen based on a pre-study test that confirmed their effectiveness as relaxants. In the main test, the scent and music chosen from the pre-study vetting procedure were lavender and instrumental music with nature sounds. The researchers found that, used separately, both music and scent significantly reduced anxiety levels in patients awaiting their appointment in a plastic surgeon's waiting room. However, when the scent and music were used together, they were ineffective at reducing patient's anxiety levels. There are three important lessons here that we can apply to our anxiety experiences:

a. a double positive can become a negative; i.e. less is sometimes more (effective);

b. not all solutions fit all scenarios; i.e. what works amazingly for calming anxiety in one situation may not work in other situations;

c. you must use those communicating sensations within your body to help you decipher if fewer calming strategies would be more effective, or if an otherwise good solution is inappropriate for this situation.

As mentioned earlier, we are also **subjecting ourselves to so much unnecessary information overload**, whether from social media, notifications going off on our mobile phones, or watching or reading or scrolling through something when we have two seconds to spare. Instead of dictating how you spend your time and taking charge of accessing digital updates when it is appropriate for you to do so, you may have notifications pinging off to lure you into checking something that's probably not even important or urgent. Instead of using those tiny pockets of time for mini moments of calm and inner peace, we stuff them with information. Everything in moderation, right? You may love consuming information and you may need to for your work...but you also need energy, mental clarity and mental well-being. Always being busy is not the sign of a winner, it's the sign of your life being out of balance.

Overextending yourself in one area of life means you can make less time for and effort with other people, other things, and yourself. For example, when you have an argument with your loved one, is it because you have overwhelmed yourself in the day by draining your limited energy resources on things that really aren't as important as your health, relationships, career and so on? Too tired to connect properly with your spouse? Not being truly present when you're with your kids? Feeling fragile, fatigued and weepy? Are you feeling or doing those things because you have drained your energy reserves on unimportant activities? When you are experiencing anxiety, how much partially stems from information overload, information you over-subject your senses to and over-subject your mind to?

Research shows that **low tolerance of uncertainty can trigger anxiety**. Intolerance of uncertainty about the future, people, objects, situations and even our own thoughts, can be enough to make some people worry more easily than others. Researchers have found that intolerance of uncertainty is related to an over-functioning of the 'alerting attentional network' in the brain, suggesting that if you have a low tolerance for the unknown, it's because your brain is being hypervigilant.[148] It's going overkill in an effort to help you and by doing so, is actually hindering you because it's making you overreact to things that aren't really threats. So how good is information overload for you if your brain is currently being hypervigilant? How much unnecessary hypervigilance are you forcing your brain into when you consider how social media is a gamble every time you log on, because you don't know what you are going to see, and then consequently think and feel? Do you feel anxious before you log on to your social media accounts? If so, that's a sign you may not be feeling resilient enough right now to deal with the uncertainty it can bring. So consider minimising how many times you entertain such 'risky behaviours' whilst you rewire your brain to be anxiety free and more balanced so that only situations that really warrant anxiety, trigger it – like a salivating, hungry lion chasing you. Interestingly, given this point we are addressing about over-subjecting your mind to potential 'threats', particularly when you know you currently have a really low threshold for uncertainty, research has shown that if you are nineteen to thirty-two years old and have seven to eleven social media platforms you are significantly more likely to have depression and anxiety symptoms than someone who has zero to two social media platforms.[149]

⊨ OVER TO YOU ⊨
Reduce Mental Overload

Ensure the amount of information you absorb feels enjoyable and manageable. Whether to maintain healthy well-being in general, or whether your anxiety is being caused partially or wholly by information overload (a self-generated threat), manage your information consumption thoughtfully.

If it soothes you, do it. If it distracts you, limit it.

Get serious about how you spend your limited and precious time and mental energy. If there are some things you know you do waste too much time on, set some goals for how you'll change it. Remember also that sometimes sensory overload can stem from things in your environment that you may not even consider contributory factors, such as music playing in the background, a flickering light, a buzzing electrical sound or a large downstairs window open that makes you feel constantly on-guard for your safety from strangers walking by outside.

Things to consider:

- hours spent watching TV;
- having the TV or music on in the background;
- electrical buzzing sounds from electrical goods nearby such as a TV, lamp, or refrigerator;
- open or unlocked windows and doors or open curtains at night;
- stuffing emails, social media and internet surfing into every free minute you have;
- hours spent on personal social media sites;
- having lots of notifications going off on your phone or laptop;
- worrying about things that may never happen;
- worrying about a decision you have made and now cannot change.

Set some specific written goals now, for example:

- I will spend, at most, one hour a day on social media, at the weekends only.
- I will distract myself every time I start to worry about something I cannot control, or have no way of knowing if I even need to worry about it.
- I will reduce how much time I spend on activities that provide little value but cost a lot of time, energy and focus, and that diminish my mental well-being, consciously or subconsciously, during or after.

Exercise Effect

Exercise has repeatedly been implicated as a powerful tool for easing the symptoms of anxiety disorders.[150] Some of the reasons for this that have been suggested have been the obvious stuff you might first think of. For example, exercise can help you to get a good night's sleep and reap all the rewards associated with that; or the fact that exercise releases endorphins which reduce the perception of pain and give you a feel-good rush in your physical body, too. But there also appear to be other reasons, like the reduction of anxiety sensitivity – a fear of the bodily sensations associated with anxiety itself – something that even just one bout of exercise has been found to help.[151] Or the fact that mastering exercise routines or becoming fitter, leaner or more muscular may make you feel more confident and capable of mastering other areas of your life too.

Aerobic exercise also helps you to rewire your brain for calm. A brain protein called brain-derived neurotrophic factor (BDNF) has been implicated in the the brain's ability to constantly adapt to its environment by learning new things and storing new memories and thus rewire itself (and create new habits).[152] BDNF has also been found to be effective in alleviating depression and anxiety.[153] Moderate intensity aerobic exercise, rather than resistance training, has also been found to increase BDNF.[154]

Research also suggests that stress in childhood and adulthood can reduce the amount of BDNF, which, along with the increased release of the 'stress hormone', cortisol, seem to contribute to a smaller hippocampal volume in people with a severe mental disorder,[155] the hippocampus being an area involved in learning, memory and emotion regulation. This may explain why exercise-induced BDNF production can alleviate mental health problems and make us naturally more resilient to stress.[156] It seems as though, when we help the brain to produce BDNF, we help it to resolve its anxiety or depression problems. Maybe because the brain needs the BDNF for healthy emotion regulation. Or maybe the BDNF enables you to use your brain well to problem-solve and resolve whatever's making you anxious or depressed like when you honour Calm Pillars 1, 2 and 3 (identify the cause of the anxiety, identify solutions, take thoughtful action). Or maybe because BDNF enables you to create and sustain new self-serving thinking and behaviour habits to prevent and/or resolve anxiety. Or maybe it's a combination of these factors. Either way, aerobic exercise that gets your heart rate up and helps the production of BDNF and BDNF helps alleviate mental-health problems.

In a review of research studies looking into the **effects of aerobic exercise on the volume of the hippocampus** (a region involved in learning, memory and emotion regulation), when compared with their inactive counterparts, researchers concluded that aerobic exercise was linked to retention of the volume of their left hippocampus.[157] So aerobic exercise may also prevent age-related decline in this brain region and that might in turn contribute to a healthy brain, one which we can use for learning better thinking habits, better behaviour habits, and a better ability to retrain the brain, including retraining our brain for daily calm, as we age.

Exercise soothes anxiety symptoms and aids sleep. Both aerobic and resistance training have been found to have beneficial effects on symptoms of generalised anxiety disorder in thirty clinically diagnosed women (only women were tested in this study) even though only undertaken for a relatively short six week period.[158] Many other studies producing significant effects on mood disorders have used exercise training for eight to twelve weeks. In another women-only study, resistance training was found to have a significant positive effect on sleep for women with generalised anxiety disorder.[159] Improvements were noted as a quicker onset of sleep and less time spent sleeping at the weekends. It's possible the energy expended during and after resistance training (when muscles are recuperating) leads to better sleep which in turn leads to reduced anxiety severity in generalised anxiety disorder, even if just because sleeplessness can negatively affect emotion regulation, learning, problem solving, decision-making, successful communication and energy levels.

In anther study of 106 postmenopausal women from a society where people tend to be fairly inactive, merely walking with an increase of 500 steps a week over a period of twelve weeks, was found to have a significant positive effect on depression, insomnia, and anxiety among postmenopausal women.[160] Perhaps this effect wouldn't be as pronounced if you already live a very active lifestyle but if you don't, walking can be the perfect gateway into a healthy lifestyle if the idea of exercising conjures up thoughts of too much pain. Going for a brisk walk, preferably with a bit of nature to feast your eyes and ears on, is an easy way to adopt a regular aerobic routine to help build BDNF and resilience to mental-health disorders. Brisk walks also help us to dispel anxiety symptoms when something triggers them and your body will tell you if you need to up the pace for dispelling your anxiety symptoms at that moment. One minute the anxiety can definitely be felt in your body, and then suddenly, whether ten minutes in or thirty minutes in or longer, your body will tell you when that anxiety sensation has left your body.

There is something about exerting energy and creating bodily movements that seems to be at play here; it does something for us psychologically, physiologically and neurologically.

Then there is yoga. Yoga is also starting to make waves in the world of anxiety for its ability to help us achieve inner calm, much like exercise, much like meditation…and good people, nature, sleep, and images of cute animals! Yoga is also being linked to increases in BDNF levels, suggesting improved brain health and neuroplasticity amongst people with depression[161] and those without any clinical diagnoses for mood disorders but whom reported reduced anxiety and depression levels, as well as increases in mindfulness.[162]

There are some people who are particularly affected by the sensations of anxiety within their body, referred to earlier, which is termed anxiety sensitivity; others can find it particularly difficult or scary to face negative emotions and deal with the source of them, termed low distress tolerance. People with low distress tolerance can use self-sabotaging strategies to not have to deal with problems, such as emotional eating, a means of pushing away emotions they don't want to acknowledge or confront, which ultimately leads to the problems lasting longer and often getting worse. In a study of fifty-two women who used emotional eating to deal with stress, those assigned to eight weeks of twice-weekly sessions of Bikram yoga reduced their level of emotional eating and reported an increased ability to deal with distress, more so than those in the no-treatment group.[163] In other words, the yoga sessions made them feel better able to face negative emotions rather than fear them. Therefore, if you find the symptoms of stress and worry scary, you may find yoga can help you to face your anxiety head-on rather than shy away from it, i.e. employ the Three Pillars of Calm – identify, solve and resolve your anxiety – rather than employ avoidance behaviour.

In another study, on people with schizophrenia, both thirty minutes of yoga and twenty minutes of aerobic exercise on an exercise bike were similarly found to help people reduce their anxiety levels in the moment, reduce psychological stress, and increase well-being, when compared with those offered neither yoga nor exercise.[164] Just one short session resulted in immediate psychological changes that benefited their mood and their anxiety, helping them to feel calmer. It may be that these effects were partially due to their preference for yoga or aerobic exercise or the fact that they got to have additional human-to-human communication during these single sessions, but the message I would always leave you with is to try it for yourself and see what happens. Use your body as a gauge to let you know if you feel better as a result or not. That is all you ever need to do: pay attention to what works for you, using your body as a source of communication, and then simply...do it. Life is simple:

◊ If it helps you, do it.
◊ If it hinders you, avoid it.
◊ If you're not sure, keep an open mind and try it.
◊ If you don't like it, you don't have to do it again.

Perhaps the use of exercise over the long term – aerobic, resistance and yoga – and their effects on:

◊ the brain (its plasticity, learning, memory and problem-solving ability),
◊ the body (slimming down, improved shape and tone, more flexibility, and more energy),
◊ and lifestyle (better sleep and energy)

will produce psychological well-being effects, and in the long run this could reduce the severity of your condition by helping you to feel good, confident, capable and more in control of your life.

Ultimately, based on my experience and the research to date, I would suggest you firstly use aerobic and/or resistance training for treating anxiety symptoms in the moment when you're experiencing them, to gain instant relief; it helps massively. Secondly, because aerobic exercise, and possibly yoga, appear to improve your brain's ability to learn and retain new skills by increasing BDNF levels that assist neuroplasticity, exercise will help you resolve your anxiety directly (e.g. eliminate rumination and replace it with positive thinking) and indirectly (e.g. gaining mental clarity and becoming better at problem-solving) as we'll see later in the problem-solving chapter. In other words, moderate-intensity aerobic exercise in particular, e.g. brisk walking, jogging, swimming, etc., can help you gain immediate relief from bodily sensations and psychological symptoms of anxiety and completely resolve your anxiety by helping you to implement Calm Pillars 1, 2 and 3 – identify the cause of your anxiety, identify solutions to overcome the threat, and take thoughtful action to resolve the issue.

⊨ OVER TO YOU ⊨

Use Exercise for Easing Anxiety Symptoms

Use aerobic exercise for anxiety symptom relief and mental clarity. One that gets your heart rate up e.g. brisk walking can help treat depression, low moods, anxiety symptoms and insomnia, help maintain physical health and healthy self-esteem, and boost your resilience.

Use an aerobic activity that feels pleasurable and sustainable so that you enjoy it, want to use it, can easily employ it and can easily stick at it long-term if you choose to for the health benefits. Research studies suggests that a dose of 30 minutes, 3-5 times a week is effective for treating depression mid- to long-term.[165]

Use your body as a gauge, as well as your thoughts and emotions, to help you work out how much aerobic exercise you need to do right now to help soothe your symptoms.

Nutrition Effects

Much like exercise, it seems nutrition also helps ease anxiety symptoms, thereby helping you to implement Calm Pillars 1, 2 and 3 much more easily – identify the cause of your anxiety, identify solutions, and take thoughtful action.

Besides, even when you are not solving and resolving your anxiety in that moment, sometimes you need to present your best self somewhere, like at a presentation or a meeting, and if you're feeling nauseous or dizzy, for example, what you need is some quick help.

Firstly, plant-based foods help. A large study used ten different corporate workplace sites with adults of multi-ethnic backgrounds to test the effects of diet on anxiety, depression and quality of life.[166] Five of the corporate sites were instructed to eat a low-fat vegan diet (with vitamin B12 supplements and any portion sizes, energy, or carbohydrate intake they desired), while the other five sites weren't given any instructions about food intake. After eighteen weeks (four months), those on the low-fat, plant-based, vegan diet reported significant improvements in depression, anxiety, fatigue, emotional well-being and daily functioning because of emotional health, improvement while working because of health, overall work improvement because of health, and non-work related activity improvement because of health, compared with those given free reign to eat as they desired.

Now I'm not saying you shouldn't eat meat or that there are any dangers from eating meat or meat-based products but this research certainly suggests that plant-based foods assist our health and well-being, specifically anxiety and depression symptoms. After all, nutrition is your body's fuel. The human body needs certain nutrients and minerals to do what it does and to do it well. For example, you need vitamins A and C for healing wounds on your skin, you need iron for energy and for healthy, thick hair, you need Vitamin D for a healthy brain and energy and to help with mood disorders. Some people take way more care not to put petrol in a diesel car or vice versa (because it would completely ruin the car) than they do with fuelling their own body. Possibly because the human body is so sophisticatedly resilient to all the junk we put into it, we forget about the necessary nutrients the human brain and body need. It's one of the first places you should look when you have any illness, physical or mental; just like you wouldn't build a house on shaky foundations, make sure you don't try to build your mental and physical health and fitness from the outside in, only; get the foundation right.

Healthy gut bacteria have also been linked to brain health and combatting mood disorders such as anxiety and depression. Gut bacteria affect the function of three brain regions that work together to maintain homeostasis (regulate bodily process to maintain a balanced state) and together they also coordinate and influence our body's response to stress – the hypothalamus, pituitary gland and adrenal gland – the co-working of which is referred to as the HPA axis.

Gut bacteria have been shown to (a) play a role in how the HPA axis is programmed early in life and (b) how the brain and body react to stress during our lifetime. A review of research highlights how stress impacts the composition of gut bacteria and this is turn influences the central nervous system and our brain–body response to stress.[167] The central nervous system controls and coordinates most functions of our mind and body, interpreting information from our external world through our senses such as eyes and nose as well as from internal organs such as our stomach. Foods that help maintain a healthy gut include bananas, broccoli, blueberries, oranges, bran, lentils and beans. Such foods provide good gut bacteria and are fibre-rich and so help clean out waste and toxins, thus helping you to maintain a healthy gut that can properly absorb the nutrients from the food you've eaten. This may be partially why a plant-based diet helps reduce anxiety because of the fibre and good gut bacteria-feeding compounds within many plant-based foods. If you struggle to get enough fibre into your diet or have struggled with digestive problems for many years, suggesting your gut and intestines may be working inefficiently, psyllium husk, a fibre supplement you can buy from most health food stores, can also be a fantastic cleanser.

Antioxidants also help. Foods high in vitamins A, C and E, such as berries, nuts and beans, contain antioxidants, and these have been found to lower anxiety levels in patients with generalised anxiety disorder after six weeks of increased intake.[168]

Minerals may help, too. Foods to help if you have deficiencies such as zinc[169] and magnesium[170] may also resolve anxiety-like effects as found in research on mice.

Oil the system. Omega 3, a type of fat, has been found to reduce inflammation and anxiety even in healthy youngsters.[171] Oily fish (salmon, sardines, mackerel), dark leafy green vegetables (spinach, kale), chia seeds and flaxseed are all great sources of omega-3 fatty acids.

Inflammation is another word you see pop up time and time again in research papers addressing anxiety and its link to internal states. Most nutritious foods are anti-inflammatory, such as the ones mentioned above, as well as tomatoets, olive oil, nuts (almonds, walnuts) and fruits (strawberries, blueberries, cherries, and oranges).

Other foods can be inflammatory, and in research on mice have also been linked to anxiety-like behaviour,[172] such as sugar, artificial sweeteners which we see in so many drinks these days, alcohol and fried foods; and if you have a gluten or lactose intolerance, foods that contain wheat or cheese, for example.

So as you can see, the emphasis is on unprocessed whole foods – not takeaways and ready meals! You'll also find that once you create a habit of eating nutritious foods, you will crave them much more than junk food, maybe because you train yourself into that habit and/or maybe because your brain learns to associate those nutritious foods with so many benefits and so much more satisfaction as a result.

Stay hydrated. Drink plenty of water, aim for three litres a day and you'll notice how it can instantly lift your mood, make you more alert, give you more energy and make you look healthier, brighter and younger...for real!

Everything has a consequence. When you remember that the brain and body and our external environment are all connected and influence each other and communicate with each other, you begin to look at problems you experience in life in a whole different way. For example, it's not just what someone says to you, it's how those words and their meanings impact your brain and body internally in ways you can't see but most definitely are affected by. The food you eat also affects how your brain and body function. Self-care or a lack thereof also affects how your brain and body function, whether you see it or not. Viewing, smelling and seeing nature affect your brain and body's functioning, in unseen ways as we noted a short while ago. Your thoughts affect your brain and body in amazing ways as we saw in the thoughts chapter. I can't urge you enough to seriously recognise that nothing happens in isolation and everything has a ripple effect. This realisation has been at the core of my work as a coach from the day I began my coaching practice and it's one of the reasons I help my clients to achieve incredible changes in their life, in such a short space of time. The sooner you realise that everything has a consequence, whether seen, heard, felt, or neither of the three, the sooner you'll treat your own brain and body, and other people, with much more care and by doing so, reap huge rewards very quickly.

So make smart nutrition choices as a long-term strategy for prevention of anxiety symptoms and use it as an immediate symptom-reliever by keeping some healthy snacks to hand wherever you go, e.g. fruits and nuts and vegetables.

Self-Compassion

Be kind to yourself. It makes a huge difference. So does being hurtful towards yourself. From this point on you get to choose in every minute of every day whether you're going to be kind to yourself or hurtful towards yourself. If you wouldn't talk to a friend the way you talk to yourself, stop talking to yourself that way. When you lack self-compassion it's as if you're with a bully, harassing you with negative comments, judgements and impatience, making it difficult for you to identify the cause of your anxiety, identify solutions and take thoughtful action (Calm Pillars 1, 2 and 3). When you have self-compassion, it's as if you're with a supportive friend who soothes, encourages and congratulates you. To successfully overcome anxiety you need to be able to make mistakes during any trial and error process you go through as you set about identifying and implementing the Three Pillars of Calm. If you make identifying and implementing Calm Pillars 1, 2 and 3 uncomfortable, you'll be stuck with your anxiety. On the other hand, if you're self-compassionate, you'll accept that mistakes are a natural part of the anxiety solving and resolving process.

Self-compassion is vital for good mental health and happy, healthy relationships. Romantic partners can even notice when their partner is being self-compassionate or not because of how self-compassion alters our behaviour.[174] Self-compassionate people make warmer, more considerate and more affectionate partners, whilst people lacking self-compassion make detached and self-critical partners who ruminate on negative feelings about themselves. So be gentle, compassionate and patient with yourself and with the world, and allow yourself to be fallible, as all humans are. By doing so:

◊ you'll be much happier,
◊ you'll be much more productive,
◊ you'll have better relationships with others,
◊ and you'll overcome any bouts of anxiety, much more easily.

Remember, if you and others aren't allowed to make mistakes then you won't be able to solve and resolve your anxiety problem. Always welcome mistakes and failures as learning curves and stepping stones that are directing you towards inner peace and calm.

Pampering and Cleanliness

When you pamper yourself (e.g. massage or manicure) and keep your body clean, you remind your brain of your worth and goodness. After all, that's how you treat anyone or anything you care about, isn't it? In your own way, you pamper people and animals that you value and you aim to maintain the smartness and cleanliness of any person or object you value. Cleanliness is something we have seen linked to goodness and godliness for centuries, and as a society we tend to link clean to good and dirt to bad: 'My conscience is clean so I feel good', 'They give off a dirty image, they're probably bad people'.

Research has also demonstrated the 'Macbeth effect'; that cleaning the body cleans the mind or reinstates our moral purity again[175] and thus helps us to feel better about ourselves. In one study, researchers found that recalling a moral transgression motivated people to want to clean their hands afterwards (when given the choice) and that when they did, they felt absolved of their guilt.[176] Research has also found that enacting an immoral act, such as lying, not only motivates people towards a preference for cleansing products over and above non-cleansing products when offered both, but their brain scans also show that even just imagining immoral behaviour makes us feel literally dirty. Wow! So there is a mind–body connection there in terms of what we do with our mind and how it makes us feel about our body and what we do with our body and how it influences our mind and our self-image, i.e. how we feel about ourselves. Never again must you be casual about how you treat your body in terms of care and cleanliness. Your brain is paying attention so remind it of your worth with good care and cleanliness, both in terms of your own physical body and your environment, so that you then feel more at peace within your own skin.

⊨ OVER TO YOU ⊨

Create a Positive Mind–Body Connection

Build a more positive self-image from this point on:

1. Keep your body and immediate environment clean and tidy every day. A shower can work as a wonderful 're-set button' for your emotions and physical tension.
2. Make yourself feel valuable by treating and pampering yourself as often as required. This can be once a month, once a week, or three times in one week if you really need a big burst of self-love. You could get a massage, a manicure, a haircut or new clothing; have a soak in the bath; soak your feet; paint your toenails; shave your stubble, and so on. This stuff is especially helpful to do regularly if you suffer from low self-esteem and also if your resilience ever feels dangerously low.
3. Once or twice a year, it can be good to do a spring clean if you have a habit of hanging on to old, worn-out things. Whether annually, bi-annually or as and when necessary throughout the year, throw out tatty clothes, shoes, acces-

sories and other such possessions that you attach to your
own body or personal environment, for these items shape
our self-image by reinforcing either a low self-worth ('this
is all I'm worth') or a healthy self-worth. Start right now:
schedule and complete a spring clean during the next
seven days. It's fun, feels good immediately afterwards
and has an overall positive effect on your self-image and
outlook as the weeks and months go by.

Time to Relax / Me Time

Spending time alone in your own company:

◊ recharges you,
◊ refocuses your mind with clarity, and
◊ reinforces your self-worth.

Me time allows you to have time out from people, their
demands, questions and opinions. You get to have time out from
work commitments and personal commitments. You also get to
have time to spend as you want to, reminding yourself that life is
not just about work and goals and being there for other people.
Sometimes it's about just playing, just being in the moment, and
just being there for yourself so you can just relax, have fun, smile
and be happy in that moment, doing what you want to do, exactly
as you want to do it. Life's stresses will be there when your me
time is done. In the meantime, for a portion of time every day,
have some time out for yourself to just enjoy being alive and your
mental health will thank you for it. Your anxiety will also thank
you for it when you much sooner solve and resolve it with Calm
Pillars 1, 2 and 3, because you recharged your mind, brain and
body and thus also reinforced your worth.

Me time is a crucial re-energiser. When you abandon these personal wants for the sake of a partner, boss, child or someone else, your brain doesn't forget; instead, it is repeatedly reminded by you that you must not be worthy of even simple pleasures because perhaps you are not a valuable human being. You are valuable so reinforce your self-worth by carving out time for yourself, and your mind, body and brain will thank you for it with a more positive self-image, energy, focus and resilience for solving and resolving your anxiety.

When your thoughts or body suggest you can't take on or process much more, e.g. 'They asked me another question, I don't think I can cope with another question', or 'I can't listen to any more noise, I desperately need some silence', or your body feels like it is shaking internally or it feels exhausted, that is a sign that you need time out, fast. Listen to it. Obey it.

Me time is time spent by ourselves in the following ways:

a. Just 'being': like when we mindfully enjoy the present moment by focusing only on what we are absorbing through our senses.
b. Pampering ourselves, e.g. massage, retail therapy, manicure, etc.
c. Doing what we want to do just because we want to do it, like reading a book or creating some art.
d. Spending some time thinking about things:
    i. Reliving good memories for happiness.
    ii. Thinking about life and consolidating good memories for recalling later.
    iii. Thinking about life to learn from it: what we have learned about ourselves, human nature, the important people in our lives, and so on.
    iv. Thinking about ourselves and our goals, what we're doing and not doing and why, and how these choices are moving us closer to our goals or further away.

⊨ OVER TO YOU ⊨

Having 'Me Time' is Vital

Make a habit of spending time alone every day to rest and have a mini-recharge, even if it's only for thirty minutes.

If need be, carve out a specific time of day and place, for you to commit to some quality me time so that life and your loved ones don't get in the way of this all-important routine. You may have to contract this time-out with your partner and find a place of sanctuary away from the family and all their daily hustle and bustle in the home.

If others want your time or you want to give your time to others, you need to recharge yourself by having some time to yourself, frequently. It can be important to let your loved ones know you need this for you to be more loving and attentive with them and achieve your shared goals.

SUMMARY

Proper self-care can soothe, prevent or completely eliminate anxiety in the moment and long term, and help you to honour the Three Pillars of Calm.

Self-care builds a positive self-image, boosts your self-esteem, helps you to feel calm and happy, and replenishes your resilience for facing life's stresses and solving and resolving your anxiety.

Ensure you improve any areas of self-care that have been neglected or outright abandoned, including living conditions, any drug habits, sleep, nature, time to relax and switch off ('unplug' from the world), exercise, nutrition, self-compassion, pampering and cleanliness, and me time.

Make self-care a natural part of your everyday life and when you're struggling to honour the Three Pillars of Calm (identify, solve, resolve) because you're so tense, overwhelmed, or foggy-headed from the anxiety, make sure you indulge some self-care then, too.

Use Problem-Solving Thoughts
and Behaviours

*'The formulation of the problem is often more essential
than its solution, which may be merely a matter
of mathematical or experimental skill.'*
Albert Einstein

Your anxiety is alerting you to a problem – a threat that is real or
imagined, self-generated or externally generated, major or minor
– and to solve and resolve it, you need to do something about that
threat or 'threat'. You should seek medical advice first to
determine what sort of anxiety is affecting you, but generally
speaking whether you have generalised anxiety disorder, social
anxiety disorder, obsessive compulsive disorder, phobias, health
anxiety, perinatal anxiety or post-traumatic stress disorder, only by
using your thoughts and behaviours differently from how you are
currently using them will you solve and resolve your anxiety. Let's
look at some examples:

Generalised anxiety disorder is especially perpetuated by
repetitive negative thinking which can become a habit that sucks
you into a downward spiral where everything becomes a trigger.
You can start to feel like you're losing your mind and life becomes
miserable because you're feeling almost constantly tense, stressed
out and not happy. Undoing this wiring requires retraining your
brain to replace negative, self-sabotaging thinking and behaviours
with positive, self-serving thinking and behaviours (including

rewiring with mindfulness meditation) so that you rewire it for calm. You will then also still need to resolve any other actual threats that your anxiety is alerting you to, if any.

One of my clients, Anne, was a loving first-time mum, and she found herself feeling *very* anxious about the safety of her young toddler when the little girl was being cared for by Anne's partner, her daughter's father. Tom had previously given Anne some cause for concern on occasion and other times they simply disagreed about best child safety practices. They found themselves arguing all the time over how to safely care for their daughter and Anne was so worried about everything that could endanger her child when she was in Tom's care that she had also abandoned all her me time and socialising time in favour of ensuring her daughter's safety. This, of course, had a negative knock-on effect on her mental well-being. Over time, Tom's parenting triggered Anne's anxiety even when it didn't warrant it, and this in turn resulted in contempt for Tom. Anne had begun verbally criticising virtually every little childrearing method Tom employed and Tom had begun zoning out and ignoring Anne's repetitive negative comments and safety-related instructions, whether on the phone, via text or face-to-face. Anne's instructions and criticising comments seemed endless but so was her anxiety and this was why she was resorting to the only tactics she felt she could employ to protect her child from illness or death. Remember that 'trying to solve anxiety with endless worry' strategy we discussed (pp.22–4)? She didn't want to hurt Tom with her words or actions and she didn't want to feel this way, she just wanted to ensure her child's safety, but that endless worry method had, over months, resulted in incessant anxiety that had taken over Anne's life and was ruining both Anne and Tom's calm and happiness.

A few solutions helped to resolve Anne's anxiety. Firstly, I encouraged her to view Tom's parenting behaviour over the space of a week, give or take, so that she would give him the opportunity to grow as a father instead of stunting his growth with constant criticism. This would also allow her to gain a realistic view of Tom's parenting skills and any dangers he posed to their child, so that she could then give him parenting advice but only if she still thought it was required, not every few minutes. This in turn would allow her to feel calmer because she would finally be addressing safety concerns in a much smarter, goal-serving way (the goal being to protect their daughter) rather than causing conflict and poor mental clarity with constant criticism which would only sabotage their goal of protecting their daughter by much more likely resulting in unnecessary mistakes and dangers. I also asked Anne to commit to thirty-minute mindfulness meditations at least three times a week to rewire her brain back from anxious most of the time, to calm most of the time, as she had told me that mindfulness meditation had helped her previous period of anxiety. I also asked Anne to take her health and happiness seriously by indulging proper self-care such as me time, time at the gym (which she enjoyed but wasn't doing much of) and socialising with friends which she was barely doing but craving.

These simple changes transformed her daily anxiety to daily calm, allowed Tom the space to prove himself as the loving, attentive, great father he was, allowed them to become a better parenting team and a happy couple again, and achieved the goal of creating a safe environment for their daughter, the ultimate threat Anne sought to resolve all along. Though Anne was being sucked into a downward spiral of anxiety because of her incessant negative thinking ('I'll keep worrying to protect my child') which then resulted in a lot of conflict and a big ripple effect on her and her loved ones, there was something important that she was worrying about, a real threat which we needed to find a solution for, and once we did, the anxiety eventually dissipated.

Social anxiety disorder requires you to retrain your brain to (re) learn that social interactions, in general, are not scary or dangerous.

By using self-serving thoughts and behaviours you rewire your brain for calm at least most of the time, you stop being anxious about social interactions that don't warrant anxiety and you actually reap rewards from social interactions. For example, give yourself enough time to get ready before you go out and make sure you feel happy with how you're dressed, thus creating calm and confidence. Then, when you are out, put a smile on your face so that people know you are approachable, look ahead instead of down, make an effort with others and make respectful eye contact with them. Position yourself near the middle of where people are milling about, instead of sitting on the perimeter indirectly telling people with your body language and behaviours that you don't want them to approach you. What *you* do makes a difference to how others respond to you, and what you do and how they respond to you will either reinforce social anxiety or social confidence. If your social anxiety is also connected to how you view yourself, ensure your thoughts about yourself and the situation are realistic and self-nurturing and do other things that boost your self-esteem.

Obsessive compulsive disorder is when you let intrusive thoughts take over your life as though they are holding a gun to your head. They are not. They are thoughts. They may come, but you can ask them to leave or ignore them if they won't leave. Although obsessive compulsive disorder can stem from a desire for control, compulsive behaviours in response to intrusive thoughts isn't giving you control so it is important to break that pattern and instead address other underlying concerns you may have, such as something you need to take control over that you're not taking charge of currently that is threatening your well-being. To retrain your brain so that you're no longer at the mercy of your thoughts (a) stop paying attention to intrusive thoughts that you know in your heart are not based in reality and are just worries/fears (e.g. 'My husband will be harmed in some way if I don't wash my hands ten times) and (b) certainly do not reinforce those thoughts by giving into them (e.g. do not wash your hands ten times in response to that thought). Remember, the brain creates habits out of anything it does repeatedly and to lose a habit we have to force the neurons that have been firing together, to fire apart. Also use mindfulness meditation and exercise to help your brain to learn and rewire new habits.

Phobias require you to retrain your brain to feel calm in the presence of that thing you are phobic of. This can mean progressively and repeatedly facing that fear in an environment in which you feel safe, so that over time you rewire your brain to associate that thing with zero fear because 'neurons that fire together wire together and neurons that fire apart wire apart'. For example, if you have a phobia of snakes, try being in close proximity to and then handling a small non-venomous snake in a room that feels warm, uplifting and safe and in the presence of someone who knows how to handle snakes well and has a positive attitude towards them. You may instead prefer repeatedly pairing that feared thing with something positive so that over time you associate the feared thing with something pleasant.

Post-traumatic stress disorder requires you to retrain your brain to react appropriately to anything that triggers an association with a previous trauma (such as sexual abuse, being in a dangerous environment, or losing friends or family), rather than maintaining a state of fight-or-flight as your 'new normal' – like that 'trying to solve anxiety with endless worry' strategy. This can involve learning how to regulate your thoughts and emotions with intention, reappraising the situation, or practising behaving in a calm way in the presence of a safe person whilst imagining the trigger for your anxiety. For example, if you suffered abuse in the past and now have a fear of physical intimacy, you could progressively face your fear with a person you feel safe with, so that you can rewire your brain to associate that trigger with alertness but zero fear because 'neurons that fire together wire together'.

Health anxiety is sometimes worry about one's health and mortality because of physical ailments that have appeared and are perhaps undiagnosed, but sometimes the worry is stemming from an underlying self-generated or externally generated threat that is causing anxiety symptoms, e.g. worry about what you are not achieving in your life, or an old trauma suddenly causing PTSD symptoms, or feeling distressed because you're not living life authentically, or someone sabotaging your self-esteem at work, etc. Either you need to get your health checked by a doctor or multiple doctors and then retrain your brain to think calm thoughts so that instead of facing every twitch/sniffle/pain with 'I might be dying', you instead rewire your brain for calm thinking like, 'Oh, no biggie, just a twitch/sniffle/ache'. OR you need to address the underlying true cause of your anxiety such as any situation that you feel stuck in or any situation you feel is sabotaging your important life, well-being or safety goals. Sometimes the true cause of your anxiety has nothing to do with health anxiety, you just identify it as health anxiety after you fail to identify anything else and simply attach the anxiety to health because you are experiencing physical anxiety symptoms and you're worried about what they mean.

Perinatal anxiety is treated in a way that is similar to health anxiety. If you feel actual harm is coming to you or your baby, get a health check from a doctor or multiple doctors and when you have the all-clear, retrain your brain to think calm thoughts whenever you experience a twitch or pain as well as using behaviours that keep your brain and body, safe calm and relaxed, e.g. listening to relaxing music, smelling lavender, napping to catch up on sleep, dancing, nature walks, or any other exercises in the emotions, relationships and self-care chapters. That way, you prevent dangers and don't exacerbate or actually create any physical or mental-health problems because you're then using self-serving thoughts and behaviours (instead). OR you need to take action to address the things you're really worried about when you think about becoming a parent, e.g. resolving relationship issues with your partner, ensuring you maintain your identity by maintaining the hobbies/lifestyle that make you happy and healthy and give you your sense of identity, or learning parenting skills, etc.

Of course there are many different experiences of anxiety and for that reason I am showing you how you will solve and resolve your own anxiety now and for the rest of your life, regardless of the label society wants to give it. You don't need a label, you just need to employ your anxiety-busting formula, the Three Pillars of Calm: identify the cause of your anxiety, identify solutions, resolve with action. If you need additional outside help to completely resolve your anxiety, like advice from a doctor, fitness trainer, relationship coach, or whomever, get that help. That is still you solving and resolving your anxiety yourself; after all, we all need help from others from time to time in order to achieve our goals, personal or business. That's called life. But for most of you, you'll completely resolve your anxiety with just this book, once you've honoured the Three Pillars of Calm:

1. Identify the cause of your anxiety,
2. Identify solutions to overcome the threat,
3. Take thoughtful action to resolve the issue;

and complemented your efforts with the five calm strengthening habits:

1. Create self-serving, positive thoughts.
2. Regulate your emotions with intention.
3. Build positive relationships, prune away negative ones.

4. Indulge proper self-care.
5. Use problem-solving thoughts and behaviours.

Problem-Solving in a Nutshell

Now let's look at how you are going to solve your anxiety for once
and for all, now and every time your anxiety sounds the alert to
say that something is threatening you.

Problem-solving requires that you:

a. clearly know what the problem is ('A'),
b. clearly know what the goal is ('B'), and
c. search for the answers you need to move you from 'A' to
    'B' until you have succeeded.

That's it. That is problem-solving in a nutshell. Coaching –
whatever type of client I am working with – is all about
problem-solving and so it goes for permanently resolving anxiety
and it works every time; it's ultimately just problem-solving to
establish what the cause of your anxiety is (Calm Pillar 1), what
the solutions for overcoming the threat are (Calm Pillar 2), and
then taking thoughtful action to completely resolve the issue
(Calm Pillar 3). Even just first identifying Calm Pillar 1 or Calm
Pillars 1 and 2 reassure our brain that we are dealing with the
threat (even if not yet completely resolved), providing us with
instant relief to some degree. Your mind and body will
communicate this relief to you, instantly.

One of my clients, Jessica, had found herself in an unexpectedly
threatening situation when, unbeknown to her, the home she had
so generously allowed someone else to live in, had been sub-let to
some very unsavoury types. She had items she loved in that house,
including sentimental and expensive possessions, and now they
seemed to be in someone else's control. When she confronted
them, they were aggressive in their manner. Jessica came to me

feeling extremely anxious, upset and panicky. I felt gutted for her as she didn't deserve this misfortune, particularly as she had found herself in this situation because of her kindness. She had been prescribed anxiolytic (anti-anxiety) drugs which she said had helped somewhat to reduce her anxiety symptoms but she was (visibly) still very much experiencing the anxiety. Determined to get to the root of her anxiety so that I could help her resolve it, I asked Jessica a few straightforward questions and it transpired within about five minutes why she was feeling so anxious. She desperately wanted her home and possessions back, as most of us would, and so she was considering getting the police properly involved and pursuing them for what was hers, but the problem with that approach was, it would potentially put her and her loved ones in a precarious position.

When she considered how it made her feel to not pursue them, thereby not puting herself and her loved ones, including her beloved dog, in the line of danger, the anxiety visibly drained from her face and body, her eyes and tone of voice changed and she sensed huge instantaneous relief. You see, her subconscious mind knew she was in very real danger, those people could physically hurt her, and psychologically hurt her through fear and abuse, whether by threatening her verbally or killing her dog, for example. The choice became instantly clear because the bodily sensations (physical anxiety symptoms) and the psychological worry (the psychological anxiety symptoms) disappeared as quickly as you could click your fingers. Jessica chose to let it go, to close the chapter, regardless of losses incurred (financial and sentimental) because her physical well-being and safety, and that of her loved ones, were more important than any of those things. The losses deeply hurt, particularly the loss of sentimental items they had stolen from her and the feeling of being unappreciated by the one whom she had leant her house to in the first place, but she walked away with her well-being and safety in tact, which meant the anxiety was now almost if not completely gone. Within about ten minutes she had honoured Calm Pillars 1, 2 and 3 (identify the cause of your anxiety, identify solutions, take thoughtful action to resolve the issue), as Calm Pillar 3 was simply deciding to not pursue those guys legally and then following through with action which in this case was inaction on trying to recoup possessions from inside the house itself in exchange for her well-being and safety and a once again calm mind.

So, when you are problem-solving your anxiety, you will find that on one day the upcoming problem-solving strategies may not make much of a difference, another day you might struggle to write down your ideas and solutions fast enough! Because the answers (ideas and solutions) that you're looking for, will always eventually come to you given time and effort, all you need to do is just keep **reflecting**, **introspecting** and **searching for answers** and when you do, the solutions you've been searching for will reveal themselves to you. Some problem-solving sessions will be fruitful, others won't be – whether in your mind, on paper, whilst going about your day-to-day life or during time dedicated to it. As you can't predict which moments will be fruitful, you just do it, and the more motivated/desperate you are to resolve your anxiety for once and for all, the more time you will naturally spend thinking about what Calm Pillars 1 and 2 are and implementing Calm Pillar 3 (identify the cause, identify solutions, take thoughtful action).

Of course, sometimes you will get it wrong. Don't worry, you'll still be closer to resolving your anxiety anyway. You just start again. If after implementing Calm Pillar 3 (take thoughtful action), you realise by assessing your thoughts, emotions and bodily sensations that you have not solved your anxiety, you simply 'go back to the drawing board' to look at Calm Pillar 2 again, and maybe even Calm Pillar 1 again, if you feel you've not only misidentified solutions for overcoming the threat (Calm Pillar 2) but also the actual cause of your anxiety (Calm Pillar 1).

Remember, just one great idea can change your life so keep going until your work is done, i.e. your anxiety has been resolved because you've successfully identified and implemented the Three Pillars of Calm (identify, solve and resolve).

Solving Your Anxiety for Once and for All

As we have seen, anxiety is actually helping you to fix issues in your life so that you keep moving towards your happiness and health and all other goals. That alert system is your friend, the one who tells you how it is. A great quote by Arnold H. Glasow sums this up well: 'A true friend never gets in your way unless you happen to be going down.'

Just as you appreciate your alarm clock for doing its job, however much you sometimes wish it wasn't sounding, your anxiety is the same, however much you may wish it wasn't there. Imagine if it didn't tell you how to keep yourself happy, healthy and alive, then you'd be mega miserable – or dead! So always remember to appreciate your in-built alert system, and friend – anxiety – and use the Three Pillars of Calm every time you encounter anxiety:

Identifying Calm Pillar 1:
When I am with clients, a few questions asked usually helps them to unveil Calm Pillar 1 – the cause of their anxiety – very quickly and easily. All you need to do is ask yourself some good questions (see p.224).

Identifying Calm Pillar 2:
Once you've identified the cause – Calm Pillar 1 – it's usually fairly quick and easy to identify Calm Pillar 2 – solutions to overcome the threat. Again, some simple questions that you can ask yourself will usually help you to unveil Calm Pillar 2 very quickly and easily.

Implementing Calm Pillar 3:

Once you've identified the cause and possible solutions – Calm Pillars 1 and 2 – all you then need to do is take thoughtful action. Not worry relentlessly or avoid repeatedly, simply take thoughtful action. In other words, do something and do it thoughtfully. The aim is to resolve the issue that your brain is alerting you to in the form of anxiety, whether self-generated or externally-generated, and so you need to act thoughtfully. This is, after all, your well-being and survival that is under threat, this is not a time for acting haphazardly or doing things half-heartedly. This is a time for serious but calm thinking and action.

You can revisit the section called 'You Could Solve Your Anxiety Problem in The Next Few Minutes' on p.46 but we'll now go through strategies that you can employ any time without having to revisit that section or any other part of this book. The aim is to give you a handful of simple, memorable tools so that you can solve and resolve your anxiety immediately or quickly, every time it occurs and so you can retrain your brain to be calm on the whole rather than anxious all the time. Tune in to your bodily sensations as you set about problem-solving and resolving your anxiety so that you can trust yourself and reach a calm state again, relatively quickly.

Always remember:

◊ When you are relentless in your search for answers and solutions, you will find the answers and solutions.

◊ The best problem-solving strategies that I suggest to clients are all simple and highly effective. All six require patience, resolve and time.

◊ Problem-solving is always a work-in-progress and must be treated as such.

◊ Just trust yourself and trust in the process. When you keep searching for the answers, they invariably present themselves to you at some point, whether after minutes, days or weeks.

The following are simple, highly effective problem-solving strategies that will help you to generate-more creative problem-solving ideas than you might otherwise, something you need to help you honour Calm Pillars 1, 2 and 3 (identify the cause, identify solutions and take thoughtful action):

◊ good questions,
◊ walking,
◊ brainstorming.

Good Questions

Thoughts are powerful, they change our emotions and behaviours and what we pay attention to; you must keep that in mind when you are problem-solving anything in life. Thoughts can also make our brain and body do things we might not even expect or even conceive as possible as we established earlier when looking at placebo research. Therefore, we have to give our brain permission to search for, and find, answers. This permission comes in the form we talk to ourselves. When you talk to yourself in statements, you tell your brain that you have made your mind up and the topic isn't open for discussion or exploration. However, if you ask your brain a question, you tell your brain to go and search for the answer. If you keep asking your brain the same question, sometimes in different settings (nature, cafe, shower), sometimes by phrasing it in different ways, and allow all answers to come without fear of negative judgement from ourselves, then like a good servant, the brain will respond and present the answers it has found in due course. You just want to keep prompting your brain with your questions and wait for the brain to connect the dots and eventually the answers you're looking for will reveal themselves. However, any old question will not do either. How you phrase the question will determine what sort of answer you get and will also influence your emotions positively or negatively. Remember the importance of having positive, self-serving thoughts which then result in positive, self-serving emotions, behaviours and outcomes, rather than negative, self-sabotaging thoughts which will result in negative, self-sabotaging emotions, behaviours and outcomes. Here's what a difference positive and negative thoughts make to your problem-solving approach.

Let's assume Charlotte is feeling anxious. Every time she logs on to social media, she feels tension in her chest and then experiences a depressed mood for a while after logging off. She doesn't yet realise that the cause of her anxiety (Calm Pillar 1) is her comparing her own career successes with the successes of friends and social media 'friends'. Charlotte is desperate to fix her anxiety. She tries to establish the cause of her anxiety (Calm Pillar 1) so that she can then work out solutions for resolving it (Calm Pillar 2) and then take action to resolve it (Calm Pillar 3). She sets out to solve and resolve the anxiety puzzle by asking one of these two questions. The first is problem-focused and disempowering; the second is solution-focused and empowering:

◊ 'Why is it that nothing I do makes me feel calm and optimistic about my career?'
◊ 'What would make me feel calmer and more optimistic about my career?'

Problem-focused questions focus the mind on the problem. Solution-focused questions focus the mind on the possible solutions.

Empowering questions highlight that we have responsibility over our own lives, and they nurture our well-being and make us proactive. Disempowering questions suggest that we lack control of our own lives, hindering our well-being and making us inactive.

Your body will tell you if you are asking yourself a solution-focused, empowering question or a problem-focused, disempowering question. The former will make you feel lighter and more relaxed; the latter will make you feel heavier and more tense. Your mind will also tell you which one you're asking: the former will make you feel in control and optimistic; the latter will make you feel somewhat helpless and pessimistic. So asking yourself solution-focused, empowering questions is vital because it gives your brain permission to search for answers and solutions to your problems. Plus, negative words can put you into fight-or-flight mode in less than a second, which then sabotages your ability to think and problem-solve well. So ask yourself questions that are (a) solution-focused, (b) empowering and (c) positively worded to help you establish what the cause of your anxiety is, how you can solve it and steps you need to take to resolve it (Calm Pillars 1, 2 and 3).

You can ask questions in your mind or on a piece of paper (the latter is better if you have the opportunity to do it), either as a series of questions or as one main overarching question. If you are asking questions in your mind, make sure you make a note of any important ideas or answers that do come up, either by logging them on paper or, if you're out and about and travelling light, in your mobile phone.

Ask yourself questions that begin with who, what, where, when, why, how, for example:

◊ Who or what makes me feel apprehensive/nervous/worried/anxious?
◊ What was happening when this bout of anxiety got triggered?
◊ Where can I get help with this type of threat to my well-being/safety?
◊ When else do I normally feel anxious like this?
◊ Why does this type of event or situation make me feel anxious?

◊ How does this situation that makes me feel anxious, differ from other situations that don't?

Keep asking, keep mulling it all over, the answers always reveal themselves when you are relentless in your search...and when it comes to anxiety, it rarely takes that long to complete because we usually know what's bothering us when we start to give it some thought.

Walking

Walking helps us to generate more creative ideas when problem-solving, both during (an immediate effect) and after (a residual effect), whether on a treadmill facing a blank wall or out and about in an urbanised setting.[177] So it doesn't have to be pretty or relaxing or spacious as walking itself has been shown to have a special power when it comes to problem-solving.

Walking in **nature,** of course, can be even better given nature's mental and physical health benefits.

Walking in **open spaces** can also feel even easier to problem-solve in, so long as you feel physically safe and unthreatened where you are, perhaps because there is less high-definition sensory detail for your brain to process leaving it with more focus and energy for mental creativity. Open spaces can also feel like they allow you more mental brainstorming room, as if the space is like a big sheet of paper that you're brainstorming on, or as though you have plenty of space to throw ideas around in. Maybe it's that confined spaces, by making you feel physically confined, naturally make you feel psychologically restricted or confined and/or emotionally restricted, possibly because it makes the brain access the mental association we have with space or lack thereof. Or perhaps it's the flow of energy that makes open spaces feel different, aside from the psychological and emotional effects shapes and colours and nature itself can have on us. Whatever the reason, there is something about space that changes your emotions, clarity and creativity so just pay attention to your internal bodily sensations, looking out for signs of tension or relaxation to guide you, like antennas from the heart, towards what feels relaxed or good and away from tense or bad. Trust the feeling. Learn from the feeling. Use the feeling to your advantage.

Movement of any kind in fact, can help, from changing the part of the room you're sitting in to face a different direction from a different spot, to moving to another part of the building you are in, e.g. home, cafe or office. Even just going for a short walk can help inspire new thoughts instantly, e.g. getting up from your seat and walking around the room, walking to another room and back, or walking up and down some stairs. Dancing is another one. I often have epiphanies when dancing, and usually pretty quickly, especially if I've just been actively thinking about that topic. Just remember these two phrases:

◊ 'movement in the body creates movement in the mind'.
◊ 'a stagnant body creates a stagnant mind'.

Struggling to think your way out of problems? Struggling to come up with any new ideas for the challenge you're facing? Stuck in a rut in one particular area of your life or life in general? Go for a walk or otherwise move around or change your routine somehow. If you go for a walk somewhere new and unfamiliar, you also provide your brain with new information to blend (from the five senses) with existing information it already has access to (short- and long-term memories) and can thus come up with new ideas more easily. Remember this phrase:

◊ 'something new in, something new out'.

Walking and bodily movement definitely help problem-solving, immediately and residually (after you've stopped moving) so just get moving when you need to problem-solve your anxiety (Calm Pillars 1 and 2 – identify the cause of, and solutions for, your anxiety). You'll love what it can do for you. Make sure you have a notepad and pen to jot ideas down; whilst you're out walking you can probably record them in your mobile phone or just carry a small notepad and pen with you. Oh, and be careful you don't trip or pull a muscle in your leg whilst frantically jotting ideas down, I have on occasion but it's worth it!

Brainstorming

Brainstorming helps us to start afresh with no prior agenda when we need to and allows us to develop ideas we've already generated. Get a blank sheet of paper and in the middle (or wherever it pleases you) write either the overarching question you're trying to answer or some keywords for generating ideas. For example:

◊ Why might I be feeling anxious; what might my mind be worrying about?
◊ What makes me feel anxious when attending work-related events?
◊ How can I protect my self-esteem around that group of people?

Or:

◊ Possible anxiety sources;
◊ Work anxiety, people, situation;
◊ Protect self-esteem.

By logging ideas on paper you are more likely to forge long-term memories of them, and can then also stop worrying about forgetting them, thereby conserving more energy and focus for generating ideas and solutions. Get inspiration from the internet, library, shops, local services, professionals, loved ones and any other places or people happy to help. Also, as per advice from Alex Osborn, a high-flying advertising executive who wrote an influential book on creative problem-solving in the mid-twentieth century, immerse yourself in a self-compassionate environment in which all ideas are welcomed and no ideas are judged, allowing for significantly better ideas-generation, and ultimately a better and quicker ability to solve problems. When you allow yourself to ponder seemingly silly or even ludicrous thoughts about the possible causes of, and solutions for, your anxiety (Calm Pillars 1 and 2), and what if anything is stopping you from taking thoughtful action (Calm Pillar 3), you can much more quickly, easily and pleasantly resolve your anxiety.

Most creative problem-solving is a work-in-progress and you can easily make it so by leaving the brainstorming paper somewhere easily accessible with a pen nearby, so that as and when you have epiphanies, you can add them to the paper. You'll find that as you spend some time consciously mulling over thoughts, questions and ideas, your mind will continue problem-solving your anxiety subconsciously and you'll experience this as answers, ideas or epiphanies suddenly popping into your mind in moments when you are not even actively (consciously) thinking about the answers and solutions you are seeking! Remember, your subconscious mind processes way more in any given minute than your conscious mind does, because otherwise you wouldn't be able to concentrate on the matter in hand if you were paying conscious attention to every little thing that your brain was sensing, processing, planning and executing.

Daydreaming

There are three additional things that can help you to be better at problem-solving itself:

◊ daydreaming,
◊ perspective tweaking,
◊ sleeping.

Research suggests daydreaming helps us to achieve our important goals. You might think of daydreaming as a dreamy or disengaged state of mind where we're kind of on auto-pilot, yet, perhaps surprisingly, research finds that when we are daydreaming, we actually engage both the brain's 'default network', which handles easy, routine tasks *and* the brain's 'executive network', which handles complex problem-solving.[178] So it appears that when we are daydreaming, though we may not be paying full attention to the task in hand, we may be subconsciously problem-solving the bigger puzzles in our life. And yet how much do we even allow ourselves to daydream anymore in this hyperconnected world? We've abandoned so much of our valuable free time only to replace it with consuming, and mentally or verbally critiquing, the unimportant. Instead of solving your important life puzzles, are you squandering away your precious, limited thinking-time on unimportant endeavours that are not benefiting you, your loved ones or mankind? If so, redress the balance, for it will help you to prevent anxiety, soothe anxiety symptoms and problem-solve and resolve your anxiety (Calm Pillars 1, 2 and 3 – identify cause, identify solutions, take action).

To induce daydreaming on purpose to help you problem-solve your anxiety, focus on a simple task and then allow your brain to wander; for example, have a shower, clean your home, play a computer game, or do some gardening. Hot showers, perhaps because they are a routine task that allow you to daydream and simultaneously relax your mind and body, are brilliant for problem-solving your anxiety.

Perspective Tweaking

Sometimes, a change in perspective is all you need. Like when people ask, 'What would your ten-year-older self say to your current self?' Notice how when you take on a different set of thoughts and tweak the lens of your mind differently, you come out with a different view altogether? Just like physically moving your body to a different spot with a different view over a landscape, move your thoughts and go get a different view over your life. What I mean by that is, when generating ideas and looking for solutions to things, in particular when you're trying to identify the cause of your anxiety and possible solutions to overcome the threat, you can imagine what your older self would say to your current self, and you can also pretend you're giving advice to someone else or that you are someone else giving advice to you, for example:

◊ 'What advice would I give my sibling/friend in this situation?'
◊ 'What would my mum/dad suggest I do?'

How about when you feel like you are 'too close to the problem'? Again you can change your perspective by looking at things from a different point, this time from a different point in time, like when you feel 'too close to the problem'. One study found that even when the task in-hand has nothing to do with 'time', you can enhance your insights and creativity, for example, by imagining your life a year later and/or imagine working on the current task a year later to gain perspective and, subsequently, increase how many creative ideas or solutions you generate.[179]

Interestingly, whilst the distant-time perspective can help creative thinking ('divergent thinking') to generate ideas, it can actually hinder logical thinking ('convergent thinking') when trying to come up with specific action steps to move us to our end goal. So, if you are going to play around with time to help you with the aforementioned strategies – good questions, brainstorming and walking/movement:

◊ think from a distant-time perspective to help creative problem-solving when you want to generate ideas (like for

Calm Pillars 1 and 2, identify the cause of, and solutions for, your anxiety);

◊ think from a current or near-future time perspective to help concrete thinking when you need to be analytical, logical and organise ideas into a flow of action (like when preparing a plan for Calm Pillar 3, take thoughtful action).

Once you know which perspective to use depending on the type of problem you're trying to solve, you then simply ask yourself a question to help you tap in to either one of those perspectives, for example:

◊ Distant-time perspective: 'If I was ten years older, what solutions for resolving my anxiety would I advise myself to consider right now?'

◊ Current or near-future time perspective: 'What would be helpful next steps for preventing him from sabotaging my mental well-being?'

The great thing about all of these problem-solving ideas is that you can use them at the same time, completely separately, or one after the other, especially given that walking has been found to have a residual effect on creative problem solving. If you wished to use them together, simultaneously, or one after the other, you could for example use:

◊ walking coupled with good questions;
◊ good questions coupled with brainstorming;
◊ walking followed by brainstorming;
◊ brainstorming followed by walking;
◊ walking followed by a simple task that allows your brain to wander to daydream.

Sleeping

Lastly, it is always important to get a good night's sleep. Firstly, because as we noted earlier (see pp.180–84), the brain needs sleep to consolidate memories and gain perspective on stressful events. Secondly, the brain also benefits from sleep when trying to solve a problem. In one study, more than twice as many participants who slept for eight hours, compared with those who were not allowed to sleep in between a problem-solving task and a retest, gained insight into a hidden rule that helped them to complete the tasks much quicker than they could have otherwise.[180] It's possible that our brain restructures memories during sleep, helping us to gain new insights from old information. You've likely experienced this at some point yourself where you've tried hard to solve a problem for hours, completely failed to, only to find that the answer effortlessly popped into your head the following day after you had slept well. Sleeping on a problem really can help! For example, it may be just what you need to correctly identify the true cause of your anxiety (Calm Pillar 1) or to work out why your attempts to resolve it (Calm Pillar 3) haven't worked.

In another study, some participants were asked to nap and some to stay awake to see if it affected their ability to solve a complex problem in a video game.[181] Results showed that those who had napped were twice as likely to solve the problem than those who had stayed awake for the same amount of time. So even a nap can help our problem-solving ability despite a number of studies linking improved problem-solving ability to Rapid Eye Movement sleep (REM sleep). It seems there is something about sleep in general that is important for our brain to be able to solve problems and napping may be a useful way of using this in-built problem-solving function when you are struggling to get a good night's sleep when trying to solve and resolve your anxiety.

Although one night of sleep deprivation may not hinder your ability to put together a plan of action – linear (convergent) thinking – it will likely hinder your ability to use creative (divergent) thinking[182] so when you need to get creative, do yourself a favour and get a good night's sleep, or at least nap more often. Of course, a lot of people suffer from both anxiety and sleep problems at the same time; sleep problems likely being a by-product of Calm Pillars 1 and/or 2 not yet having been identified (identifying the threat and the solution) or Calm Pillar 3 not yet having been implemented (taking thoughtful action), all three of which would lead to an underlying concern your brain would struggle to switch off from because the anxiety alarm is still ringing. After all, it's usually when we're worried about something that we struggle to get a quality night's sleep. So I appreciate that when you're still trying to resolve the anxiety, whichever stage you're at, getting a good night's sleep may feel inherently difficult, but that is why you should use the tips on sleep from the last chapter to help you (see pp.184–85), and why you must take your anxiety alarm seriously from the moment it arises and start working immediately and persistently until you have fully solved and resolve your anxiety:

◊ **Identify the cause** of your anxiety (Calm Pillar 1).
◊ **Identify solutions** to overcome the threat (Calm Pillar 2).
◊ **Take thoughtful action** to resolve the issue (Calm Pillar 3).

Remember, regardless of the stage you're at when it comes to implementing the Three Pillars of Calm, in order to overcome your anxiety and become calm, you can do things to help you de-stress and/or fatigue your mind or body to help you get some quality sleep, e.g. writing things down so that you give your brain permission to let go, a hot shower or hot drink of milk before bedtime, physical exercise, or reading a story (and see more ideas on pp.184–85).

So sleep is our recharge function and our re-set button, as we saw in the last chapter, and it can also be our upgrade button, as we are seeing in this chapter.

⊨ OVER TO YOU ⊨

Problem-Solving So You Can Honour the Three Pillars of Calm

To utilise the Three Pillars of Calm (identify the cause of your anxiety, identify solutions to overcome the threat, take thoughtful action to resolve the issue) you will need to use at least some of the problem-solving strategies discussed. Use them to help you answer the following questions:

1. What is the cause of my anxiety?
2. What solutions will resolve the threat?
3. What do I need to do proactively to eliminate this threat and when or when by?

Every day, spend five to thirty minutes (or longer) solving and then resolving your anxiety. The more motivated you are to resolve your anxiety quickly, the more often you'll spend time problem-solving in your head, on paper, as you go about your day or during time specifically set aside for it. When you're highly motivated, you'll usually do a lot of this problem-solving in your head as you're going about the rest of your day-to-day life, pausing only to make notes as required.

Today and every subsequent day, use the following techniques:
- Ask yourself goal-focused, solution-focused, empowering questions that start with who, what, when, where, why and how.
- Brainstorm your answers and any other notable thoughts you have, with pen and paper. Welcome and capture all ideas with self-compassion.
- Further explore the thoughts and ideas that stand out as

the best and most likely to be useful. Ask yourself further questions, or brainstorm further on new sheets of paper, for each of these.

- Use physical movement to get your creative juices flowing.
- Use others' perspectives and distant-time perspectives for generating creative ideas and possible solutions (for Calm Pillars 1 and 2 – identify cause, identify solutions).
- Use near-time perspectives for creating actionable steps to resolve the anxiety completely (Calm Pillar 3).
- Practise activities that help to induce daydreaming.
- Use SMART goals as and when required, e.g. to help you set goals around the thoughtful actions you need to take to resolve your anxiety (Calm Pillar 3). SMART goals are Specific, Measurable, Attainable, Relevant and Time-bound and tell you at a glance, what specifically you are going to do and when or when by, e.g. 'I will talk to my partner during our dinner this Tuesday night about my need to be with someone who does want to have children.'

Treat all problem-solving as a work-in-progress and keep your brainstorming papers somewhere accessible with a pen by them at all times so you can add to them as you go. Feel free to do more than thirty minutes' problem-solving at any one time.

Persistence is vital and pays off when you keep asking good questions and keep searching for answers, sometimes consciously, other times subconsciously. The more time you spend thinking consciously about your goals and any challenges to overcome, the more time your subconscious mind will spend thinking about them.

Watch your anxiety symptoms reduce and then dissipate as you problem-solve further and further until you actually solve the anxiety problem and resolve the threat completely.

Use Your Intuition

The final tip I want to cover to help you become calm and anxiety free very quickly, is the use of your intuition, a skill anyone can hone so long as they have a healthy (non-damaged) brain.

Intuition will allow you to correctly identify Calm Pillars 1 and 2 (identify the cause of your anxiety, identify solutions to overcome the threat) and help you to quickly know whether Calm Pillar 3 is working (taking thoughtful action to resolve the issue). Using your intuition alongside the critical thinking, planning, problem-solving part of your brain, will enable you to make great decisions quickly and easily and with confidence. Intuition will allow you to trust yourself further and then feel calm; and over time you will see just how spot on your intuition is and what a positive effect it has on your life when you effortlessly and confidently make the right decisions for you, including about your anxiety, its causes and its solutions.

Intuition is your ability to understand or know something instinctively, without conscious reasoning. It allows you to access information that your brain and body know subconsciously that you don't yet know consciously. Research demonstrates that our subconscious mind makes decisions before we consciously become aware of those decisions and then 'consciously make' those same decisions.[183] There is a huge amount of calculating and evaluating going on inside your brain and body that you don't get to see but intuition lets you take a sneak peak.

Research suggests intuition works by the brain:

◊ using information absorbed via our senses (ears, eyes, etc),[184]
◊ accessing information stored in memory from our distant past or recently,[185]

◊ identifying any patterns occurring,
◊ using information detected by the heart and the skin.

What your brain does is evaluate very quickly all the information it has access to, and uses patterns it notices, past experiences and new information, to form a rapid decision on something and sometimes even take action on something based on that information. To access your intuition, particularly useful are the heart area and that voice in your head that often answers at lightening speed, too quick for it to be conscious thought. When someone asks you to do yet another work task and your schedule is already busy with work commitments, your intuition will tell you, rapidly, if you should say yes or no to the request to take on more work. Your intuition will likely have calculated the answer by taking into account various factors such as your well-being, your existing schedule, your goals, past experiences, your skill set, and more. Your conscious critical thinking brain on the other hand might overlook some factors and be swayed more by feelings of guilt or habits wired into the brain. The great thing about getting into the habit of using your intuition is that you are practising being present, being mindful, rather than at the mercy of a panicky, chaotic, nervous, self-defeating brain, wired this way over time through repetition, whether it once served you but no longer does (as with PTSD) or whether it has been perpetuated over time through habit (as with OCD or generalised anxiety disorder).

What you'll find is that when you dare to trust yourself and follow your intuitive hunches, over time you'll know whether you are tuning into your intuition or not because you'll later find out if your intuitive decisions were the right decisions for you to make or the wrong decisions. You see, initially, we don't consciously know the reason for the feeling; we just know that something felt good or felt bad, or felt right or felt wrong. Whether we trust the feeling or not, moments, hours, or even weeks later, our conscious mind is able to pinpoint in words specifically why we had experienced that intuitive feeling, whether it was about something that has happened, is happening right now or a decision we had to make about the future. So research suggests your body physically reacts to information it has access to consciously and subconsciously and that you can tune in to that bodily reaction, even when you don't yet know what specifically it is reacting to. By doing so, you use your body as a conduit of knowledge that helps you to make correct decisions when identifying Calm Pillars 1 and 2 (identify the cause and identify solutions) and take the correct course of action, quickly and easily, when implementing Calm Pillar 3 (take thoughtful action). Trusting your intuition can help you to instantly tap into information and answers that can help you, protect your well-being and even prove to be potentially life-saving!

Intuitive thoughts and answers almost don't feel real. And because intuition works so fast and so accurately, it makes it easy for people to reject their intuition as silly guess work or even paranoia when in reality that is one of your in-built well-being and survival tools at your disposal. So allow me to give you some helpful tips on how you can tune in to and hone your intuitive skills.

OVER TO YOU

Tuning in to Your Intuition

When you want to decipher which decision is right for you, whether you have multiple options to choose from or a relationship to pursue or distance yourself from, use the upcoming tips to help you tune in to your intuition and make great decisions quickly and easily.

Do what it takes to relax yourself and quiet your mind of distractions, as it's usually difficult to tune in to your intuition when you are not relaxed. A **quick pick-me-up** or **soothe-me session** to ease waves and storms and calm internal waters, at least temporarily, will help you to create the conditions necessary for accurately tuning in to your intuition. For example, lighting some candles, going for a brisk walk, taking a hot soak in the bath, having a positive word with yourself, or one of the other emotion-regulation strategies or self-care strategies we have discussed.

Focus your heart and mind on the thing you want answers about so you can tune in to the feeling, or perhaps the energy. Think of it like focusing your eyesight on something far away or listening out closely for something.

Very often it's the first answer that pops into your head before you've had time to consciously over-think it or even finish asking yourself the question! The answer rapidly flashes through your mind and feels detached from your conscious evaluating process.

Use bodily sensations or **physical signs** to establish how you feel about each possible option. For example, let's assume you need to make a decision and you have three options to choose from: 'X', 'Y' and 'Z':

- Imagine yourself pursuing one of the three possible options.
- As you wholeheartedly imagine pursuing that option, pay attention to the sensations you feel within your body and any involuntary body movements you notice.
- Repeat this exercise for each of the three options.
- You'll usually find that one of the options triggers the most relaxed feeling or physical state compared with the other options, as you vividly imagine each one separately. The presence of a relaxed state is a good indicator as to which decision may be the right one for you. The presence of tension is a good sign that something may not be right for you.

- The internal bodily sensations may be felt around your chest, back, neck, shoulders, scalp, stomach or elsewhere. Your most obvious tell-tale sign regions will be specific to you. Certainly, though, the heart area is a useful one to tune in to as you can sometimes detect beat-to-beat changes, and general tension and relaxation, which can help signpost you towards the right decision.

- The external physical indicators might be involuntary body movements like clenching your fist, shaking your leg, tapping your feet or rubbing your head, which might represent anxiety about the option that you are considering in that moment.

- Consider the physiological and/or physical response as your subconscious mind's way of telling you, 'I've scanned all the information, stored and new, and I suggest this option is safe or right for you and that option is unsafe or wrong for you.' When you have the courage to follow your gut feeling, watch how hours, days or weeks later, your conscious mind delivers the specific reasons that support your intuitive hunch.

Monitor your results to build your self-belief, even if you don't always have the courage to follow your gut feeling (your intuition). To do this, regardless of whether you follow through on your intuitive hunch, use any opportunity you can to make an intuitive decision about something important, like whether to date someone or go to an event, or intuitively guess something silly like how much the supermarket shopping is going to cost or how many grapes are in the bowl. As you monitor the outcomes after some minutes or weeks have passed – whichever time period might be necessary – you'll hone your skill and increase your confidence.

Use common sense when applying these tips. If you're feeling tense about something, use conscious reasoning and questions to decipher if the tension is due to your anxiety about doing something new (e.g. public speaking) or due to the option being fraught with problems (e.g. you don't have enough time to prepare and do well).

———

Just to leave you with an idea of how sophisticated your brain and body are, research has found your heart even reacts to information from a future event that it couldn't possibly have any foreknowledge of or identify patterns for.[186] That's mind-blowing. Yet there's something in it. Entrepreneurs and leaders often use this heightened sense to help them get ahead and lead others to success and victory. Stock-brokers, too. Remember how, in the self-assessment chapter, we noted that those who performed better over time on the stock markets and earned more money were those who were better at interoception, the ability to sense the internal state of our body. You can hone the same skill with practice and you'll likely find that focusing your mind on your heart area is especially useful when you want to 'listen in to' information your heart is communicating. It's like intercepting the message from your heart to your brain, listening in to the conversation they're having. If you can focus your mind on your heart area when you need to problem-solve, plan or make a decision, then you can tap into a sci-fi-like awareness that will help you to protect your well-being and survival. That will help you massively when implementing the Three Pillars of Calm in order to become calm and anxiety-free (identify the cause, identify solutions, take thoughtful action). Use your intuition to help you prevent and fight off all threats to your mental and physical well-being, whether real or imagined, self-generated or externally-generated, major or minor.

SUMMARY

Whenever you have a problem, life requires that you solve and resolve it in order to move towards your goals, happiness, health and survival. Anxiety is your brain alerting you to a problem that threatens your mental or physical well-being or survival. Regardless of whether that threat is real or imagined, self-generated or externally-generated, you need to solve and resolve that threat.

All three steps of the Three Pillars of Calm require problem-solving thoughts, whether creative problem-solving where you generate ideas and solutions (as with Calm Pillars 1 and 2, identify the cause and identify solutions) or linear problem-solving where you're planning actions (in preparation for Calm Pillar 3, take thoughtful action).

Problem-solving benefits from asking yourself good questions, walking and movement, brainstorming, daydreaming, tweaking your perspective and sleeping.

When you know the cause of your anxiety, the solution can be quite obvious because then it's just about working out what will help you to regain your mental and/or physical well-being and safety again.

Problem-solving mostly takes place in your mind as you go about day-to-day life; your body, with its intuitive signals, can help you to solve and resolve your anxiety within just a few minutes or a few weeks.

Part 3:
The Anxiety Free
Four-Week Plan

Four Weeks to Anxiety Free

*'Survival is not about being fearless. It's about making a
decision, getting on and doing it, because I want to see
my kids again, or whatever the reason might be.'*
Bear Grylls

So remember, guys and girls, anxiety is your friend alerting you to
a threat to your mental or physical well-being or survival. Your job
is to be grateful for the alert and find the threat and resolve it.
That threat can be real or imagined, and either self-generated
(stemming from your thoughts and/or behaviours) or externally
generated (stemming from a **P**erson, **O**bject, **S**ituation or **E**vent),
or a combination.

Anxiety can be treated in a few minutes or a few weeks, when
you immediately and relentlessly face anxiety with the Three
Pillars of Calm:

1. **Identify the cause** of your anxiety,
2. **Identify solutions** to overcome the threat,
3. **Take thoughtful action** to resolve the issue,

and help yourself to do so with the Five Calm Strengthening
Habits covered in Part 2:

1. Create self-serving, positive thoughts.
2. Regulate your emotions with intention.
3. Build positive relationships, prune away negative ones.

4. Indulge proper self-care.
5. Use problem-solving thoughts and behaviours.

Importantly, always facing anxiety with the Three Pillars of Calm retrains your brain to habitually face anxiety with a calm, solution-focused, proactive response so that rather than be unnerved by your anxiety symptoms, you instead feel grateful and in control and can then think more clearly about how you're going to resolve the threat they are alerting you to.

Write down your three-point anxiety-busting formula, the Three Pillars of Calm, along with the Five Calm Strengthening Habits, and keep them to hand to help you immediately remember and employ them. You may prefer to write them simply as:

Three Pillars of Calm:
identify cause —> identify solutions —> take action.

Five Calm Strengthening Habits: positive thoughts, positive emotions, positive relationships, good self-care and good problem-solving.

Becoming anxiety free will take **a few minutes** if the cause of your anxiety requires a one-off solution and can be implemented right away; **a few weeks** if the cause of your anxiety needs a series of actions over time.

Self-generated anxiety that stems from your **thoughts** can take a few minutes or a few weeks to calm depending on whether you need to (**A**) change the focus of your unnecessary negative thoughts right now (e.g. distract yourself from worrying about future events that may never happen); (**B**) retrain your brain to rewire it for calm (e.g. calm, confident thoughts).

Self-generated anxiety that stems from your **behaviours** can take a few minutes or a few weeks to calm depending on whether you need to (**A**) change what you're doing right now (e.g. taking more time over the task in hand); (**B**) retrain your brain into better behaviour habits, (e.g. not using social media to compare yourself to others).

Externally-generated anxiety that stems from a **P**erson, **O**bject, **S**ituation or **E**vent can take a few minutes or a few weeks to calm because again it depends on whether you just need to (**A**) take one or two actions and can do so immediately (e.g. end a friendship with someone who has been mistreating you and sabotaging your mental well-being for some time); (**B**) take action over time on something or someone (e.g. rehearse a presentation until you feel confident and calm about delivering it, or build a better relationship with someone you have to spend time around); (**C**) retrain your brain to rewire it for calm (e.g. for a calm association with a clown doll, a loud sound, a certain room, or groups of people).

The upcoming table explains which type of threat requires which type of approach. Within the table you are signposted to the numbered 'Over To You' exercises on pages 254 onwards that will most likely especially help you to resolve each type of threat. On pages 254 onwards, you are signposted to all the 'Over To You' exercises within the book to help you complement your journey to becoming anxiety free within minutes or weeks.

Creating a planner and/or daily to-do lists can help. Of special importance to be included in your daily and/or weekly routines are the activities/habits that help generate feelings of calm consistently and for the long-term: problem-solving your anxiety, positive thoughts, positive relationships, exercise, nature, me time, making progress.

Type Of Threat	Become Anxiety Free In a Few Minutes	Become Anxiety Free In Four Weeks
Self-Generated Threats		
Repetitive negative thinking (e.g. self-criticism, worry and rumination)	You get instant relief when you distract your brain from the thing that you're worrying about, whether something real or imagined and whether you're still identifying the cause of your anxiety (Calm Pillar 1) or are still in the throes of resolving the threat with action (Calm Pillar 3). **SOLUTIONS** 'Over To You' exercises: 4 (distraction) 5 (positive self-talk) 8 (music) 9 (dancing) 10 (art) 21 (exercise)	It takes just a few weeks to 'lose' the old wiring of negative-focused, self-sabotaging thoughts like worry and self-criticism whilst you 'use' the new habit of positive-focused, self-serving thoughts that make you feel calm and confident to rewire your 'use it or lose it' brain. **SOLUTIONS** 'Over To You' exercises: 2 (mindfulness meditation) 3 (rewire brain) 5 (positive self-talk) 11 (happiness-building) 21 (exercise) 22 (mind–body connection) 23 (me time) **and maybe also especially helpful:** 6 (focus towards desires) 4 (distraction) 8 (music) 9 (dancing) 10 (art) 19 (nature)

Type Of Threat	Become Anxiety Free In a Few Minutes	Become Anxiety Free In Four Weeks
Self-image (i.e. how you view yourself)	You can change how you view yourself in the present moment by doing right by yourself and doing right by others. If you feel you have let yourself down or have let someone else down in some way, right the wrong. You can make reparations by improving or fixing the very thing you've done 'wrong' or doing something else to compensate for the mistake in how you've treated yourself or someone else.	You can change how you view yourself by changing your thoughts to be more positive about yourself, indulging positive self-care habits, surrounding yourself with positive relationships only, taking charge of your life by making progress on your goals and building confidence by achieving new things.
	SOLUTIONS	**SOLUTIONS**
	'Over To You' exercises: 13 (self-image) 14 (identity) 15 (protect self online) 16 (guard social networks) 11 (happiness-building) 18–23 (self-care) 24 (tune into your body) 25 (problem-solving)	'Over To You' exercises: 13 (self-image) 14 (identity) 15 (protect self online) 16 (guard social networks) 11 (happiness-building) 18–23 (self-care) 3 (rewire brain)

Type Of Threat	Become Anxiety Free In a Few Minutes	Become Anxiety Free In Four Weeks
Authenticity (i.e. whether you behave in line with your true inner self)	You get instant relief when you live life the way you truly want to live it, in a way that feels right for your personality and motivations and how you want to experience your life, regardless of what the world expects of you. **SOLUTIONS** 'Over To You' exercises: 14 (identity) 15 (protect self online) 16 (guard social networks) 22 (mind–body connection) 24 (tune into your body) 25 (problem-solving)	Living life the way you truly want to live in a way that feels right for your personality and motivations and how you want to experience your life, regardless of what the world expects of you, gives an increasing sense of calm and well-being over time, as you then start living more and more aspects of your life as you want to, having the sort of relationships you want to have, spending your time as you want to and where you want to, and pursuing a career that suits your personality. Freedom to make our own choices for our own life, feels euphoric. **SOLUTIONS** 'Over To You' exercises: 14 (identity) 15 (protect self online) 16 (guard social networks) 22 (mind–body connection) 24 (tune into your body) 25 (problem-solving) 3 (rewire brain)

Type Of Threat	Become Anxiety Free In a Few Minutes	Become Anxiety Free In Four Weeks
Overload (i.e. taking on too many tasks or mentally processing too much information)	Giving yourself more time for the task in hand or the day ahead, will give you instant relief from anxiety as you give yourself more mental clarity and emotional calm for better thinking and performance because you're not overwhelming, and thus sabotaging, yourself with too much to do or too much to think about. **SOLUTIONS** 'Over To You' exercises: 15 (protect self online) 18–23 (self-care) 24 (tune into your body) 25 (problem-solving)	Minimising overload, over time, allows you to perform better and achieve more in life, and feel calmer and happier minute to minute, day to day. **SOLUTIONS** 'Over To You' exercises: 3 (rewire brain) 6 (focus towards desires) 15 (protect self online) 18–23 (self-care) 24 (tune into your body) 25 (problem-solving)

Type Of Threat	Become Anxiety Free In a Few Minutes	Become Anxiety Free In Four Weeks
Externally-Generated Threats		
People (e.g. negative relationships)	Feel calm in the very moment that you take instant control over your self-worth and self-respect and thus maintain healthy self-esteem and a positive self-image. Your kindness towards others must not be greater than your self-respect, and care and kindness for yourself. **SOLUTIONS** 24 (tune into your body) 25 (problem-solving) 14 (identity) 15 (protect self online) 16 (guard social networks) 21 (exercise) 22 (mind–body connection) 23 (me time)	Feel calm, happy and deserving of good fortune day to day when you take ongoing control over your self-worth and self-respect and thus maintain healthy self-esteem and a positive self-image. To help you with this, prune away negative relationships that you can't change which reinforce low self-esteem, and look after your mind and body with good self-care. **SOLUTIONS** 24 (tune into your body) 25 (problem-solving) 14 (identity) 15 (protect self online) 16 (guard social networks) 3 (rewire brain) 21 (exercise) 22 (mind–body connection) 23 (me time)

Type Of Threat	Become Anxiety Free In a Few Minutes	Become Anxiety Free In Four Weeks
Objects (e.g. fear of clown dolls)		Feel calm in the presence of an object by repeatedly and consistently pairing its presence with a safe environment, thereby teaching your brain that being in its presence per se feels safe as this poses no danger. Displace the old wiring of negative associations with the item and overreacting to it, and replace it with the new habit of feeling calm and unthreatened by its presence in safe situations. **SOLUTIONS** 'Over To You' exercises: 2 (mindfulness meditation) 3 (rewire brain) 5 (positive self-talk) 21 (exercise)

Type Of Threat	Become Anxiety Free In a Few Minutes	Become Anxiety Free In Four Weeks
Situations (e.g. life goals seeming out of reach, temporarily living with your in-laws, dark alleyways)	You get instant relief when you successfully prevent a danger in your life that threatens your well-being or safety, mentally or physically, and sometimes that danger only requires one or a few actions to resolve it that can be executed quickly and easily. **SOLUTIONS** 'Over To You' exercises: 24 (tune into your body) 25 (problem-solving) 5 (positive self-talk) 6 (focus towards desires) 13–16 (relationships with self and others) 18–23 (self-care)	Sometimes you need to commit to a few actions or changes over time which help your brain to feel reassured that the threat is being dealt with in a timely and successful manner and so do not feel like a threat anymore (as reasonable progress is being made). Even if the issue may take longer than four weeks to complete, your brain will usually tell you, through the absence or presence and the strength of the anxiety, whether you are making reasonable, timely progress on the issue, whether that issue is a life goal you desperately want to achieve or a danger you desperately want to avoid. Ensuring you indulge in positive, self-serving thoughts most of the time will also assist. **SOLUTIONS** 'Over To You' exercises: 24 (tune into your body) 25 (problem-solving) 3 (rewire habits) 5 (positive self-talk) 6 (focus towards desires) 13–16 (relationships with self and others) 18–23 (self-care) 2 (mindfulness meditation)

Type Of Threat	Become Anxiety Free In a Few Minutes	Become Anxiety Free In Four Weeks
Events (e.g. a presentation, job interview, social occasion, your own impending wedding that you're having second thoughts about)	As above, you get instant relief when you successfully prevent a danger in your life that threatens your well-being or safety, mentally or physically, and sometimes that danger only requires one or a few actions to resolve that can be executed quickly and easily. **SOLUTIONS** 'Over To You' exercises: 24 (tune into your body) 25 (problem-solving) 26 (intuition) 5 (positive self-talk) 6 (focus towards desires) 15 (protect self online) 16 (guard social networks) 20 (overload)	Again, sometimes you need to take actions over a period of time to prevent a threat or resolve it somehow if it is inevitable. Even if the issue may take longer than four weeks to complete, your brain will usually tell you, with the absence or presence of anxiety, whether you are making reasonable progress on the issue, whether that issue is a goal you desperately want to achieve or a danger you desperately want to avoid. Again, ensuring you indulge positive, self-serving thoughts most of the time will also assist and may be the last piece of the anxiety puzzle you're looking to solve. **SOLUTIONS** 'Over To You' exercises: 24 (tune into your body) 25 (problem-solving) 26 (intuition) 3 (rewire habits) 5 (positive self-talk) 6 (focus towards desires) 15 (protect self online) 16 (guard social networks) 20 (overload)

Calm Strengthening Habit 1: Create self-serving, positive thoughts

1. *The Effects Thoughts Have on My Life*
Your objective: Understand the impact of negative and positive thoughts.
Dose: As and when required.
How to: Use the 'Over To You' exercise on page 74.

2. *Train Your Brain to Become Calm with Mindfulness Meditation*
Your objective: To rewire your brain from anxious to calm.
Dose: As and when required.
How to: Use the 'Over To You' exercise on page 80.

3. *Rewire Your Brain for Calm and any Good Habits*
Your objective: To eliminate bad habits and create good habits, including a habit of calm.
Dose: As and when required.
How to: Use the 'Over To You' exercise on page 89.

4. *Create and Use Distraction Exercises*
Your objective: To distract yourself from repetitive negative thinking, e.g. worry, rumination, self-criticising.
Dose: As and when required.
How to: Use the 'Over To You' exercise on page 93.

5. *Create a Habit of Talking Positively to Yourself*
Your objective: To use your self-talk to steer your life in a desirable direction, only.
Dose: Every second of every day.
How to: Use the 'Over To You' exercise on page 97.

6. *Focus Your Mind in the Direction You Want to Go in*

Your objective: To focus your mind on your desires and goals frequently.

Dose: Most of the time.

How to: Use the 'Over To You' exercise on page 103.

Calm Strengthening Habit 2: Regulate your emotions with intention

7. Reappraise a Memory or Situation to Release Its Hold Over Your Life

Your objective: To re-evaluate a memory/situation to regulate your emotions and improve your relationship with yourself (e.g. self-esteem, authenticity) and others.

Dose: As and when required.

How to: Use the 'Over To You' exercise on page 111.

8. Use Music to Soothe

Your objective: To use music to help quell your anxiety symptoms and to help you problem-solve.

Dose: As and when required.

How to: Use the 'Over To You' exercise on page 116.

9. Use Dancing to Soothe and Problem-Solve

Your objective: To use dancing to help quell your anxiety symptoms and to help you problem-solve.

Dose: As and when required.

How to: Use the 'Over To You' exercise on page 121.

10. Use Art to Soothe and Problem-Solve

Your objective: To use art to help quell your anxiety symptoms and to help you problem-solve.

Dose: As and when required.

How to: Use the 'Over To You' exercise on page 123.

11. *Use Happiness-Building Activities to Soothe and Build Resilience*
Your objective: To have a regular timetable of
happiness-maintenance activities to help sustain fairly
consistently positive emotions long term.
Dose: Daily, two to three times a week, or weekly.
How to: Use the 'Over To You' exercise on page 125.

12. *Use Sensory Changes*
Your objective: To identify and use sensory changes to help
transform your emotional state.
Dose: As and when required.
How to: Use the 'Over To You' exercise on page 128.

Calm Strengthening Habit 3: Build positive relationships,
prune away negative ones

13. *Ways to Raise Your Self-Image*
Your objective: To take care with, and take charge of, the
associations you create with yourself.
Dose: Daily.
How to: Use the 'Over To You' exercise on page 136.

14. *Embrace Your Identity*
Your objective: To embrace the multiple identities that you hold
as one person.
Dose: Daily.
How to: Use the 'Over To You' exercise on page 142.

15. *Protect Your Vulnerability and Self-Esteem Online*
Your objective: To protect your well-being online and feel as
safe as possible in a digital space.
Dose: Daily.
How to: Use the 'Over To You' exercise on page 149.

16. *Nurture Positive Relationships, Prune Away Negative Ones*
Your objective: To build and nurture positive relationships and
eliminate or reduce time around negative relationships.
Dose: Daily.
How to: Use the 'Over To You' exercise on page 155.

17. *A Quick Breathing Technique for Achieving a Calm, Coherent*
State
Your objective: To get yourself into a calm state, on cue, when
needed or desired.
Dose: As and when required.
How to: Use the 'Over To You' exercise on page 161.

Calm Strengthening Habit 4: Indulge in proper self-care

18. *Get a Good Night's Sleep*
Your objective: To allow your body to perform its necessary
functions for mental and physical health and well-being.
Dose: Daily.
How to: Use the 'Over To You' exercise on page 180.

19. *Use Nature to Soothe*
Your objective: To use nature to help quell your anxiety
symptoms and improve happiness and well-being.
Dose: Daily and as and when required.
How to: Use the 'Over To You' exercise on page 184

20. *Reduce Mental Overload*
Your objective: To help quell anxiety symptoms or eliminate
anxiety altogether, recoup wasted energy and focus and gain
more calm and resilience.
Dose: Daily.
How to: Use the 'Over To You' exercise on page 188.

21. Use Exercise for Easing Anxiety Symptoms

Your objective: To use exercise to help quell your anxiety symptoms and to help you problem-solve and to help eliminate your anxiety long term.

Dose: Three to five times a week for at least thirty minutes. Additionally, use as and when required for as long as required for problem-solving or for shifting the feeling of anxiety or tension from your body and relaxing your mind.

How to: Use the 'Over To You' exercise on page 195.

22. Create a Positive Mind–Body Connection

Your objective: To elevate your self-image and self-worth with proper cleanliness and self-love.

Dose: Maintain cleanliness daily. Pamper yourself as required.

How to: Use the 'Over To You' exercise on page 202.

23. Having 'Me Time' Is Vital

Your objective: To take ownership of how much time and space you need to feel calm, rested, resilient and ready for the world.

Dose: Daily.

How to: Use the 'Over To You' exercise on page 205.

Calm Strengthening Habit 5: Use problem-solving thoughts and behaviours

24. Tune into Your Body's Communication of Your Subconscious Thoughts

Your objective: To be skilled at using your body as a communication device, communicating your thoughts and emotions to you, including who or what or when you feel anxious or calm, tense or relaxed, threatened or safe, unsure or confident, overwhelmed or energetic, weak or resilient, and so on.

Dose: Daily and as and when required.
How to: Use the 'Over To You' exercise on page 62.

25. Problem-Solving So You Can Honour the Three Pillars of Calm

Your objective: To problem-solve relentlessly anything you need ideas or answers for, including how to correctly identify and implement Calm Pillars 1, 2 and 3 (identify the cause of your anxiety, identify solutions to overcome the threat, take thoughtful action to resolve the issue).
Dose: Daily, or near daily, to problem-solve, overcome challenges, resolve anxiety, achieve goals and regulate emotions.
How to: Use the 'Over To You' exercise on page 231.

26. Tuning Into Your Intuition

Your objective: To use your intuition to help you learn about people and situations, identify threats and safety, and make good decisions for you.
Dose: As and when required.
How to: Use the 'Over To You' exercise on page 235.

You Can Be Anxiety Free in as Little as Four Minutes or Four Weeks

You are now equipped to solve and resolve your anxiety within a few minutes or a few weeks (except where an externally-generated threat cannot be resolved within four weeks due to reasons out of your control).

Remember, anxiety is your friend. It's your brain's way of saying, 'Warning, something is or might sabotage your goals, health, happiness and survival – find it, fix it!' to which your mental response should be, 'Gee, thanks, I'm on it!'

All you then have to do, is:

◊ honour The Three Pillars of Calm (identify cause, identify solutions, take action),
◊ and help yourself to do this by employing the Five Calm Strengthening Habits (positive thoughts, positive emotions, positive relationships, good self-care and good problem-solving).

To become anxiety-free in four minutes, identify, solve and resolve the anxiety-causing threat (apply the Three Pillars of Calm).

To become anxiety-free in four weeks, identify, solve and resolve the anxiety-causing threat (apply the Three Pillars of Calm) AND rewire your brain for calm and self-serving habits.

Don't let the negativity or confusion of others shape your life. It's up to you to make yourself calm and anxiety free in minutes or weeks. My clients have achieved this time and time again. You can too – and that makes me very excited for you!

References

1. Na, H.-R., Kang, E.-H., Lee, J.-H., and Yu, B.-H. (2011). The genetic basis of panic disorder. *Journal of Korean Medical Science*, 26(6), 701–710. http://doi.org/10.3346/jkms.2011.26.6.701; Waszczuk, M. A., Zavos, H. M. S., and Eley, T. C. (2013). Genetic and environmental influences on relationship between anxiety sensitivity and anxiety subscales in children. *Journal of Anxiety Disorders*, 27(5), 475–484. http://doi.org/10.1016/j.janxdis.2013.05.008.

2. Mind (2016). 'What Causes Depression?' Available at: https://www.mind.org.uk/information-support/types-of-mental-health-problems/depression/causes/#childhood.

3. Harvard Medical School (2011). 'What Causes Depression?' Available at: https://www.health.harvard.edu/mind-and-mood/what-causes-depression.

4. Steimer, T. (2002). The biology of fear- and anxiety-related behaviors. *Dialogues in Clinical Neuroscience*, 4(3), 231–249.

5. Meeten, F., Davey, G. C. L., Makovac, E. (2016). Goal directed worry rules are associated with distinct patterns of amygdala functional connectivity and vagal modulation during perseverative cognition front. *Hum. Neurosci.*, https://doi.org/10.3389/fnhum.2016.00553

6. Weich, S., Pearce, H., Croft P., Singh S. et al. (2014). Effect of anxiolytic and hypnotic drug prescriptions on mortality hazards: retrospective cohort study. *BMJ*, 348:g1996.

7. Locke, E. A. and Latham, G. P. (2002). Building a practically useful theory of goal setting and task motivation: A 35-year odyssey. *American Psychologist*, 57(9):705–17.

8. Locke, E. A., Shaw, K. N., Saari, L. M. and Latham, G. P. (1981). Goal setting and task performance: 1969–1980. *Psychological Bulletin*, 90(1):125–52.

9. Hirsch, C., Meynen, T. and Clark, D. (2004). Negative self-imagery in social anxiety contaminates social interactions. *Memory*, 12:496–506.

10. Collier, L. (2017). 'Using objective data to improve performance'. Available at: http://www.apa.org/monitor/2017/06/data-performance.aspx.

11. Lackner, R. J., and Fresco, D. M. (2016). Interaction effect of brooding rumination and interoceptive awareness on depression and anxiety symptoms. *Behaviour Research and Therapy*, 85:43–52. http://doi.org/10.1016/j.brat.2016.08.007.

12. Kandasamy, N. et al. (2016). Interoceptive ability predicts survival on a London trading floor. *Sci. Rep.*, 6, 32986; doi: 10.1038/srep32986.

13. Yang, M., Kim, B., Lee, E., Lee, D., Yu, B., Jeon, H. J. and Kim, J. (2014). Worry and rumination. *Psychiatry Clin Neurosci*, 68:712–720. doi:10.1111/pcn.12193.

14. Spinhoven, P., Drost, J., van Hemert, B., and Penninx, B. W. (2015). Common rather than unique aspects of repetitive negative thinking are related to depressive and anxiety disorders and symptoms. *J. Anxiety Disord.*, 33:45–52. doi: 10.1016/j.janxdis.2015.05.001.

15. Gustavson, D. E., du Pont, A., Whisman, M. A., and Miyake, A. (2018). Evidence for transdiagnostic repetitive negative thinking and its association with rumination, worry, and depression and anxiety symptoms: A commonality analysis. *Collabra: Psychology*, 4(1), 13. DOI: http://doi.org/10.1525/collabra.128.

16. Ruscio, A. M., Gentes, E. L., Jones, J. D., Hallion, L. S., Coleman, E. S., and Swendsen, J. (2015). Rumination predicts heightened responding to stressful life events in major depressive disorder and generalized anxiety disorder. *Journal of Abnormal Psychology*, 124(1), 17–26. http://doi.org/10.1037/abn0000025.

17. Wolfgang H. R. Miltner, Otto W. Witte. (2016). Neural plasticity in rehabilitation and psychotherapy. *Zeitschrift für Psychologie*, 224:2, 59–61.

18. Hölzel, B. K., Carmody, J., Vangel, M., Congleton, C., Yerramsetti, S. M., Gard, T., and Lazar, S. W. (2011). Mindfulness practice leads to increases in regional brain gray matter density. *Psychiatry Research: Neuroimaging*, 191(1):36–43.

19. Hölzel, B. K., Carmody, J., Evans, K. C., Hoge, E. A., Dusek, J. A., Morgan, L., Pitman, R. K., and Lazar, S. W. (2009). Stress reduction correlates with structural changes in the amygdala. *Social Cognitive and Affective Neuroscience*, 5(1): 11–17.

20. Doidge, N. (2007). *The Brain That Changes Itself: Stories of Personal Triumph from the Frontiers of Brain Science*. New York, USA: Penguin Group.

21. Ibid.

22. Pascual-Leone, A., Amedi, A., Fregni, F., and Merabet, L. B. (2005). The plastic human brain cortex. *Annual Review of Neuroscience*, 28: 377–401.

23. Lieberman, M. D., Eisenberger, N. I., Crockett, M. J., Tom, S. M., Pfeifer, J. H., Way, B. M. (2007). Putting feelings into words: affect labeling disrupts amygdala activity in response to affective stimuli. *Psychol Sci.*, 2007 May; 18(5):421–428. doi: 10.1111/j.1467-9280.2007.01916.

24. Eagleson, C., Hayes, S., Mathews, A., Perman, G. and Hirsch, C. (2016). The power of positive thinking: Pathological worry is reduced by thought replacement in Generalized Anxiety Disorder. *Behaviour Research and Therapy*, 78. 10.1016/j.brat.2015.12.017.

25. Hatzigeorgiadis, A., Zourbanos, N., Galanis, E. and Theodorakis, Y. (2011). Self-talk and sports performance: A meta-analysis, *Perspectives on Psychological Science*, 6(4):348–56.

26. Hatzigeorgiadis, A., Zourbanos, N., Mpoumpaki, S. and Theodorakis, Y. (2009). Mechanisms underlying the self-talk–performance relationship: The effects of self-talk on self-confidence and anxiety, *Psychology of Sport and Exercise*, 10(1):186–92.

27. Lane, A. M., Totterdell, P., MacDonald, I., Devonport, T. J., Friesen, A. P., Beedie, C. J. and Nevill, A. (2016). Brief online training enhances competitive performance: Findings of the BBC Lab UK Psychological Skills Intervention Study. *Frontiers in Psychology*, 7, 413. http://doi.org/10.3389/fpsyg.2016.00413.

28. Shi, Xi., Brinthaupt, T. and Mccree, M. (2015). The relationship of self-talk frequency to communication apprehension and public speaking anxiety. *Personality and Individual Differences*, 75:125–129. 10.1016/j.paid.2014.11.023.

29. Moser, J. S., Dougherty, A., Mattson, W. I. and Katz, B. (2017). Third-person self-talk facilitates emotion regulation without engaging cognitive control: Converging evidence from ERP and fMRI. *Scientific Reports*, Vol. 7, Art. No.: 4519

30. Chadwick, A. E., Zoccola, P. M., Figueroa W. S. and Rabideau, E. M. (2016). Communication and stress: Effects of hope evocation and rumination messages on heart rate, anxiety, and emotions after a stressor. *Health Communication*, 31:12,1447-1459, DOI: 10.1080/10410236.2015.1079759

31. Benedetti, F., Carlino, E. and Pollo, A. (2011). How placebos change the patient's brain. *Europsychopharmacology*, Vol. 36, 339–354.

32. Petrovic, P. et al. (2005). Placebo in emotional processing–induced expectations of anxiety relief activate a generalized modulatory network. *Neuron*, Vol. 46, Issue 6, 957–969.

33. Colloca L., Sigaudo M. and Benedetti F. (2008). The role of learning in nocebo and placebo effects. *Pain*, 2008 May; 136(1-2):211–8. doi: 10.1016/j.pain.2008.02.006. Epub 2008 Mar 26.

34. Crum, A. J. and Langer, E. J. (2007). Mind-set matters: Exercise and the placebo effect. *Psychological Science*, 18, No. 2:165–171.

35. Weger, U. W. and Loughnan, S. (2013). Mobilizing unused resources: Using the placebo concept to enhance cognitive performance. *The Quarterly Journal of Experimental Psychology*, 66:1, 23–28.

36. Lieberman, M. D., Eisenberger, N. I., Crockett, M. J., Tom, S. M., Pfeifer, J. H., Way, B. M. (2007). Affect labeling disrupts amygdala activity in response to affective stimuli. *Psychol. Sci.*, 18 (5), 421–428.

37. Kalokerinos, E. K., Greenaway, K. H. and Denson, T. F. (2015). Reappraisal but not suppression downregulates the experience of positive and negative emotion. *Emotion*, 15(3):271–5.

38. Skånland, M. S. (2013). Music, health, and well-being. *International Journal of Qualitative Studies on Health and Well-being*, 8:1, DOI: 10.3402/qhw.v8io.21780.

39. Hou, J., Song, B., Chen, A. C. N., Sun, C., Zhou, J., Zhu, H., and Beauchaine, T. P. (2017). Review on neural correlates of emotion regulation and music: Implications for emotion dysregulation. *Frontiers in Psychology*, 8:501. http://doi.org/10.3389/fpsyg.2017.00501.

40. Panteleeva, Y., Ceschi, G., Glowinski, D., Courvoisier, D. S. and Grandjean, D. (2017). Music for anxiety? Meta-analysis of anxiety reduction in non-clinical samples. *Psychology of Music*, Vol. 46, Issue 4, 473–487.

41. Thoma, M. V., La Marca, R., Brönnimann, R., Finkel, L., Ehlert, U., and Nater, U. M. (2013). The effect of music on the human stress response. *PLoS ONE*, 8(8), e70156. http://doi.org/10.1371/journal.pone.0070156.

42. Feng, S., Suri, R. and Bell, M. (2014). Does classical music relieve math anxiety? Role of tempo on price computation avoidance. *Psychol. Mark.*, 31:489–499. doi:10.1002/mar.20710.

43. Carlson, E., Saarikallio, S., Toiviainen, P., Bogert, B., Kliuchko, M., and Brattico, E. (2015). Maladaptive and adaptive emotion regulation through music: a behavioral and neuroimaging study of males and females. *Frontiers in Human Neuroscience*, 9:466. http://doi.org/10.3389/fnhum.2015.00466.

44. Croom, A. (2015). Music practice and participation for psychological well-being: A review of how music influences positive emotion, engagement, relationships, meaning, and accomplishment. *Musicae Scientiae*, 19:44–64. 10.1177/1029864914561709

45. Jayakar, J. P., Alter, D. A. (2017). Music for anxiety reduction in patients undergoing cardiac catheterization: A systematic review and meta-analysis of randomized controlled trials. *Complementary Therapies in Clinical Practice*, Vol. 28, 122–130, ISSN 1744-3881, https://doi.org/10.1016/j.ctcp.2017.05.011.

46. Bradt J, Dileo C, Shim M. (2013). Music interventions for preoperative anxiety. *Cochrane Database of Systematic Reviews* 2013, Issue 6. Art. No.: CD006908. DOI: 10.1002/14651858.CD006908.pub2.

47. Kwo-Chen, L., Yu-Huei C. et al. (2012). Evidence that music listening reduces preoperative patients' anxiety. *Biological Research For Nursing*, Vol. 14, Issue 1, 78–84.

48. Kovac, M. (2014). Music interventions for the treatment of preoperative anxiety. *Journal of Consumer Health on the Internet*. 18: 193–201. 10.1080/15398285.2014.902282.

49. Miyata, K., Odanaka, H., Nitta, Y., Shimoji, S., Kanehira, T., Kawanami, M. and Fujisawa, T. (2016). Music before dental surgery suppresses sympathetic activity derived from preoperative anxiety: A randomized controlled trial. *JDR Clinical & Translational Research*, Vol. 1, Issue 2, 153–162.

50. Akbas, A., Gulpinar, M. T., Sancak, E. B., Karakan, T., Demirbas, A., Utangac, M. M., Dede, O., Sancaktutar, A. A., Simsek, T., Sahin, B. and Resorlu, B. (2016). The effect of music therapy during shockwave lithotripsy on patient relaxation, anxiety, and pain perception. *Renal Failure*, 38:1, 46-49, DOI: 10.3109/0886022X.2015.1096728; Rossetti, A., Chadha, M., Torres, B. N., Lee, J. K., Hylton, D., Loewy, J. V., Harrison, L. B. (2017). The impact of music therapy on anxiety in cancer patients undergoing simulation for radiation therapy. *International Journal of Radiation Oncology/Biology/Physics*, Vol. 99, Issue 1, 103–110, ISSN 0360-3016, https://doi.org/10.1016/j.ijrobp.2017.05.003.

51. Chang, M.-Y.; Chen, C.-H.; Huang, K.-F. (2008). Effects of music therapy on psychological health of women during pregnancy. *J. Clin. Nurs.*, 17: 2580–2587.

52. Labrague, L. J. and McEnroe-Petitte, D. M. (2014). Use of music intervention for reducing anxiety and promoting satisfaction in first-time Filipino fathers. *American Journal of Men's Health*, Vol. 10, Issue 2, 120–127.

53. Hallam, S. and Creech, A. (2016). Can active music making promote health and well-being in older citizens? Findings of the music for life project. *London Journal of Primary Care*, 8:2, 21–25, DOI: 10.1080/17571472.2016.1152099.

54. Monteiro, N. and Wall, D. (2011). African dance as healing modality throughout the diaspora: The use of ritual and movement to work through trauma. *Journal of Pan African Studies*, 4:234–252.

55. Quiroga Murcia, C., Kreutz, G., Clift, S. and Bongard, S. (2010). Shall we dance? An exploration of the perceived benefits of dancing on well-being. *Arts & Health*, 2:149–163. 10.1080/17533010903488582.

56. Harvard Mahoney Neuroscience Institute (2018). Dancing and the brain. Available at: http://neuro.hms.harvard.edu/harvard-mahoney-neuroscience-institute/brain-newsletter/and-brain-series/dancing-and-brain.

57. Verghese, J., Lipton, R. B., Katz, M. J., Hall, C. B., Derby, C. A., Kuslansky, G. and Buschke, H. (2003). Leisure activities and the risk of dementia in the elderly. *The New England Journal of Medicine*, 348:2508–2516. http://dx.doi.org/10.1056/NEJMoa022252.

58. Ibid.

59. Muro, A. and Artero, N. (2017). Dance practice and well-being correlates in young women. *Women & Health*, 57:10, 1193–1203, DOI: 10.1080/03630242.2016.1243607.

60. Duberg A., Hagberg L., Sunvisson H. and Möller M. (2013) Influencing self-rated health among adolescent girls with dance intervention a randomized controlled trial. *JAMA Pediatr.*, 167(1):27–31. doi:10.1001/jamapediatrics.2013.421.

61. Ibid.

62. Aaron, R. E., Rinehart, K. and Ceballos, N. (2011). Arts-based interventions to reduce anxiety levels among college students. *Arts & Health*, 3:27–38. 10.1080/17533015.2010.481290.

63. Sandmire, D., Gorham, S., Rankin, N. and Grimm, D. (2012). The influence of art making on anxiety: A pilot study. *Art Therapy*, 29:10.1080/07421656.2012.683748.

64. Triantoro, S. and Yunita, A. (2014). The efficacy of art therapy to reduce anxiety among bullying victims. *International Journal of Research Studies in Psychology*, 3:10.5861/ijrsp.2014.829.

65. Quoidbach, J., Mikolajczak, M. and Gross, J. J. (2015) Positive interventions: An emotion regulation perspective. *Psychological bulletin*, 141:655–693.

66. Lyubomirsky, S. and Layous, K. (2013). How do simple positive activities increase well-being? *Current Directions in Psychological Science*, Vol. 22, Issue 1, 57–62.

67. Küller, R., Ballal, S., Laike, T., Mikellides, B. and Tonello, G. (2006). The impact of light and color on psychological mood. *Ergonomics*, 49(14) 1496–507.

68. Galatzer-Levy, I. R., Brown, A. D., Henn-Haase, C., Metzler, T. J., Neylan, T. C. and Marmar, C. R. (2013). Positive and negative emotion prospectively predict trajectories of resilience and distress among high-exposure police officers. *Emotion*, 15:545–553.

69. Gerson, J., Plagnol, A. and Corr, P. J. (2016). Subjective well-being and social media use: Do personality traits moderate the impact of social comparison on Facebook? *Computers in Human Behavior*, 63:813–822. doi: 10.1016/j.chb.2016.06.023.

70. Kirkpatrick, L. A. and Hazan, C. (1994). Attachment styles and close relationships: A four-year prospective study. *Personal Relationships*, 1(2):123–42.

71. Hulme, N., Hirsch, C. and Stopa, L. (2012). Images of the self and self-esteem: Do positive self-images improve self-esteem in social anxiety? *Cognitive Behaviour Therapy*, 41:2, 163–173, DOI: 10.1080/16506073.2012.664557.

72. McNaughton, N. and Corr, P. J. (2004). A two-dimensional neuropsychology of defense: Fear/anxiety and defensive distance. *Neurosci. Biobehav. Rev.*, 28:285–305.

73. Hirsh, J. B. and Kang, S. K. (2015). Mechanisms of identity conflict: Uncertainty, anxiety, and the behavioral inhibition system. *Personality and Social Psychology Review*, Vol. 20, Issue 3, 223–244.

74. Ørjasæter, K. B., Stickley, T., Hedlund, M., and Ness, O. (2017). Transforming identity through participation in music and theatre: Exploring narratives of people with mental health problems. *International Journal of Qualitative Studies on Health and Well-Being*, 12(sup2), 1379339. http://doi.org/10.1080/17482631.2017.1379339.

75. Erickson, T. M., Granillo, M. T., Crocker, J., Abelson, J. L., Reas, H. E. and Quach, C. M. (2018). Compassionate and self-image goals as interpersonal maintenance factors in clinical depression and anxiety. *J Clin Psychol.*, 74:608–625. https://doi.org/10.1002/jclp.22524.

76. Aknin, L. B., Broesch, T., Hamlin, J. K. and Van de Vondervoort, J. W. (2015). 'Prosocial Behavior Leads to Happiness in a Small-Scale Rural Society', Journal of Experimental Psychology: General, 144(4):788–95.

77. Piferi, R. L. and Lawler, K. A. (2006). Social support and ambulatory blood pressure: An examination of both receiving and giving. *International Journal of Psychophysiology*, 62(2):328–36.

78. Williams, M. T., Chapman, L. K., Wong, J. and Turkheimer, E. (2012). The role of ethnic identity in symptoms of anxiety and depression in African Americans. *Psychiatry Research*, 199(1), 31–36. http://doi.org/10.1016/j.psychres.2012.03.049.

79. Hopkins, P. D. and Shook, N. J. (2017). A review of sociocultural factors that may underlie differences in African American and European American anxiety. *Journal of Anxiety Disorders*, Vol. 49, 104–113.

80. Remes, O., Brayne, C., van der Linde, R. and Lafortune, L. (2016). A systematic review of reviews on the prevalence of anxiety disorders in adult populations. *Brain and Behavior*, 6(7), e00497. http://doi.org/10.1002/brb3.497.

81. Zurbriggen, E. L., Ben Hagai, E. and Leon, G. (2016). Negotiating privacy and intimacy on social media: Review and recommendations. *Translational Issues in Psychological Science*, 2. 10.1037/tps0000078.

82. Vogel, E., Rose, J., Roberts, L. and Eckles, K. (2014). Social comparison, social media, and self-esteem. *Psychology of Popular Media Culture*, 3:206–222. 10.1037/ppm0000047.

83. Vendemia, M.A., High, A. C. and DeAndrea, D. C. (2017). "Friend" or Foe? Why People Friend Disliked Others on Facebook. *Communication Research Reports*, 34:1, 29–36, DOI: 10.1080/08824096.2016.1227778.

84. Chou, H.-T. and Edge, N. (2012). "They are happier and having better lives than I am": The impact of using Facebook on perceptions of others' lives. *Cyberpsychology, Behavior, and Social Networking*, 15:2, 117–121.

85. Mineo, L. (2017). 'Good genes are nice, but joy is better'. *The Harvard Gazette*. Available at: https://news.harvard.edu/gazette/story/2017/04/over-nearly-80-years-harvard-study-has-been-showing-how-to-live-a-healthy-and-happy-life/; Powell, A. (2012). 'Decoding keys to a healthy life'. *The Harvard Gazette*. Available at: http://news.harvard.edu/gazette/story/2012/02/decoding-keys-to-a-healthy-life/; Shenk, J. W. (2009). 'What makes us happy?' *The Atlantic*. Available at: http://www.theatlantic.com/magazine/archive/2009/06/what-makes-us-happy/307439/.

86. Waldinger, R. (2015). 'What makes a good life? Lessons from the longest study on happiness'. Ted Talks. Available at: http://www.ted.com/talks/robert_waldinger_what_makes_a_good_life_lessons_from_the_longest_study_on_happiness/transcript?language=en.

87. Powell, A. (2012). 'Decoding keys to a healthy life'. *The Harvard Gazette*. Available at: http://news.harvard.edu/gazette/story/2012/02/decoding-keys-to-a-healthy-life.

88. Holt-Lunstad, J., Smith, T. B., Baker, M., Harris, T. and Stephenson, D. (2015). Loneliness and Social Isolation as Risk Factors for Mortality: A Meta-Analytic Review. *Perspectives on Psychological Science*, 10(2):227–37.

89. Walker, E. R., McGee, R. E. and Druss, B. G. (2015). Mortality in mental disorders and global disease burden implications: A systematic review and meta-analysis. *JAMA Psychiatry*, 72(4):334–341. doi:10.1001/jamapsychiatry.2014.2502.

90. Ahn, D. and Shin, D.-H. (2013). Is the social use of media for seeking connectedness or for avoiding social isolation? Mechanisms underlying media use and subjective well-being. *Computers in Human Behavior*, Vol. 29, Issue 6, 2453–2462, ISSN 0747-5632, https://doi.org/10.1016/j.chb.2012.12.022.

91. Seabrook, E. M., Kern, M. L. and Rickard, N. S. (2016). Social networking sites, depression, and anxiety: A systematic review. *JMIR Mental Health*, 3(4), e50. http://doi.org/10.2196/mental.5842.

92. Heart Math Institute (2012). Heart intelligence. Available at: https://www.heartmath.org/articles-of-the-heart/the-math-of-heartmath/heart-intelligence.

93. NIH. How the Heart Works: The Heart's Electrical System. Available at: https://www.nhlbi.nih.gov/node/3725.

94. McCraty, R. (2017). New frontiers in heart rate variability and social coherence research: Techniques, technologies, and implications for improving group dynamics and outcomes. *Frontiers in Public Health*, 5:267. 10.3389/fpubh.2017.00267.

95. McCraty, R., Deyhle, A. and Childre, D. (2012). The global coherence initiative: Creating a coherent planetary standing wave. *Global Advances in Health and Medicine*, 1(1), 64–77. http://doi.org/10.7453/gahmj.2012.1.1.013.

96. Campus, M. (2017). Heart rate variability: A new way to track well-being. *Harvard Health*. Available at: https://www.health.harvard.edu/blog/heart-rate-variability-new-way-track-well-2017112212789.

97. Ginsberg, J. P., Berry, M. E. and Powell, D. A. (2010). Cardiac coherence and PTSD in combat veterans. *Alternative Therapies in Health and Medicine*, 16:52–60.

98. Hearth Math (2018). Quick coherence technique. Available at: https://www.heartmath.com/quick-coherence-technique.

99. Morris, S. (2010). Achieving collective coherence: Group effects on heart rate variability coherence and heart rhythm synchronization. *Alternative Therapies*, Jul/Aug 2010, Vol. 16, No. 4.

100. Konvalinka, I., Xygalatas, D. and Bulbulia, J. et al. (2011). Synchronized arousal between performers and related spectators in a fire-walking ritual. *Proceedings of the National Academy of Sciences*, May 2011, 108 (20) 8514-8519; DOI:10.1073/pnas.1016955108.

101. Ferrer, E. and Helm, J. (2012). Dynamical systems modeling of physiological coregulation in dyadic interactions. *International Journal of Psychophysiology*, 88. 10.1016/j.ijpsycho.2012.10.013.

102. Goldstein, P., Weissman-Fogel, I., Shamay-Tsoory, S. G. (2017). The role of touch in regulating inter-partner physiological coupling during empathy for pain. *Scientific Reports*, Vol. 7, Art. No.: 3252.

103. Mitkidis, P., McGraw, J., Roepstorff, A. and Wallot, S. (2015). Building trust: Heart rate synchrony and arousal during joint action increased by public goods game. *Physiology & Behavior*, 10:1016/j.physbeh.2015.05.033.

104. Radin, D. (2004). The feeling of being stared at: An analysis and replication. *Journal of the Society for Psychical Research*, 68:245–52

105. Sheldrake, R. (2005). The sense of being stared at. *Journal of Consciousness Studies*, 12:10-13.

106. McCraty, R., Atkinson, M., Stolc, V., Alabdulgader, A. A., Vainoras, A., and Ragulskis, M. (2017). Synchronization of human autonomic nervous system rhythms with geomagnetic activity in human subjects. *International Journal of Environmental Research and Public Health*, 14(7), 770. http://doi.org/10.3390/ijerph14070770.

107. McCraty, R., Deyhle, A. and Childre, D. (2012). The global coherence initiative: Creating a coherent planetary standing wave. *Global Advances in Health and Medicine*, 1(1), 64–77. http://doi.org/10.7453/gahmj.2012.1.1.013

108. Framingham Heart Study. Available at: https://www.framinghamheartstudy.org/.

109. Fowler, J. H. and Christakis, N. A. (2008). Dynamic spread of happiness in a large social network: Longitudinal analysis over 20 years in the Framingham Heart Study. *Br. Med. J.*, 337, a2338. (doi:10.1136/bmj. a2338).

110. Hoppmann, C. A., Gerstorf, D., Willis, S. L. and Schaie, K. W. (2011). Spousal interrelations in happiness in the Seattle Longitudinal Study: Considerable similarities in levels and change over time. *Developmental Psychology*, 47(1), 1–8.

111. Rosenquist, J., Fowler, J. and Christakis, N. (2011). Social network determinants of depression. *Molecular Psychiatry*, 16(3), 10.1038/mp.2010.13. http://doi.org/10.1038/mp.2010.13.

112. Cacioppo, J. T., Fowler, J. H., and Christakis, N. A. (2009). Alone in the crowd: The structure and spread of loneliness in a large social network. *Journal of Personality and Social Psychology*, 97(6), 977–991. http://doi.org/10.1037/a0016076.

113. Coviello, L., Sohn, Y., Kramer, A. D. I., Marlow, C., Franceschetti, M., Christakis, N. A., et al. (2014). Detecting emotional contagion in massive social networks. *PLoS ONE*, 9(3):e90315. https://doi.org/10.1371/journal.pone.0090315.

114. Peen, J., Schoevers, R. A., Beekman, A. T., et al. (2010). The current status of urban-rural differences in psychiatric disorders. *Acta Psychiatr Scand*, 121:84–93.

115. Lederbogen, F., et al. (2011). City living and urban upbringing affect neural social stress processing in humans. *Nature*, 474:498–501.

116. Farris, S. G., Allan, N. P., Morales, P. C., Schmidt, N. B. and Zvolensky, M. J. (2015). Does successful smoking cessation reduce anxious arousal among treatment-seeking smokers? *Journal of Anxiety Disorders*, 36:92–98. http://doi.org/10.1016/j.janxdis.2015.07.009.

117. Holmes, A., Fitzgerald, P. J. and MacPherson, K. P. (2012). Chronic alcohol remodels prefrontal neurons and disrupts NMDAR-mediated fear extinction encoding. *Nature Neuroscience*, Vol. 15, 1359–1361.

118. Haynes, J., Farrell, M., Singleton, N., Meltzer, H., Araya, R., Lewis, G. and Wiles, N. (2005). Alcohol consumption as a risk factor for anxiety and depression: Results from the longitudinal follow-up of the National Psychiatric Morbidity Survey. *British Journal of Psychiatry*, 187(6), 544–551. doi:10.1192/bjp.187.6.544.

119. Cox, R. C. and Olatunji, B. O. (2016). A systematic review of sleep disturbance in anxiety and related disorders. *Journal of Anxiety Disorders*, Vol. 37, 104–129, ISSN 0887-6185, https://doi.org/10.1016/j.janxdis.2015.12.001.

120. Van der Helm, E. and Walker, M. P. (2009). Overnight therapy? The role of sleep in emotional brain processing. *Psychological Bulletin*, 135(5), 731–748. http://doi.org/10.1037/a0016570.

121. Klumpp, H., Roberts, J., Kapella, M. C., Kennedy, A. E., Kumar, A. and Phan, K. L. (2017). Subjective and objective sleep quality modulate emotion regulatory brain function in anxiety and depression. *Depress Anxiety*, 34:651–660. https://doi.org/10.1002/da.22622.

122. Cai, D. J., Mednick, S. A., Harrison, E. M., Kanady, J. C. and Mednick, S. C. (2009). REM, not incubation, improves creativity by priming associative networks. *Proceedings of the National Academy of Sciences*, Jun 2009, 106(25) 10130-10134; DOI:10.1073/pnas.0900271106.

123. Zalta, A. K., Dowd, S., Rosenfield, D., Smits, J. A. J., Otto, M. W., Simon, N. M. and Pollack, M. H. (2013). Sleep quality predicts treatment outcome in CBT for social anxiety disorder. *Depression and Anxiety*, 30(11), 1114–1120. http://doi.org/10.1002/da.22170.

124. Ramsawh, H. J., Bomyea, J., Stein, M. B., Cissell, S. H. and Lang, A. J. (2016). Sleep quality improvement during cognitive behavioral therapy for anxiety disorders. *Behavioral Sleep Medicine*, 14(3), 267–278. http://doi.org/10.1080/15402002.2014.981819.

125. Ramsawh, H. J., et al. (2009). Relationship of anxiety disorders, sleep quality, and functional impairment in a community sample. *Journal of Psychiatric Research*, 43, 10:926–33.

126. Baroni, A.,Bruzzese, J.-M., Di Bartolo, C. A., Ciarleglio, A. and Shatkin, J. P. (2018). Impact of a sleep course on sleep, mood and anxiety symptoms in college students: A pilot study. *Journal of American College Health*, 66:1, 41–50, http://doi.org/10.1080/07448481.2017.1369091.

127. Ewing, D. L., Manassei, M., Gould van Praag, C., et al. (2017). Sleep and the heart: Interoceptive differences linked to poor experiential sleep quality in anxiety and depression. *Biological Psychology*, Vol. 127, 163–172, ISSN 0301-0511, https://doi.org/10.1016/j.biopsycho.2017.05.011.

128. Venkatraman, V., Huettel, S. A., Chuah, L. Y. M., Payne, J. W. and Chee, M. W. L. (2011). Sleep deprivation biases the neural mechanisms underlying economic preferences. *The Journal of Neuroscience*, 31:3712–8. 10.1523/JNEUROSCI.4407-10.2011.

129. Minkel, J., Htaik, O., Banks, S. and Dinges, D. (2011). Emotional expressiveness in sleep-deprived healthy adults. *Behavioral Sleep Medicine*, 9(1):5–14. http://doi.org/10.1080/15402002.2011.533987.

130. Wang, Q., Chair, S. Y., Wong, E. and Li, X. (2016). The effects of music intervention on sleep quality in community-dwelling elderly. *The Journal of Alternative and Complementary Medicine*, 22. 10.1089/acm.2015.0304.

131. Shobeiri, F., Khaledi, S., Masoumi, S. Z. and Roshanaei, G. (2016). The effect of music therapy counseling on sleep quality in pregnant women. *International Journal of Medical Research & Health Sciences*, 5, 9S:408-416.

132. Mirbastegan, N., Ganjloo, J., Bakhshandeh Bavarsad, M., Rakhshani M.H. (2016). Effects of aromatherapy on anxiety and vital signs of myocardial infarction patients in intensive care units. *IMJM*. Vol. 15, No. 2, Dec 2016.

133. Karadag, E., Samancioglu, S., Ozden, D. and Bakir, E. (2015). Effects of aromatherapy on sleep quality and anxiety of patients. *Nursing in Critical Care*, 10.1111/nicc.12198.

134. Gould van Praag, C. D., Garfinkel, S. N., Sparasci, O., et al. (2017). Mind-wandering and alterations to default mode network connectivity when listening to naturalistic versus artificial sounds. *Scientific Reports*, Vol. 7, Art. No.: 45273.

135. Saadatmand, V., Rejeh, N., Heravi-Karimooi, M., et al. (2013). Effect of nature-based sounds' intervention on agitation, anxiety, and stress in patients under mechanical ventilator support: A randomised controlled trial. *International Journal of Nursing Studies*, Vol.50, Issue 7, 895–904.

136. Brown, D. K., Barton, J. L. and Gladwell, V. F. (2013). Viewing nature scenes positively affects recovery of autonomic function following acute-mental stress. *Environmental Science & Technology*, 47(11), 5562–5569. http://doi.org/10.1021/es305019p.

137. Shanahan, D. F., Bush, R., Gaston, K., Lin, B., Dean, J., Barber, E. and Fuller, R. (2016). Health benefits from nature experiences depend on dose. *Scientific Report*, 6:28551. 10.1038/srep28551.

138. Ochiai, H., Ikei, H., Song, C., Kobayashi, M., Takamatsu, A., Miura, T., Kagawa, T., Li, Q., Kumeda, S., Imai, M. and Miyazaki, Y. (2015). Physiological and psychological effects of forest therapy on middle-aged males with high-normal blood pressure. *International Journal of Environmental Research and Public Health*. 12:2532–42. 10.3390/ijerph120302532.

139. Ochiai, H., Ikei, H., Song, C., Kobayashi, M., Miura, T., Kagawa, T., Miyazaki, Y. (2015). Physiological and psychological effects of a forest therapy program on middle-aged females. *International Journal of Environmental Research and Public Health*, 12(12) 15222–15232. http://doi.org/10.3390/ijerph121214984.

140. Bratman, G., Hamilton, J. P., Hahn, K. S., Daily, G. C. and Gross, J. J. (2015). Nature experience reduces rumination and subgenual prefrontal cortex activation. *Proceedings of the National Academy of Sciences*, 112:8567–8572. 10.1073/pnas.1510459112.

141. Jordan, R. (2015). Stanford researchers find mental health prescription: Nature. *Stanford News*. Available at: https://news.stanford.edu/2015/06/30/hiking-mental-health-063015/

142. Berry, M., Sweeney, M., Morath, J., Odum, A. and Jordan, K. (2014). The nature of impulsivity: Visual exposure to natural environments decreases impulsive decision-making in a delay discounting task. *PLoS ONE*, 9. e97915. 10.1371/journal.pone.0097915.

143. Igarashi, M., Song, C., Ikei, H., and Miyazaki, Y. (2015). Effect of stimulation by foliage plant display images on prefrontal cortex activity: A comparison with stimulation using actual foliage plants. *Journal of Neuroimaging*, 25(1), 127–130. http://doi.org/10.1111/jon.12078.

144. Park, S.-H. and Mattson, R. H. (2008). Effects of flowering and foliage plants in hospital rooms on patients recovering from abdominal surgery. *HortTechnology*, October–December 2008, Vol. 18, No.: 4563–568.

145. Tennessen, C. M. and Cimprich, B. (1995). Views to nature: Effects on attention. *Journal of Environmental Psychology*, 15:77–85. 10.1016/0272-4944(95)90016-0.

146. Bratman, G., Daily, G., Levy, B. and Gross, J. J. (2015). The benefits of nature experience: Improved affect and cognition. *Landscape and Urban Planning*, 138:41–50. 10.1016/j.landurbplan.2015.02.005.

147. Fenko, A. and Loock, C. (2014). The influence of ambient scent and music on patients' anxiety in a waiting room of a plastic surgeon. *HERD*, 7:38–59. 10.1177/193758671400700304.

148. Fergus, T. A. and Carleton, R. N. (2016). Intolerance of uncertainty and attentional networks: unique associations with alerting. *Journal of Anxiety Disorders*, 41. 10.1016/j.janxdis.2016.03.010.

149. Primack, B., Shensa, A., Escobar-Viera, C., Barrett, E. L., Sidani, J., Colditz, J. B. and Everette, J. A. (2017). Use of multiple social media platforms and symptoms of depression and anxiety: A nationally-representative study among U.S. young adults. *Computers in Human Behavior*, 69:1–9. 10.1016/j.chb.2016.11.013.

150. Asmundson, G., Fetzner, M., DeBoer L., Powers, M., Otto, M. W. and Smits, J. (2013). Let's get physical: A contemporary review of the anxiolytic effects of exercise for anxiety and its disorders. *Depression and Anxiety*. 30. 10.1002/da.22043; Powers, M. B., Asmundson, G. J. G. and Smits, J. A. J. (2015). Exercise for mood and anxiety disorders: The state-of-the science. *Cognitive Behaviour Therapy*, 44(4), 237–239. http://doi.org/10.1080/16506073.2015.1047286; Fetzner, M. and Asmundson, G. (2014). Aerobic exercise reduces symptoms of posttraumatic stress disorder: A randomized controlled trial. *Cognitive Behaviour Therapy*, 44:1–13. 10.1080/16506073.2014.916745.

151. LeBouthillier, D. and Asmundson, G. (2015). A single bout of aerobic exercise reduces anxiety sensitivity but not intolerance of uncertainty or distress tolerance: A randomized controlled trial. *Cognitive Behaviour Therapy*, 44:1–12. 10.1080/16506073.2015.1028094.

152. Calabrese, F., Rossetti, A. C., Racagni, G., Gass, P., Riva, M. A. and Molteni, R. (2014). Brain-derived neurotrophic factor: A bridge between inflammation and neuroplasticity. *Frontiers in Cellular Neuroscience*, 8, 430. http://doi.org/10.3389/fncel.2014.00430.

153. Sleiman, S. F., Henry, J., Al-Haddad, R., El Hayek, L., Abou Haidar, E., Stringer, T., and Chao, M. V. (2016). Exercise promotes the expression of brain derived neurotrophic factor (BDNF) through the action of the ketone body ß-hydroxybutyrate. *eLife*, 5, e15092. http://doi.org/10.7554/eLife.15092.

154. Dinoff, A., Herrmann, N., Swardfager, W., Liu, C. S., Sherman, C., Chan, S. and Lanctôt, K. L. (2016). The effect of exercise training on resting concentrations of peripheral brain-derived neurotrophic factor (BDNF): A meta-analysis. *PLoS ONE*, 11(9), e0163037. http://doi.org/10.1371/journal.pone.0163037.

155. Mondelli, V., Cattaneo, A., Murri, M. B., Di Forti, M., Handley, R., Hepgul, N. and Pariante, C. M. (2011). Stress and inflammation reduce BDNF expression in first-episode psychosis: a pathway to smaller hippocampal volume. *The Journal of Clinical Psychiatry*, 72(12), 1677–1684. http://doi.org/10.4088/JCP.10m06745.

156. Kyun Jeon, Y. and Ha, C. (2017). The effect of exercise intensity on brain derived neurotrophic factor and memory in adolescents. *Environmental Health and Preventive Medicine*, 22. 10.1186/s12199-017-0643-6.

157. Firth, J., Stubbs, B., Vancampfort, D., Schuch, F., Lagopoulos, J., Rosenbaum, S. and Ward, P. (2017). Effect of aerobic exercise on hippocampal volume in humans: A systematic review and meta-analysis. *NeuroImage*, 166. 10.1016/j.neuroimage.2017.11.007.

158. Herring, M., Jacob, M., Suveg, C., O'Connor, P. J. (2011). Effects of short-term exercise training on signs and symptoms of generalized anxiety disorder. *Mental Health and Physical Activity*, 4:71–77. 10.1016/j.mhpa.2011.07.002.

159. Herring, M. P., Kline, C. E. and O'Connor, P. J. (2015). Effects of exercise on sleep among young women with generalized anxiety disorder. *Mental Health and Physical Activity*, 9:59–66. http://doi.org/10.1016/j.mhpa.2015.09.002.

160. Abedi, P., Nikkhah, P. and Najar, S. (2015). Effect of pedometer-based walking on depression, anxiety, and insomnia among postmenopausal women. *Climacteric*, 18:1–16. 10.3109/13697137.2015.1065246.

161. Halappa, Na., Varambally, S., Thirthalli, J., Rao, M., Christopher, R. and Gangadhar, B. (2016). Serum cortisol and BDNF in patients with major depression-effect of yoga. *International Review of Psychiatry*, 28:1–6. 10.1080/09540261.2016.1175419.

162. Cahn, B. R., Goodman, M. S., Peterson, C. T., Maturi, R. and Mills, P. J. (2017). Yoga, meditation and mind-body health: Increased BDNF, cortisol awakening response, and altered inflammatory marker expression after a 3-month yoga and meditation retreat. *Frontiers in Human Neuroscience*, 11:315. http://doi.org/10.3389/fnhum.2017.00315.

163. Medina, J., Hopkins, L., Powers, M., Baird, S. O. and Smits, J. (2015). The effects of a hatha yoga intervention on facets of distress tolerance. *Cognitive Behaviour Therapy*, 44(4):288–300. http://doi.org/10.1080/16506073.2015.1028433.

164. Vancampfort, D., De Hert, M., Knapen, J., Wampers, M., Demunter, H., Deckx, S., et al. (2011). State anxiety, psychological stress and positive well-being responses to yoga and aerobic exercise in people with schizophrenia: A pilot study. *Disability and Rehabilitation*, 33(8):684–9.

165. Blumenthal, J., Smith, P. J., Hoffman, B. M. (2012). 'Is Exercise a Viable Treatment for Depression', *ACSMs Health and Fitness*, 16(4).

166. Agarwal, U., Mishra, S., Xu, J., Levin, S., Gonzales, J. J. and Barnard, N. D. (2014). A multicenter randomized controlled trial of a nutrition intervention program in a multiethnic adult population in the corporate setting reduces depression and anxiety and improves quality of life: The GEICO study. *American Journal of Health Promotion*, 29. 10.4278/ajhp.130218-QUAN-72.

167. Foster, J. and McVey Neufeld, K. A. (2013). Gut-brain axis: How the microbiome influences anxiety and depression. *Trends in Neurosciences*, 36. 10.1016/j.tins.2013.01.005.

168. Gautam, M., Agrawal, M., Gautam, M., Sharma, P., Gautam, A. S. and Gautam, S. (2012). Role of antioxidants in generalised anxiety disorder and depression. *Indian Journal of Psychiatry*, 54(3):244–247. http://doi.org/10.4103/0019-5545.102424.

169. Torabi, M., Kesmati, M., Harooni, H. E. and Varzi, H. N. (2013). Effects of nano and conventional Zinc Oxide on anxiety-like behavior in male rats. *Indian Journal of Pharmacology*, 45(5):508–512. http://doi.org/10.4103/0253-7613.117784.

170. Sartori, S. B., Whittle, N., Hetzenauer, A. and Singewald, N. (2012). Magnesium deficiency induces anxiety and HPA axis dysregulation: Modulation by therapeutic drug treatment. *Neuropharmacology*, 62(1):304–312. http://doi.org/10.1016/j. neuropharm.2011.07.027.

171. Kiecolt-Glaser, J. K., Belury, M. A., Andridge, R., Malarkey, W. B. and Glaser, R. (2011). Omega-3 supplementation lowers inflammation and anxiety in medical students: A randomized controlled trial. *Brain, Behavior, and Immunity*, 25(8):1725–1734. http://doi.org/10.1016/j.bbi.2011.07.229.

172. Santos, C., Ferreira, A.,Oliveira, A. L., Chaves de Oliveira, M., Gomes, J. S. and Aguiar, D. (2016). Carbohydrate-enriched diet predispose to anxiety and depression-like behavior after stress in mice. *Nutritional Neuroscience*, 21:1–7. 10.1080/1028415X.2016.1213529.

173. Sarris, J., Logan, A. C., Akbaraly, T., Amminger, P., Balanzá-Martínez, V., Freeman, M., et al. (2015). Nutritional medicine as mainstream in psychiatry. *The Lancet Psychiatry*, 2. 10.1016/S2215-0366(14)00051-0.

174. Neff, K. D. and Beretvas, S. N. (2013). The role of self-compassion in romantic relationships. *Self and Identity*, 12(1):78–98.

175. Tang, H., Lu, X., Su, R., Liang, Z., Mai, X. and Liu, C. (2017). Washing away your sins in the brain: physical cleaning and priming of cleaning recruit different brain networks after moral threat. *Social Cognitive and Affective Neuroscience*, 12(7):1149–1158. http://doi.org/10.1093/scan/nsx036.

176. Zhong, C.-B. and Liljenquist, K. (2006). Washing away your sins: Threatened morality and physical cleansing. *Science*, 313:1451–2. 10.1126/science.1130726.

177. Oppezzo, M. and Schwartz, D. L. (2014). Give your ideas some legs: The positive effect of walking on creative thinking. *Journal of Experimental Psychology: Learning, Memory, and Cognition*, 40(4):1142–52.

178. Christoff, K., Gordon, A. M., Smallwood, J., Smith, R. and Schooler, J. W. (2009). Experience sampling during fMRI reveals default network and executive system contributions to mind wandering. *Proceedings of the National Academy of Sciences of the United States of America*, 106 (21):8719–24.

179. Förster, J., Friedman, R. S. and Liberman, N. (2004). Temporal construal effects on abstract and concrete thinking: Consequences for insight and creative cognition. *Journal of Personality and Social Psychology*, 87(2):177–89.

180. Wagner, U., Gais, S., Haider, H., Verleger, R. and Born, J. (2004). Sleep inspires insight. *Nature*, 427:352–5. 10.1038/nature02223.

181. Beijamini, F., Pereira, S. I. R., Cini, F. A. and Louzada, F. M. (2014). After being challenged by a video game problem, sleep increases the chance to solve it. *PLoS ONE*, 9(1), e84342. http://doi.org/10.1371/journal.pone.0084342

182. Horne, J. A. (1989). Sleep loss and "divergent" thinking ability. *Sleep*, 11:528–36. 10.1093/sleep/11.6.528.

183. Soon, C. S., Brass, M., Heinze, H. J. and Haynes, J. D. (2008). Unconscious determinants of free decisions in the human brain. *Nature Neuroscience*, 11(5):543–5.

184. Lufityanto, G., Donkin, C. and Pearson, J. (2016). Measuring intuition: Nonconscious emotional information boosts decision accuracy and confidence. *Psychological Science*, 27(5):622–34.

185. Voss, J. L. and Paller, K. A. (2009). An electrophysiological signature of unconscious recognition memory. *Nature Neuroscience*, 12(3):349–55.

186. McCraty, R. and Atkinson, M. (2014), Electrophysiology of intuition: Pre-stimulus responses in group and individual participants using a roulette paradigm. *Global Advances in Health and Medicine*, 3(2):16–27.

Acknowledgements

I would first like to say a massive thank you to my clients for allowing me to share a little of their personal stories within this book.

Thank you also to the amazing team at my publishing house who are so kind and calm. A huge thank you to my publisher for always letting me have a voice and to the entire team – from the editors to the publicity managers and everyone in between – who support me and my written works and work hard to help me make them a success.

A huge thank you to my talented book and TV agents and their teams for helping me to be here right now and for always making my journey so smooth.

Thank you also to all the people in the media who have given me a platform for making a positive change in the world.

And last but not least, a big, big thank you to my main lifelines – my parents, husband, the rest of my family, and my dear friends who all show me love and kindness, help me to learn and achieve, stay happy and mentally healthy, and help me to believe in myself.